An Artist's Life
New Orleans Framed

Author: Dan Wetta

Published by Daniel Wetta Publishing

Copyright 2015

Please visit Author Page:

http://www.amazon.com/Dan-Wetta/e/B00O6S0MNC

Table of Contents

Prologue

I open this book with sketches and paintings that I did over the years in Bucktown, Louisiana, which was literally wiped off the map by Hurricane Katrina in the year 2005. As usual, I intersperse doodles and cartoons here and throughout my themed sections, just to keep things interesting.

In Chapter Two, I show how I went through four stages of recollection in order to come up with a finished painting of "Mississippi's Only Alligator Farm," which I did from memory.

If this chapter bothers you, don't worry about my memory, because I have never been asked to pick out a suspect from a police line-up!

Chapters Three and Four contain most of my serious paintings with anecdotal memories. In fact, the first three chapters are the content of my e-Book entitled, *New Orleans In My Mind.* My longest anecdote is about incidents that my siblings and I experienced during the Great Depression of the 1930s, when we lived on Washington Avenue in New Orleans. (I had three brothers and two sisters.) I thought I had done a good job of painting on canvas from memory our Washington Avenue house where we lived, but my brother, Raymond, pointed out that I had put too many chimneys on the roof. I discovered that my memory of events sometimes differs from what my family remembers from those days.

The remaining chapters include sections from my last published e-Book entitled, *Last But Not The End.*

Chapter 1: Bucktown Is Gone

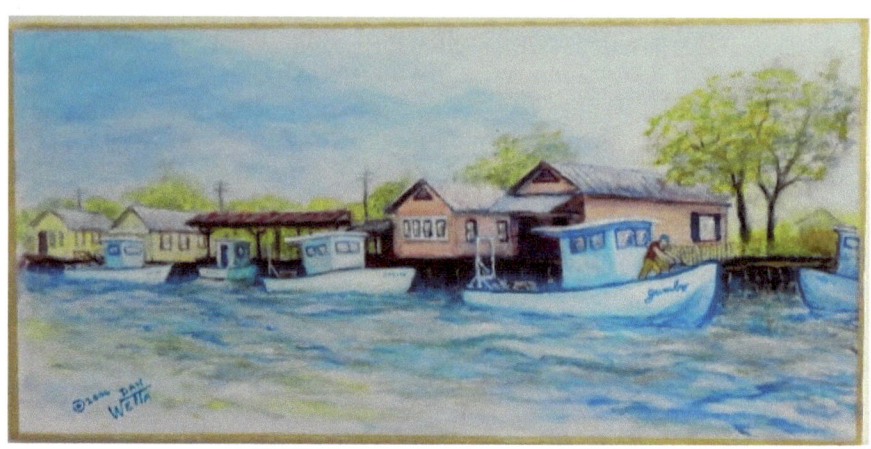

Before Hurricane Katrina, Bucktown was a little fishing village on Lake Pontchartrain, just outside of Metarie, Louisiana.

There are many legends telling how the village got the name, "Bucktown," but nobody really knows. A hundred years or so ago, Cajun fishermen and hunters began settling there. They built camp houses on stilts along the shore of Lake Pontchartrain. If nobody objected to their camp houses for a period of thirty years, they would become owners of the property under Louisiana's squatter's law.

Never-the-less, when I used to go there to paint Bucktown scenes, the quaint camp houses, boat docks and fishing boats were beginning to look rundown and in disrepair, because New Orleans business men had gone to court and obtained an eviction order. The property had become valuable because of its location on Lake Pontchartrain. Location! Location!

However, Mother Nature sent her agent, Hurricane Katrina, to Bucktown to let everybody know that she alone is the proprietor of all the land on earth, regardless of "location."

In the year 2005, Katrina completely destroyed Bucktown.

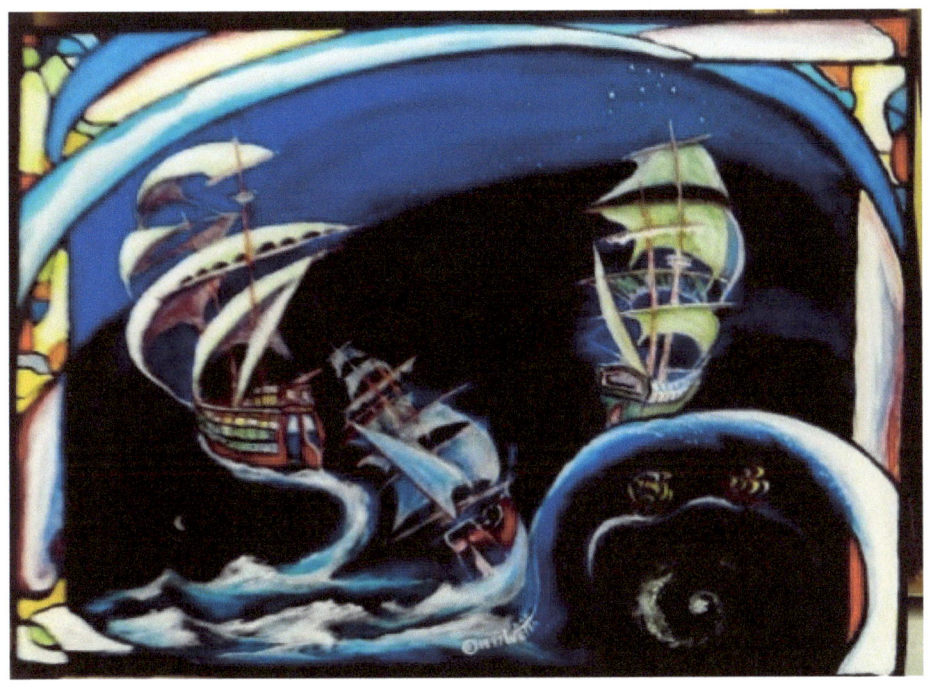

Title: (Bucktown): Don't Mess With The Wind
Size: 20x24 inches
Medium: Acrylic on canvas
Copyright by Dan Wetta 1997

When ship-builders abandoned square riggers and tall ships for faster coal-burning ships, it seemed that wind power was a thing of the past; for a while; that is, until one day the wind decided to make a comeback.

"I'll show them." said the wind, and it began to churn up the seas with storms and cyclones, and it lashed out at the land with tornadoes and hurricanes.

And eventually it showed Bucktown and New Orleans how it could create a storm surge on Lake Pontchartrain, which wiped out Bucktown and a great part of New Orleans.

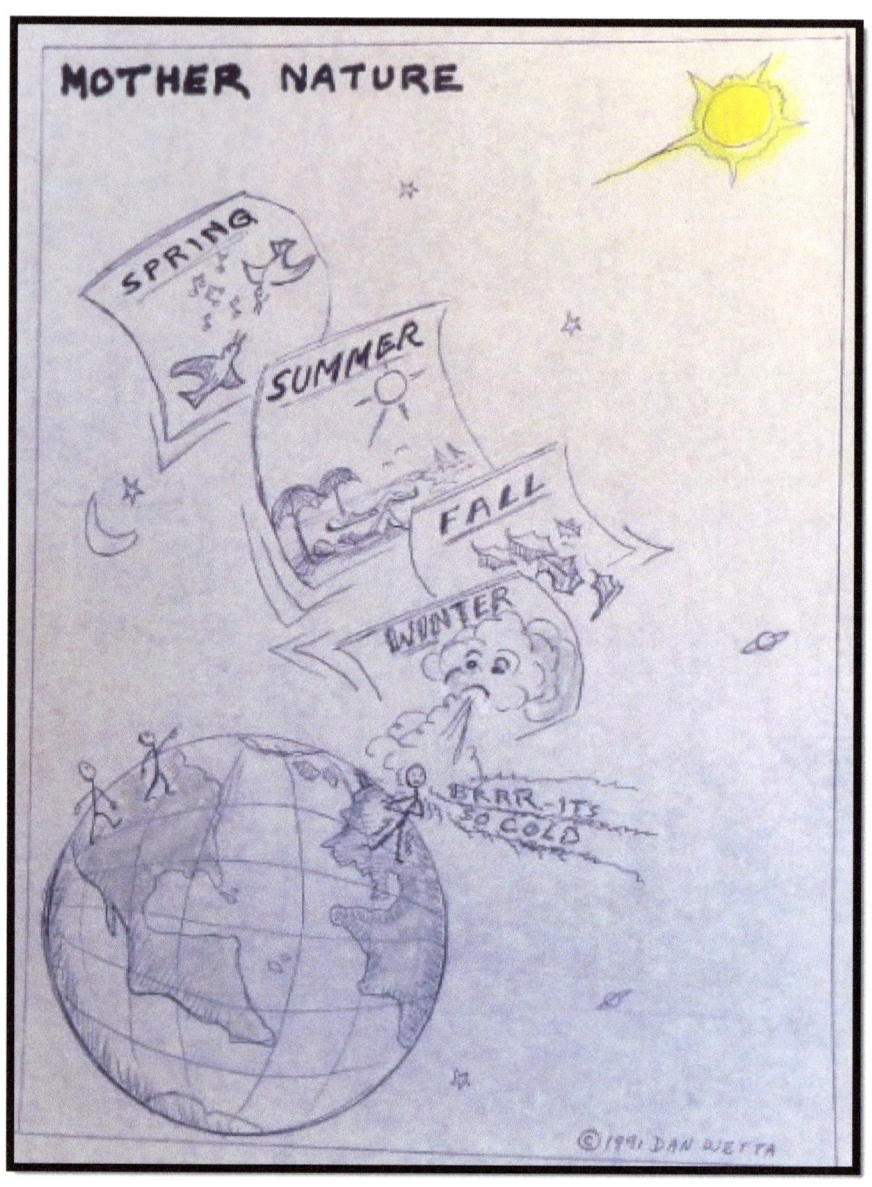

Title: (Bucktown): Calendar in Sky

"Brrr, it's so cold!" complains the man standing in Europe as he feels the icy wind of Winter in the cartoon.

Genesis 1:14: "And God said, 'Let there be lights in the dome of the sky to separate the day from the night; and let them be for signs and for seasons and for days and years.'"

Bucktown and New Orleans need a calendar in the sky to warn them about hurricanes and storm surges. Maybe it was there, but no one was paying attention.

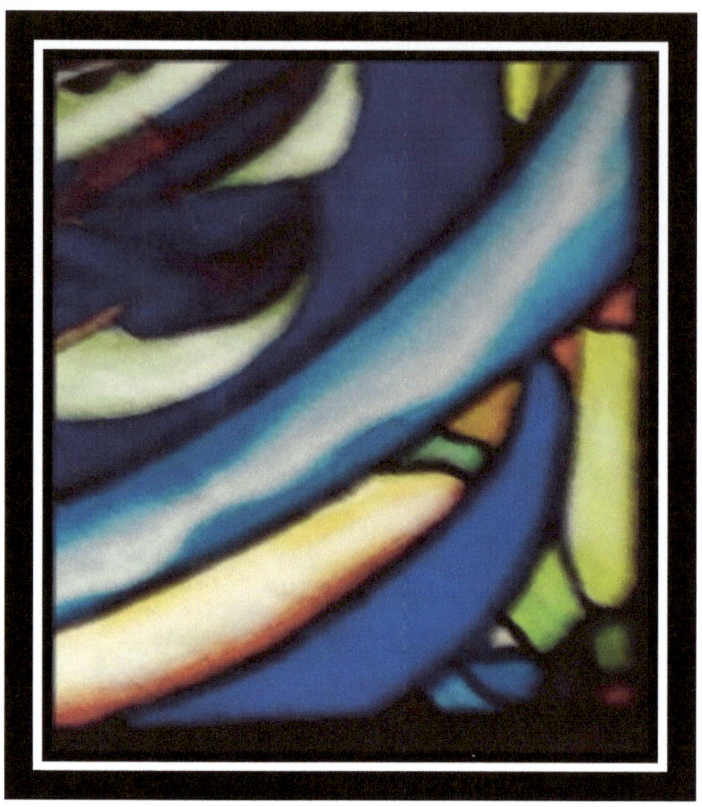

Abstract Thirty Three
Copyright by Dan Wetta 1997

This abstract is taken from my Bucktown painting, "Don't Mess With the Wind."

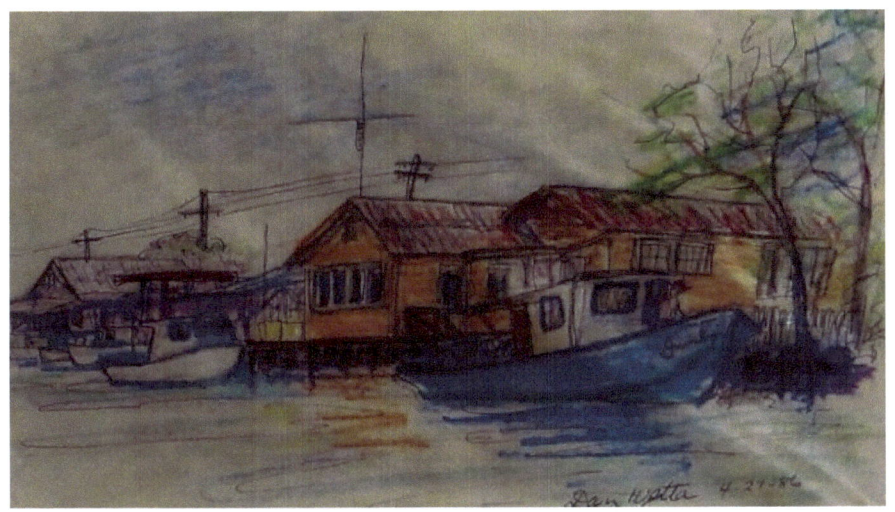

Title: (Bucktown): Cloudy Day
Size: 11 x 14 inches
Medium: Mixed media on paper

If you believe in omens, I think this cloudy-day sketch of a canal in Bucktown looks like a harbinger of Hurricane Katrina. Although this sketch was done years before Hurricane Katrina hit, my sons and I and other members of my family were vacationing in New Orleans during the week before, when Katrina was making its way towards the city. We left New Orleans on Saturday, and Katrina hit full force on Monday morning.

In the days before the hurricane, the city was sunny and almost unbearably hot and muggy. People had lost interest in the hurricane because of the prediction by meteorologists that it would pass New Orleans on a westward course across the Gulf of Mexico. The Saturday morning that we left, not many people were even talking about the hurricane. But Katrina had a cruel trick up her sleeve. She made a sudden course change for a direct hit on New Orleans. She surprised the city and the nation.

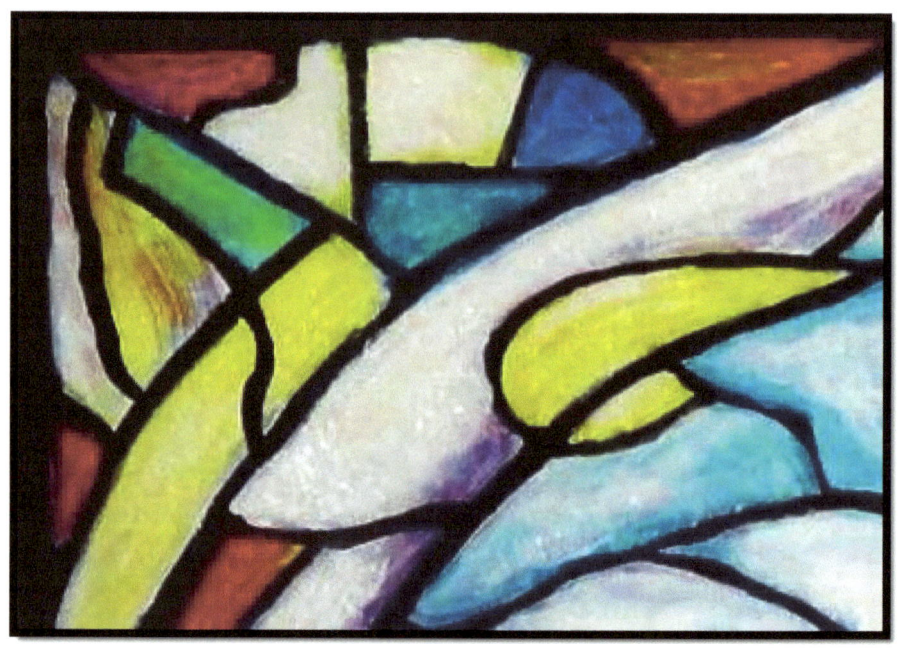

Title: Abstract, Three-Panel Garden of Eden
Copyright by Dan Wetta

This is a close-up view of a small section of my painting, "Three Panel Garden of Eden." I randomly insert abstracts such as these throughout my volumes of books. These abstracts are from sections of my paintings as identified by the titles. I never used to believe that I was capable of painting abstract art until I started noticing the details in the paintings that I did.

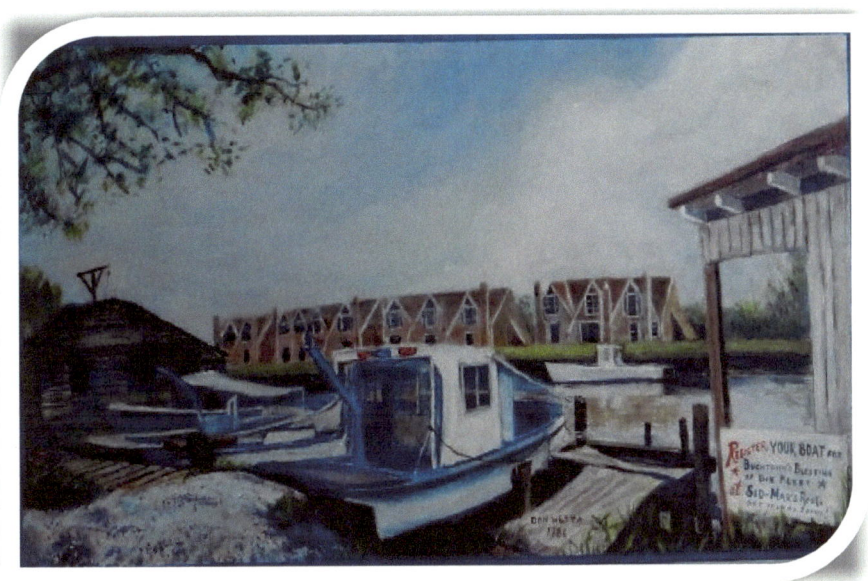

Title: Bucktown Blessing of the Fleet
Size: 12x24 inches
Medium: Acrylic on canvas
Copyright by Dan Wetta 1986

Those modern condos on the other side of the canal emphasize the contrast between old and new.

The sign in lower right of the painting tells the fishermen to register their boats for the annual "Blessing of the Fleet."

However, Mother Nature was not in a very spiritual mood when she sent Hurricane Katrina to Bucktown in 2005.

All of Bucktown and those condos across the canal are gone now.

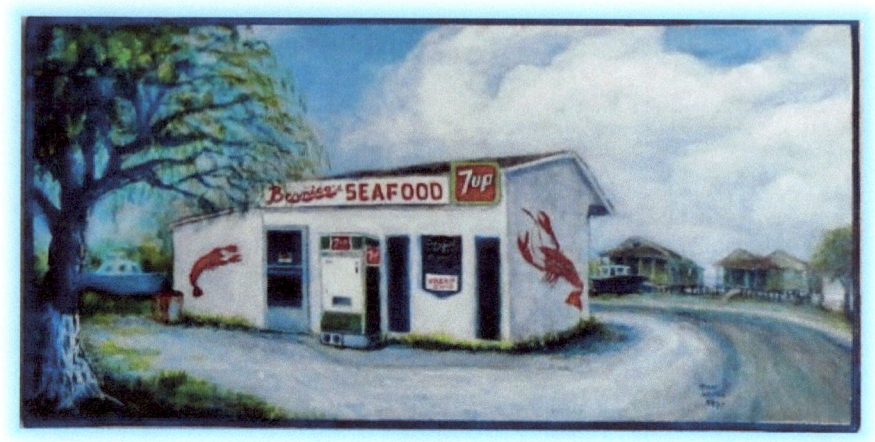

Title: Bernice's Seafood (Bucktown)
Size: 12x24 on 24x36 inch canvas board
Medium: Acrylic on canvas
Copyright by Dan Wetta 1987

Most of the places in Bucktown were rundown and dilapidated when I was sketching there in the 1980s, and Bernice's Seafood was closed because Bernice had died.

It was the painting of the crawfish on the side of Bernice's Seafood that caught my eye. We say "crawfish" in Louisiana, not "crayfish."

After Bernice died, her daughter filed a lawsuit against the adjoining Sid Mar's Restaurant over parking spaces, because space was limited in Bucktown. However, there was plenty of space after Hurricane Katrina. Nothing was left intact.

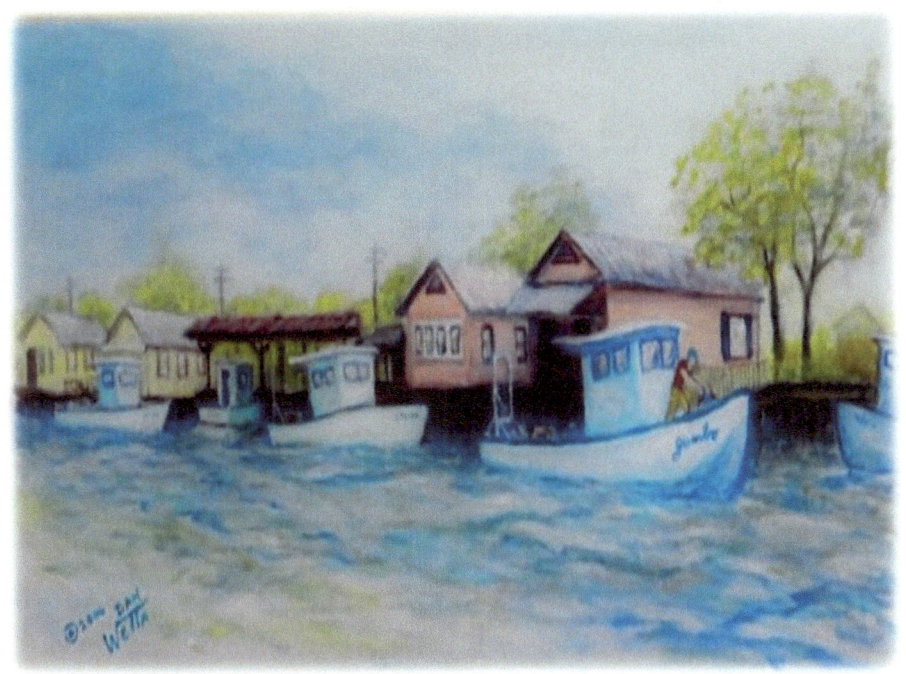

Title: Jumbo, no! Gumbo! (Bucktown)
Size: 12x24 inches
Medium: Acrylic on Canvas
Copyright by Dan Wetta 2006

I painted this a couple years after my original sketch, and I got the name wrong on that boat with the man on it. It more likely was named, "Gumbo." But I guess it doesn't matter now, because it was destroyed by Hurricane Katrina in 2005.

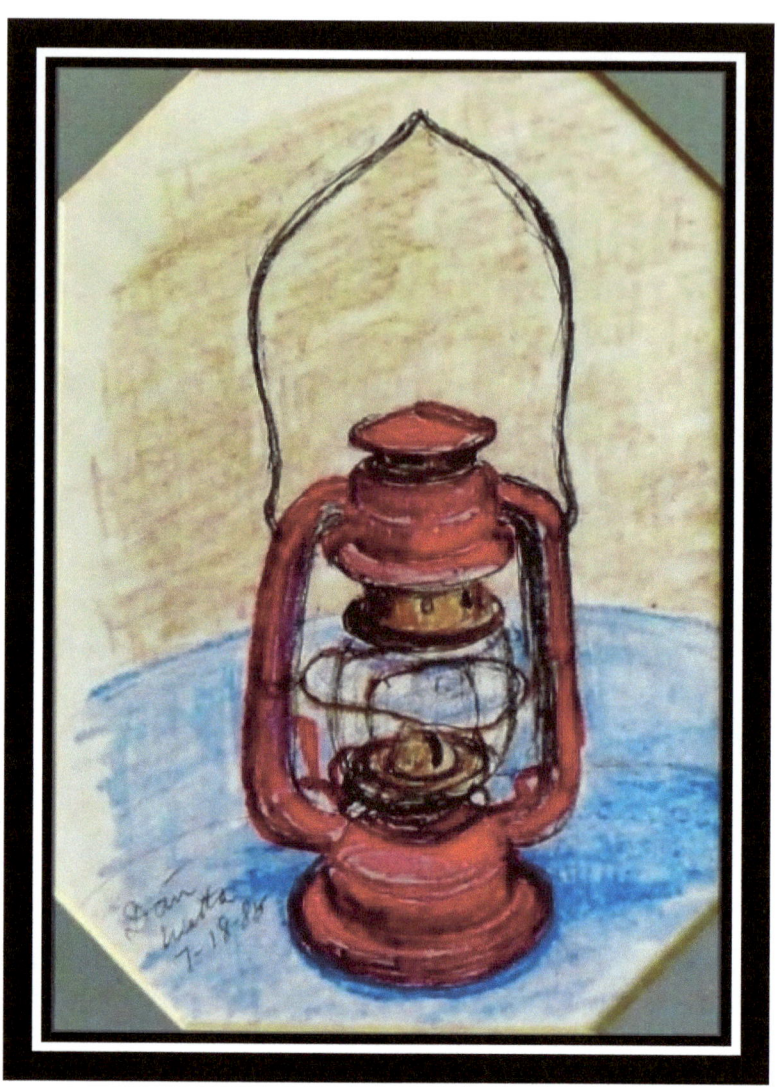

Title: Hurricane Lantern (doodle)
Copyright by Dan Wetta 1988

I think that this hurricane lantern fits in with the Bucktown paintings, since it was a hurricane that wiped out all of Bucktown and a good part of New Orleans.

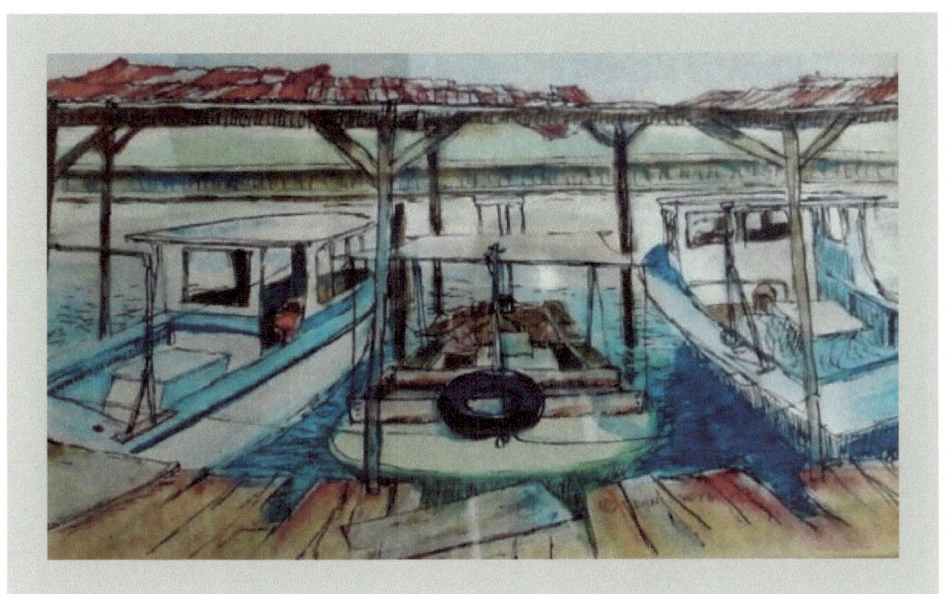

Title: (Bucktown): Three Boat Sketch
Size: 16x20 inches
Medium: Mixed media on paper
Copyright by Dan Wetta 1988

I think I was sitting in the grass when I did this preliminary sketch, and I didn't notice that fire ants had crawled up my legs until I got in my brother's car to go home. They wait until hundreds of them are on your body to start biting. You should have seen me slapping away at them!

When I got to my mom's house, there were nasty looking bite marks on my legs. Mom always had a home remedy for everything. She gave me an ointment to put on my legs, and the stings got better after a few days.

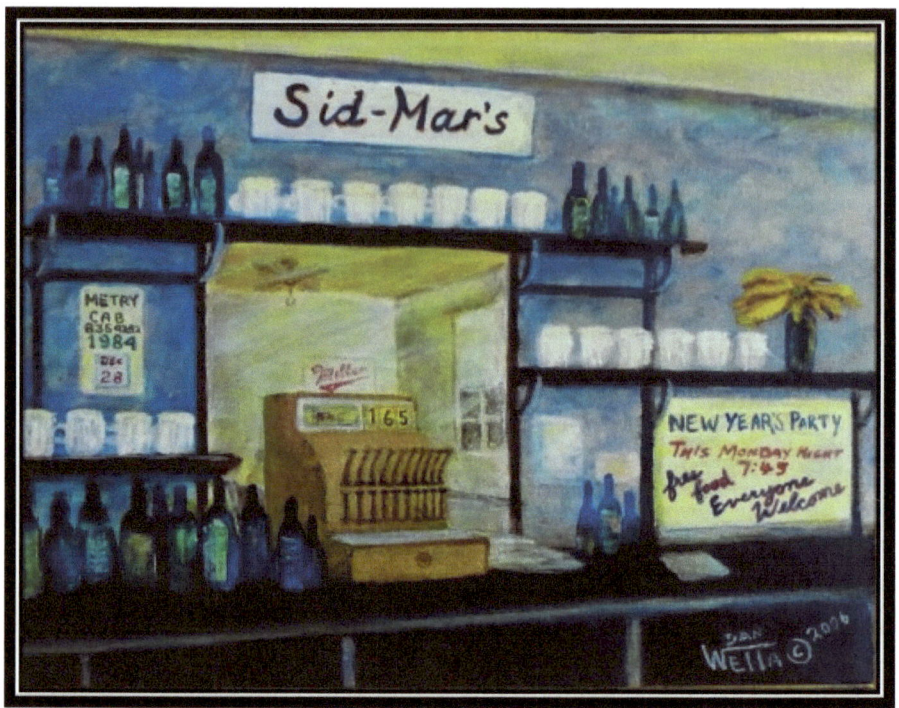

Title: Sid-Mar's (Bucktown)
Size: 12x16 inches mounted on a 16x20 frame
Medium: Acrylic on canvas
Copyright by Dan Wetta 2006

In December, 1986, my cousin, Paul, and my brother, Raymond, dropped me off in Bucktown so I could do some sketching, and they went to Sid-Mar's for a beer. They came back for me an hour later, and we all went back to Sid-Mar's. I was particularly impressed by the antique cash register, so I did a sketch of the bar, but I didn't do a finished painting until 2006.

I think Sid-Mar's started out as a gathering place for the fishermen, and then it expanded into a much larger and well-known tourist restaurant.

The fishermen used to register their boats at Sid-Mar's for the annual "blessing of the fleet." However, Mother Nature's daughter,

Hurricane Katrina, must not be very religious, because she huffed and puffed and blew Sid-Mar's to pieces, along with all the fishing boats.

P.S. Notice "the Metry Cab" calendar to the left of the cash register. "Metry" meant the town of "Metarie." We mispronounce and misspell a lot of words in Louisiana. I have seen official street signs that read "Metry" instead of "Metarie."

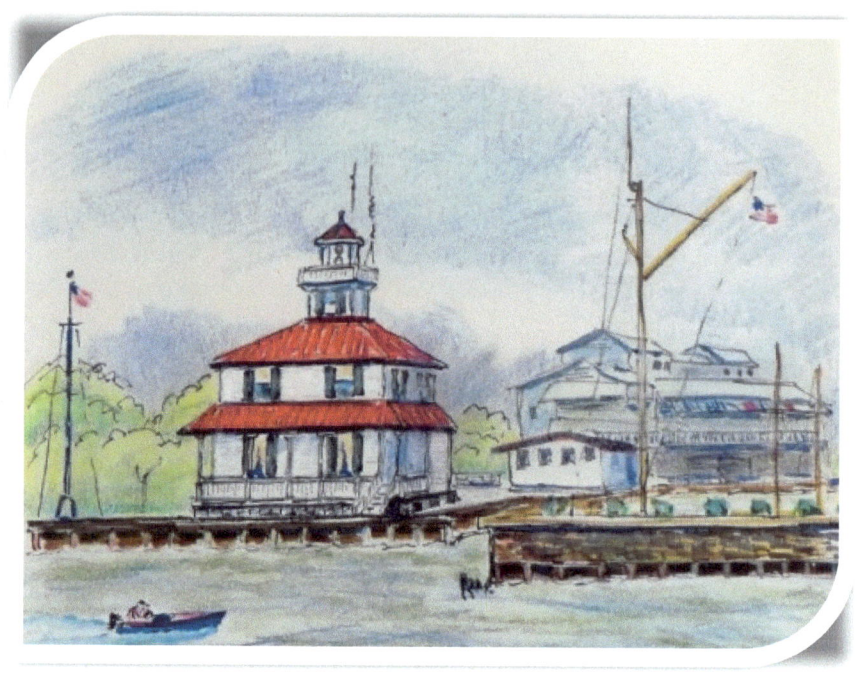

Title: Lighthouse Lake Pontchartrain
Size: 11x14 inches
Medium: Acrylic on water color paper
Copyright by Dan Wetta

This is a preliminary sketch of the Coast Guard Lighthouse on Lake Pontchartrain.

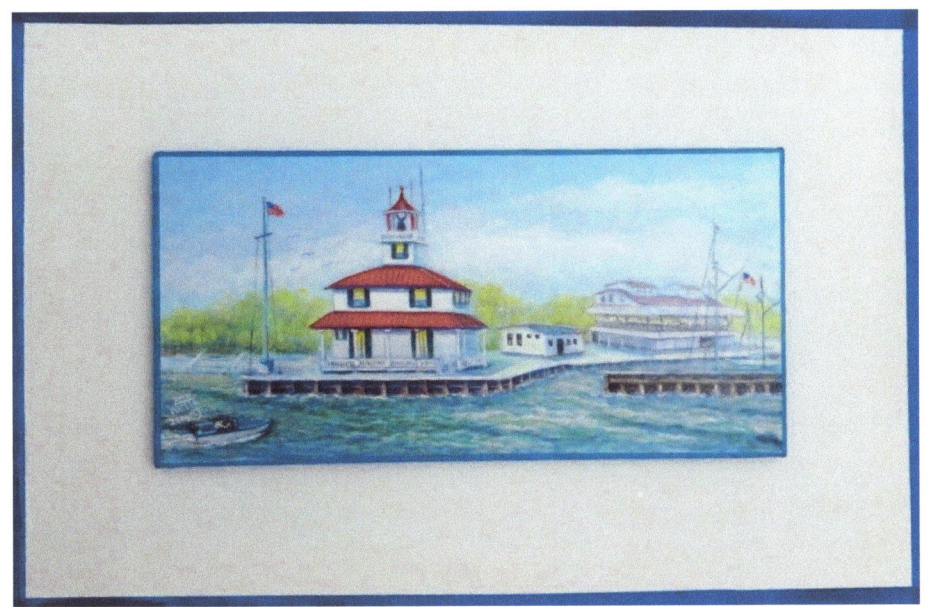

Title: (Bucktown): Lighthouse Lake Pontchartrain
Size: 12x24 on 24x36 inch canvas board
Medium: Acrylic on canvas
Copyright by Dan Wetta 2006

This is the final version on canvas board. This historic lighthouse is about a quarter mile from Bucktown.

When lighthouses became obsolete, the US Coast Guard occupied this one until 2005, when the surge created by hurricane Katrina caused Lake Pontchartrain to rise and destroy it. It has since been restored. This final painting still shows the buildings in the background, but I don't know if those have been rebuilt.

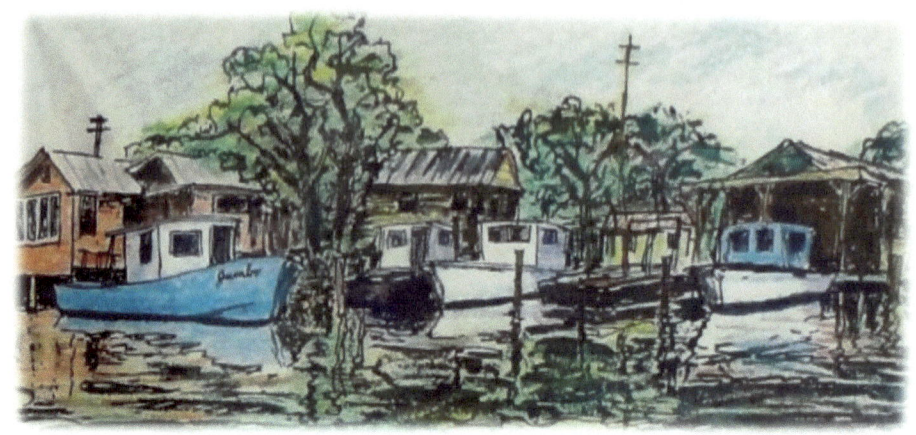

Title: "Bucktown Boats on Canal" preliminary sketch
Size: 16x20 inches
Medium: Mixed media on watercolor paper
Copyright by Dan Wetta 1988

I sketched "Jumbo" on the boat in this preliminary sketch, but it probably should be "Gumbo." In New Orleans, it's all about the "gumbo." That is a Creole dish dating back to the 18th century. There are many popular recipes for gumbo, but one with chicken, shrimp and sausage served over rice is typical. "Making a gumbo" usually refers to the preparation of the gumbo during a party for family and friends, followed by delicious eating.

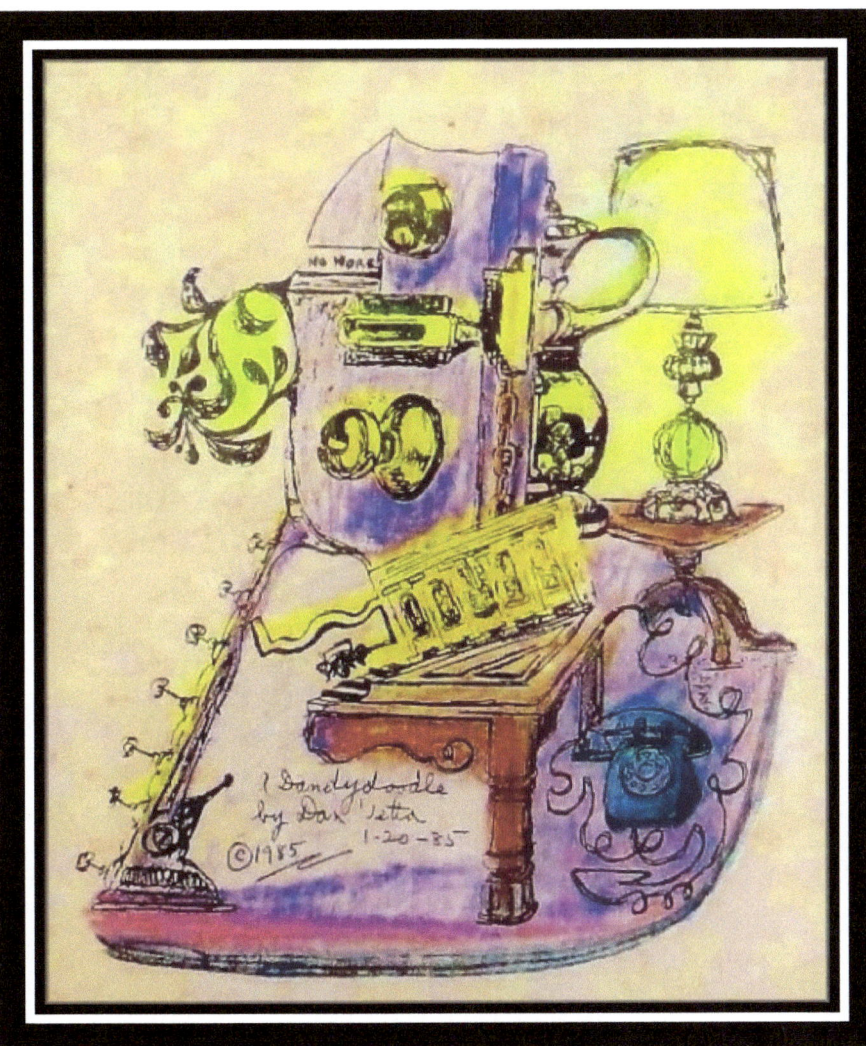

Title: Telephone Lamp and Lock (doodle)
Copyright by Dan Wetta 1985

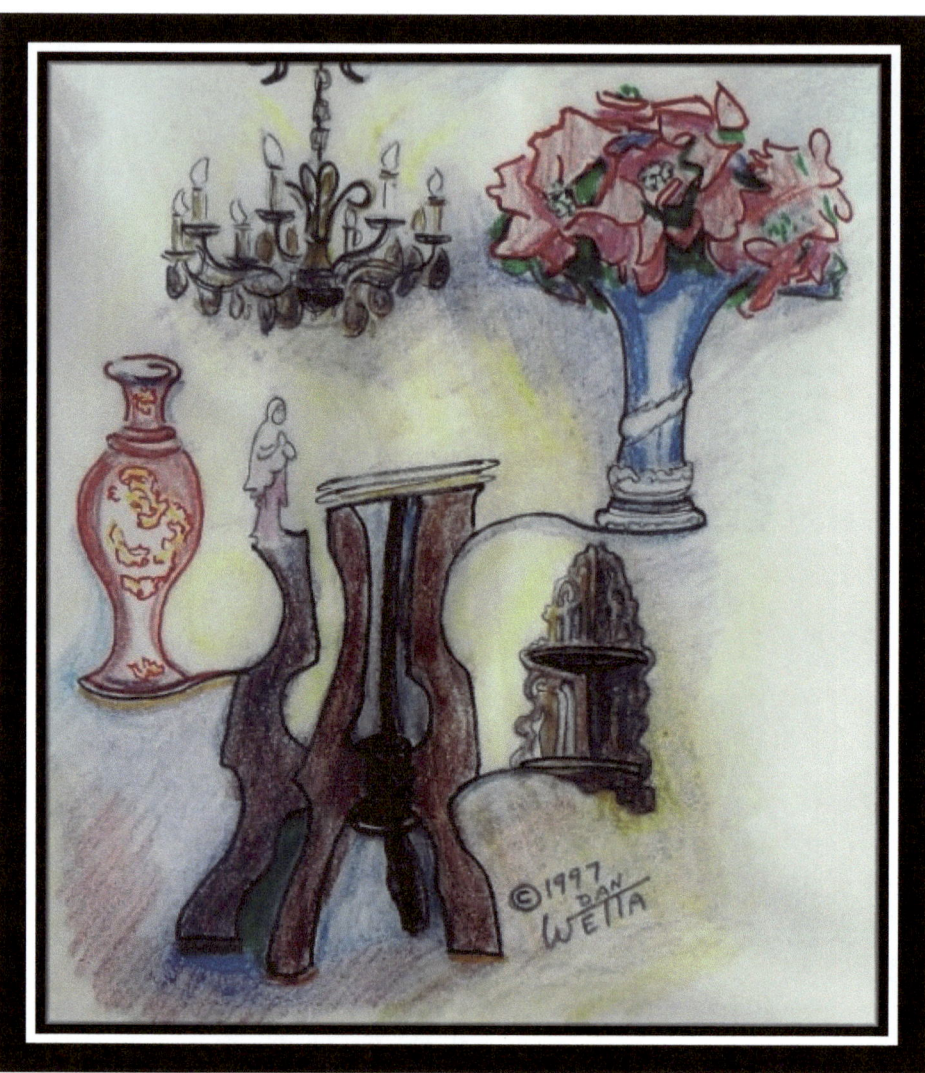

Title: Antique Medley (doodle)
Copyright by Dan Wetta 1997

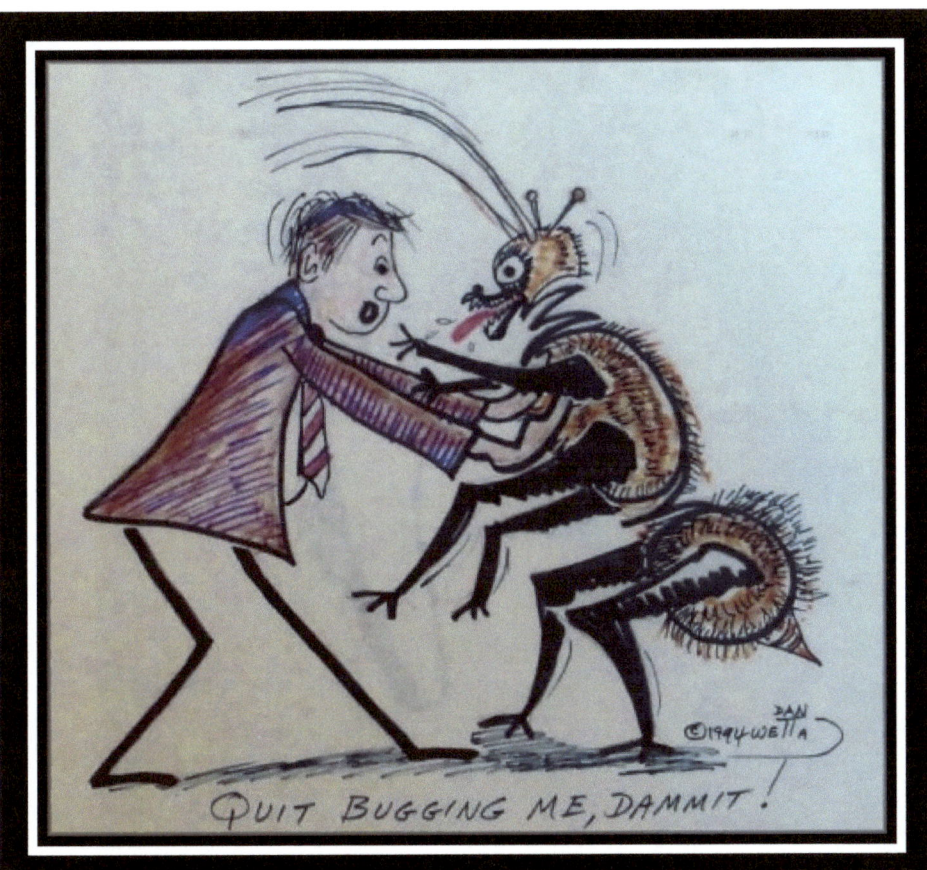

Title: Quit Bugging Me (cartoon)
Copyright by Dan Wetta

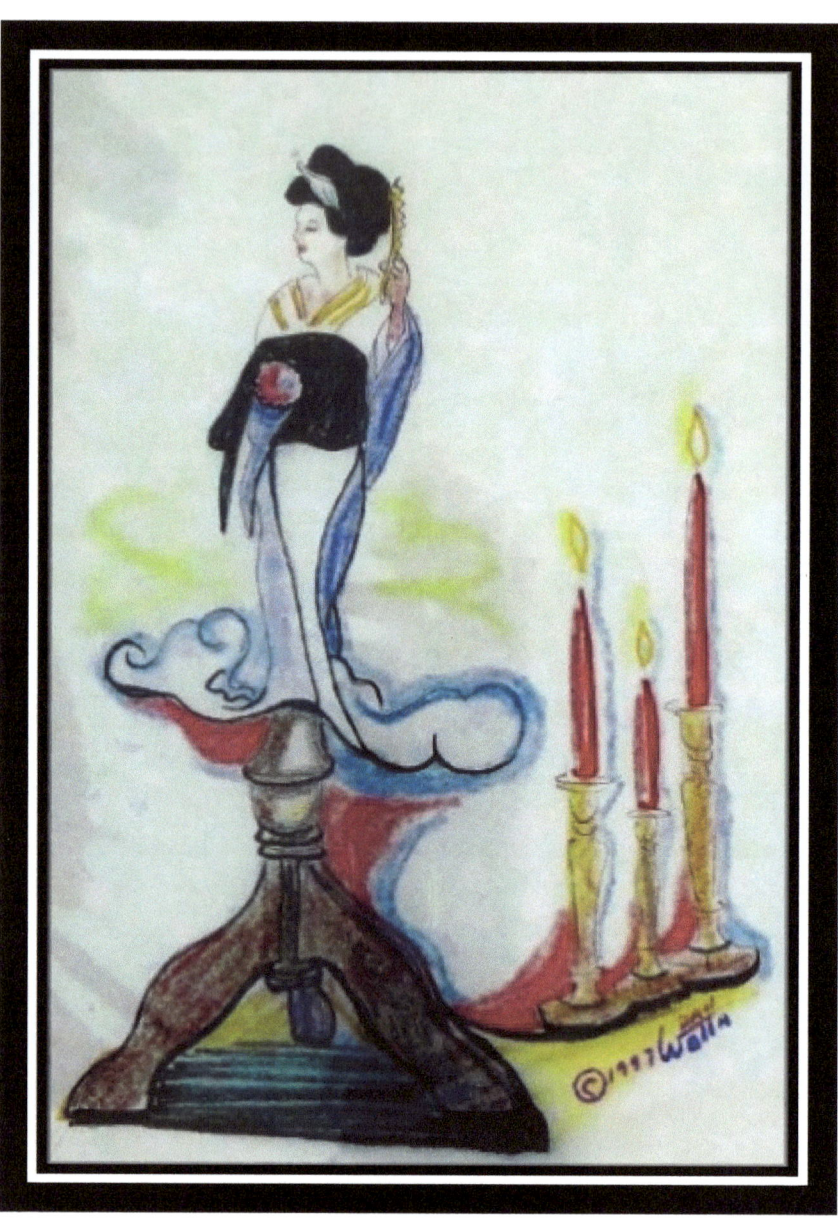

Title: Antique Lady with Three Candles (doodle)
Copyright by Dan Wetta 1997

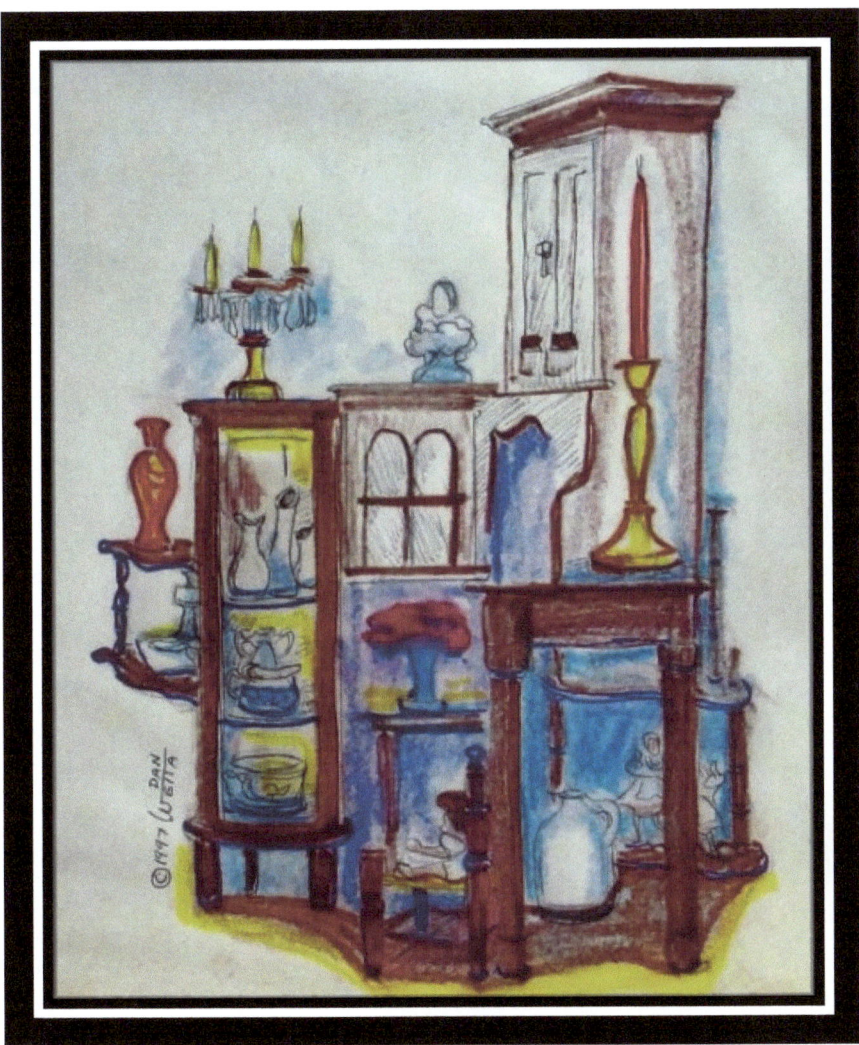

Title: Cabinet with Antique Knick-knacks (doodle)
Copyright by Dan Wetta 1997

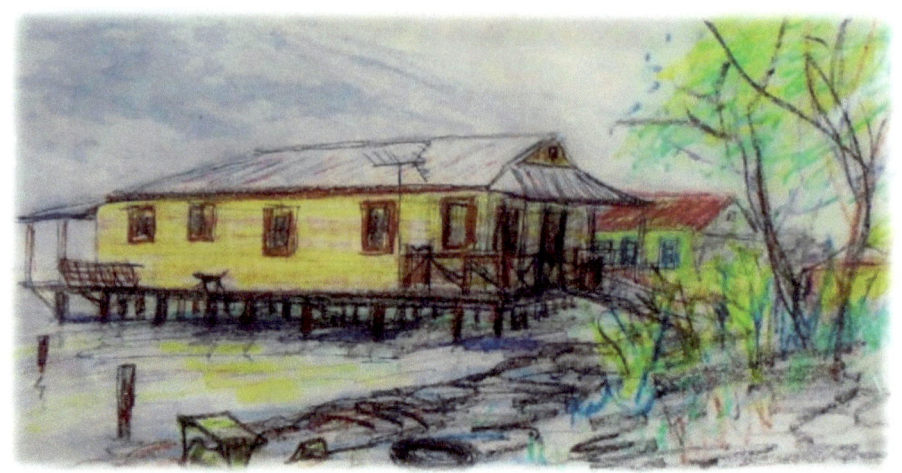

Title: Bucktown Yellow Camp House (original sketch)
Size: 16x20 inches
Medium: Mixed media on water color paper
Copyright by Dan Wetta 1986

I don't know why I sketched the trash on the beach, but I left it out in my finished painting.

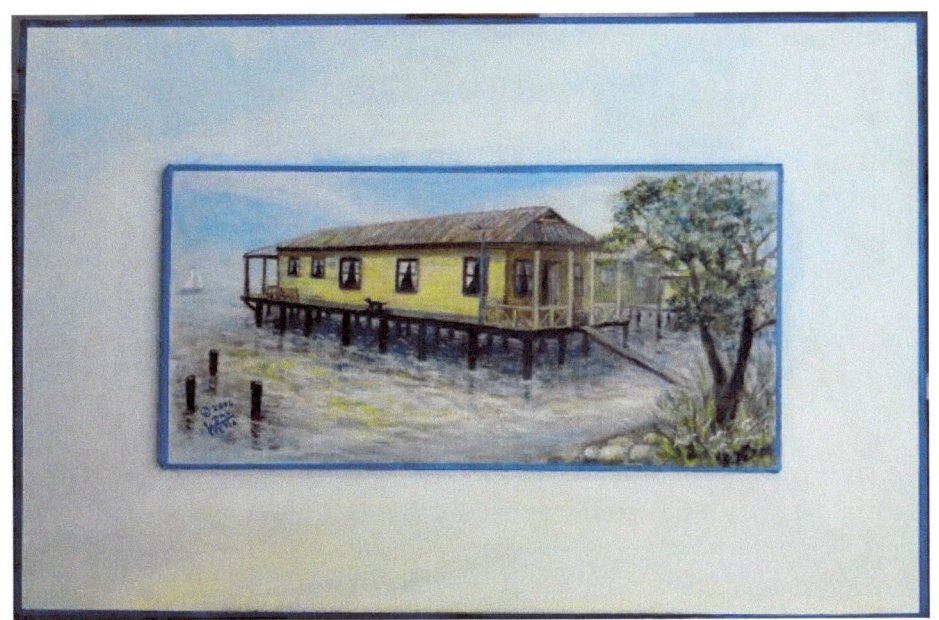

Title: Bucktown Yellow Camp House
Size: 12x24 on 24x36 inch canvas board
Medium: Acrylic on canvas
Copyright by Dan Wetta 2006

This camp house on pilings, or "stilts," was in Bucktown, but there are similar camp houses all over Louisiana. City people will rent a place like this for a week, even though there may be no electricity or running water.

Note that the "air conditioning" in Yellow Camp house is the breeze that blows off Lake Pontchartrain through those open windows.

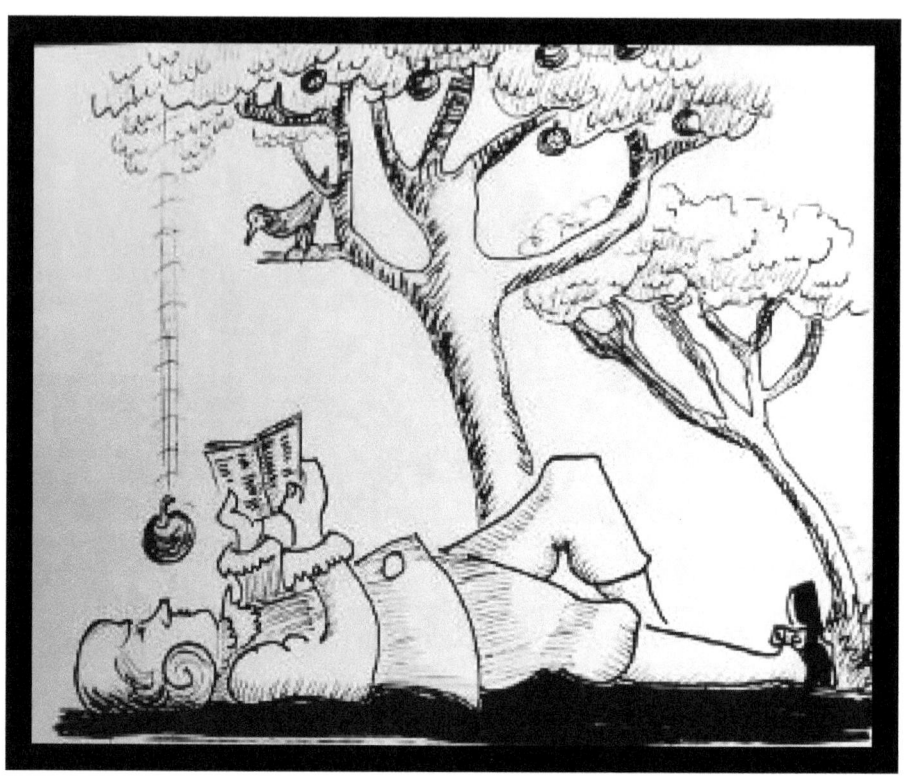

Title: Apples and Isaac (cartoon)
Copyright by Dan Wetta

The difference between me and Isaac Newton is: –
An apple falls on Isaac Newton and he discovers gravity, but...

Continued at: Apples Ouch!

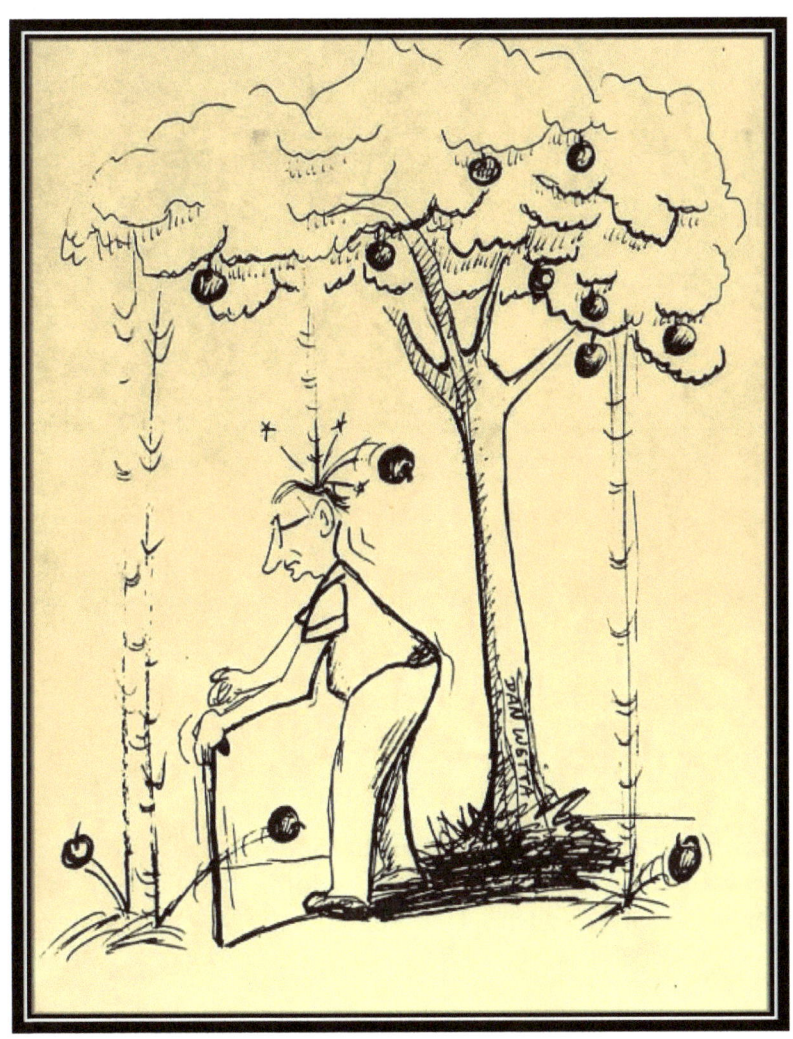

Title: Apples Ouch (cartoon)
Copyright by Dan Wetta

...Ouch! I wish them darn apples would quit reminding me about gravity!

P.S. Gravity was created instantly – not by evolution.

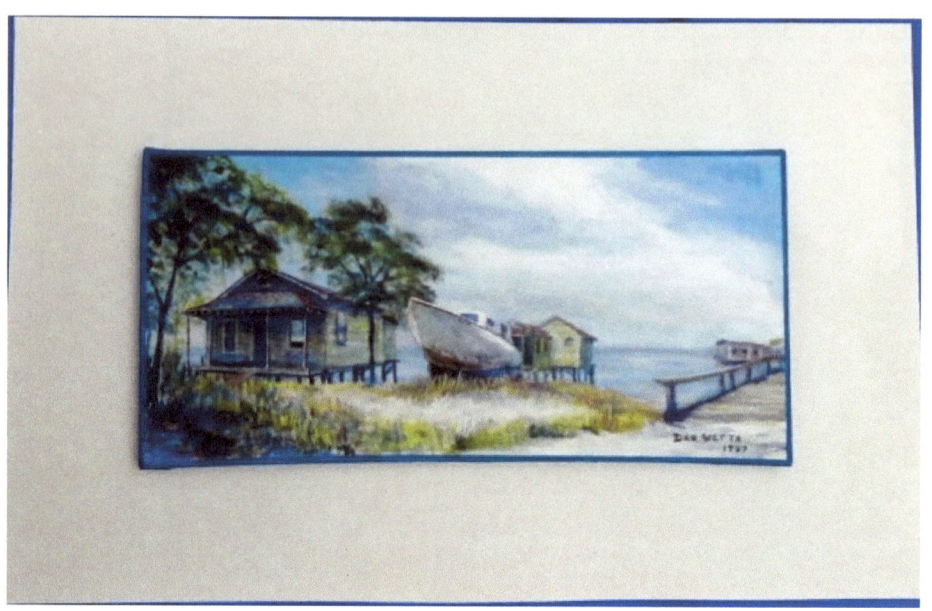

Title: (Bucktown) Foot Bridge
Size: 12X24 canvas on 24x36 inch Panel
Medium: Acrylic on canvas
Copyright by Dan Wetta 1997

That footbridge was for cars to go over to the Lighthouse area, but it became so rickety that the bridge had to be limited to foot travel. This is another piece of art where I simulated relief by mounting a smaller canvas on a larger one.

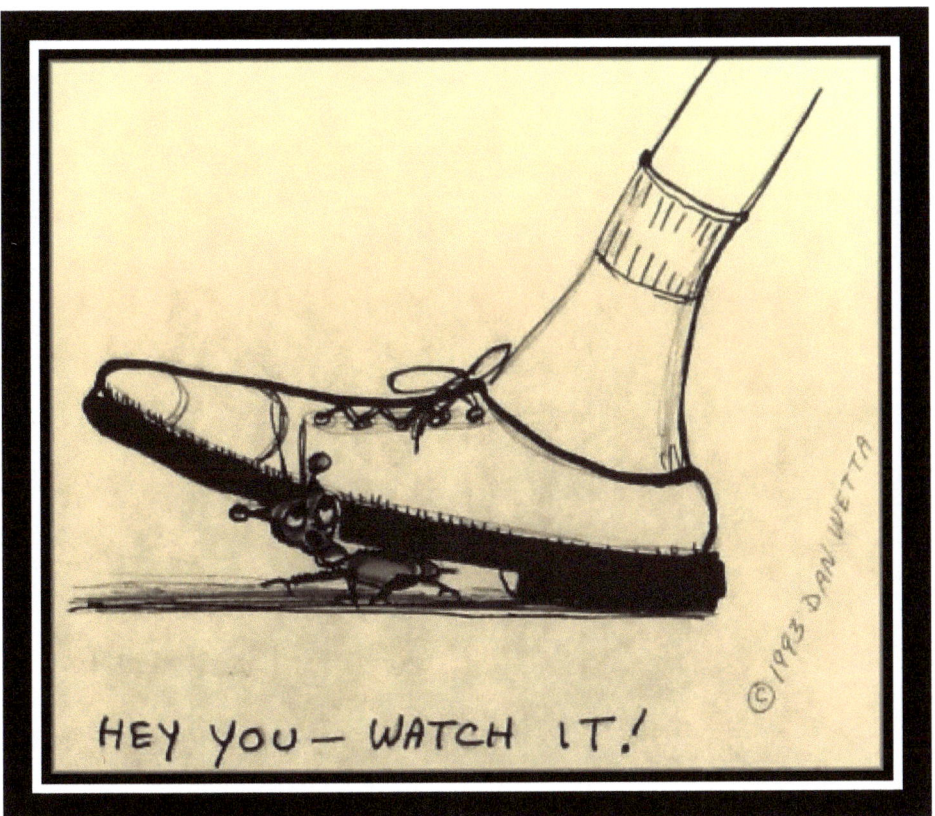

HEY YOU — WATCH IT!

Title: Watch It (cartoon)
Copyright by Dan Wetta 1993

If you want to know where Big Foot is, ask a bug.

Chapter 2: What is Memory?

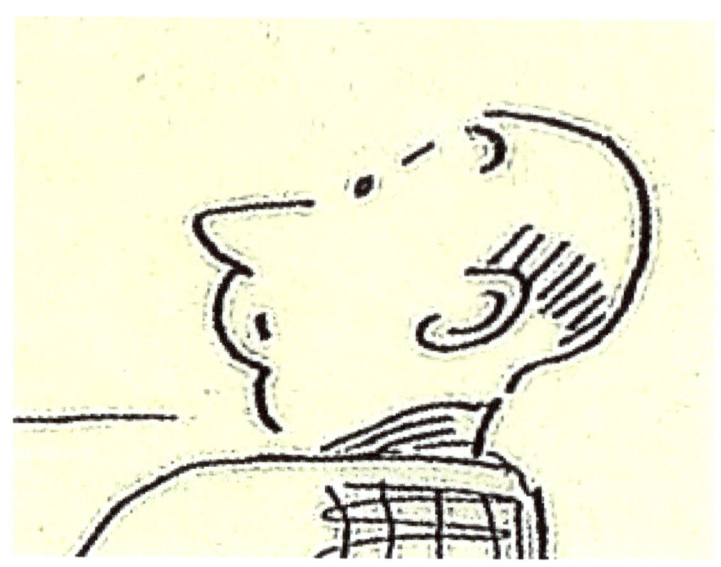

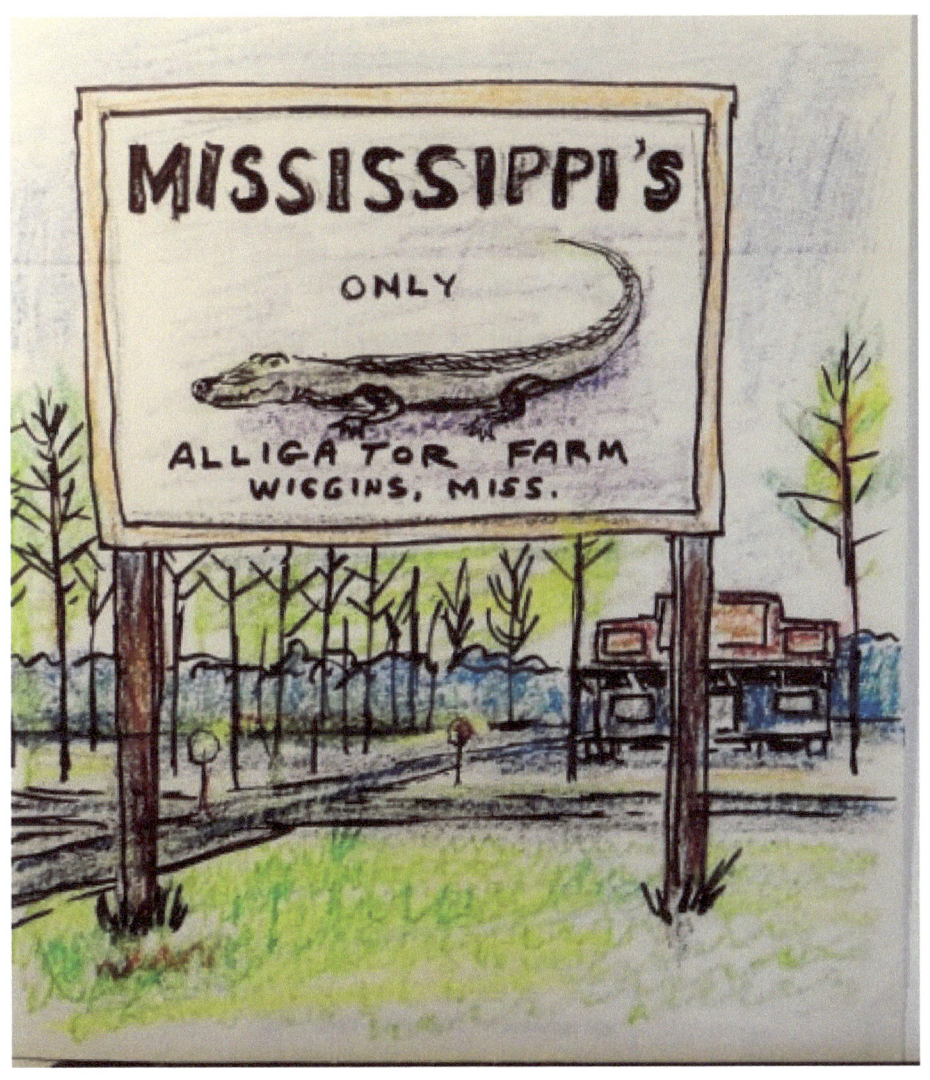

Title: "Mississippi's Only Alligator Farm" Sign
Copyright by Dan Wetta

What is memory?

When I first saw this place, it was the Alligator sign that caught my eye, and this is the very first sketch of this place that I did from memory.

Notice the signs near the top of the store in the background. In this sketch, you can't read the signs on the store. My next two versions of this scene illustrate a sign at the top of the store.

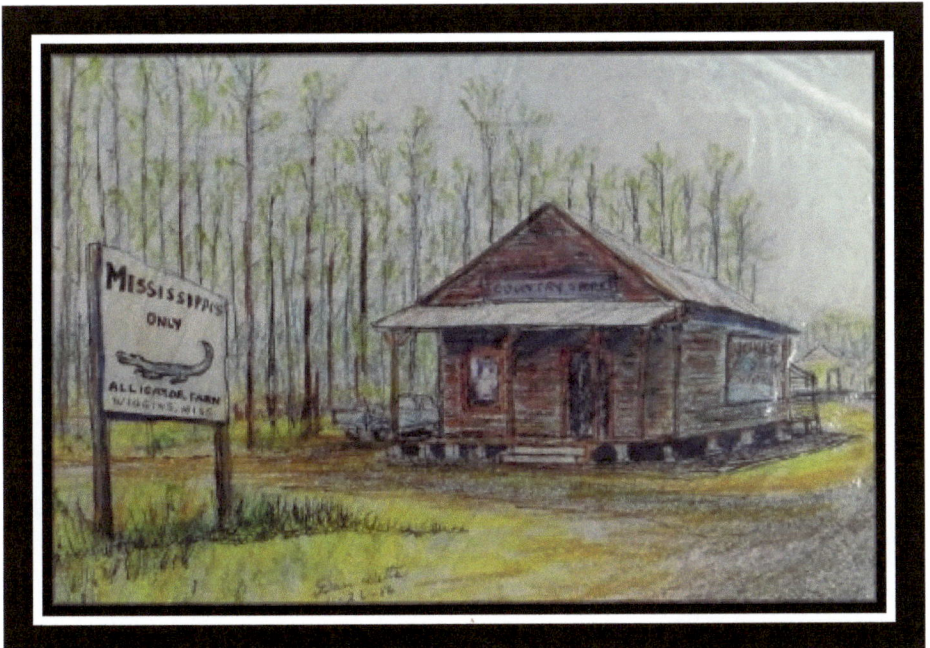

Title: First "Memory" Sketch of Mississippi's Only Alligator Farm

In this next sketch, the sign for the alligator farm is downplayed somewhat, and the store is a rival for attention, while in the background are a truck and some other buildings. This is my first "memory" sketch of "Mississippi's Only Alligator Farm" itself.

Notice that I named the store, "Country Store."

My memory seems to work in three stages, so now let's go to the second stage.

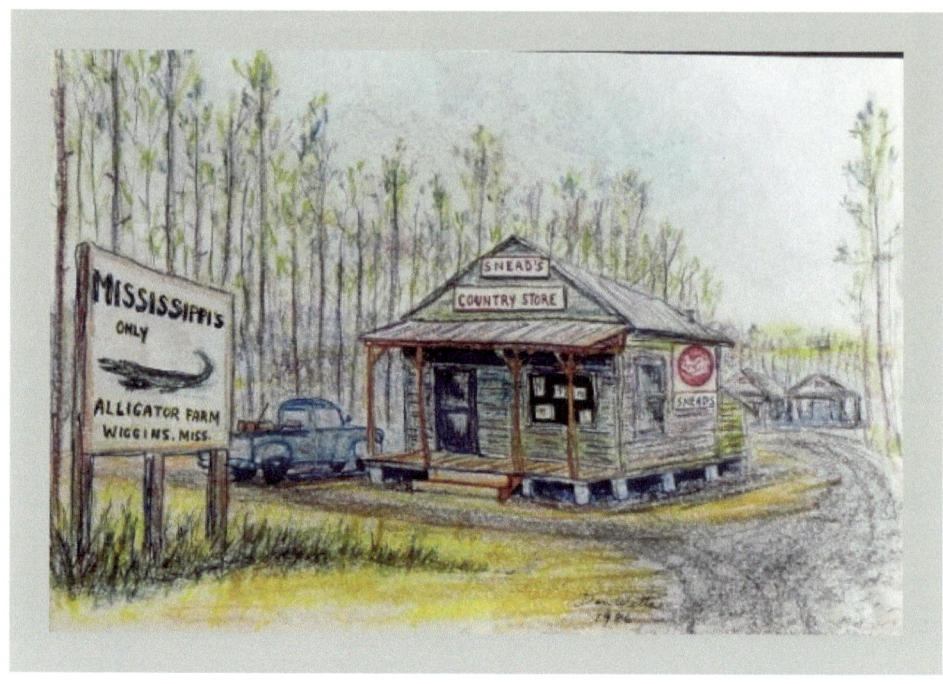

Title: Second Sketch of Mississippi's Only Alligator Farm

This is the second-stage development of my memory of "Mississippi's Only Alligator Farm."

At this point, I "remember" that the name of the store was "Snead's Country Store," instead of just plain, "Country Store." The door and window have changed position, and you can clearly see a Coke sign on the side of the store.

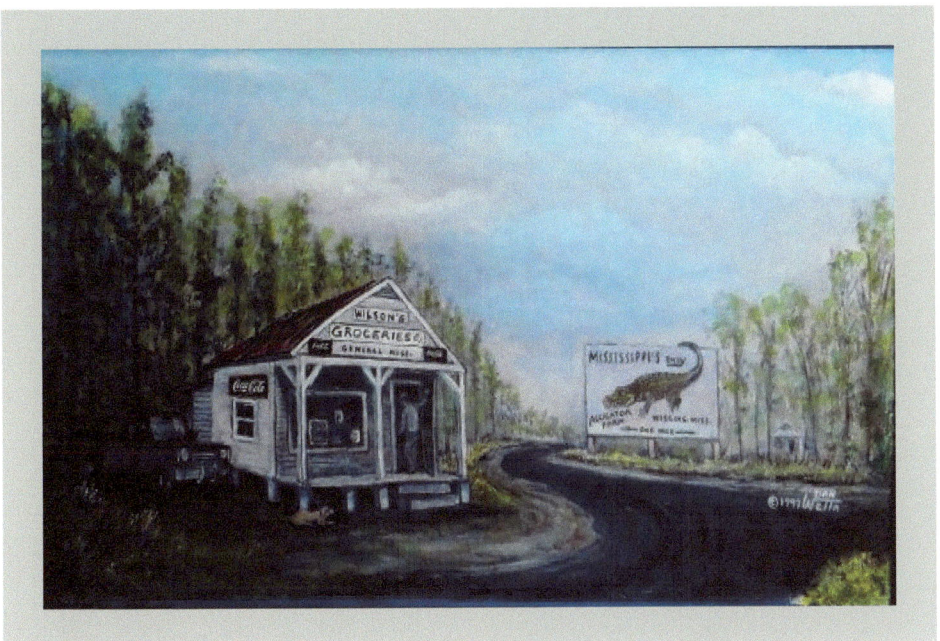

Title: Mississippi's Only Alligator Farm
Size: 12x24 inches
Medium: Acrylic on canvas
Copyright by Dan Wetta 1997

In my final version of "Mississippi's Only Alligator Farm," I have now "remembered" that the name of the store was Wilson's, not Snead's.

In other words, whenever I say that I painted something from memory, sometimes it is about 50% memory and 50% imagination.

So now the story behind this painting: I was riding in my brother's van, when I saw the sign, "Mississippi's Only Alligator Farm." We were on our way to a cabin that my brother had rented in a Mississippi state park. I knew that I just *had* to paint a picture of that sign. The year was around 1972, when there were not many alligators in Mississippi. However, I recently saw an article about a couple of guys who caught a 700-pound alligator in the wilds of Mississippi.

Alligators have now proliferated all over the southern states, so keep your little children away from the water's edge when you are down south. You won't see the alligator, but he sees you.

Speaking of Snead's Grocery Store, I provide a possible view of what that really looked like. (See the next page.) As you will see, I am not the only one with a tricky memory!

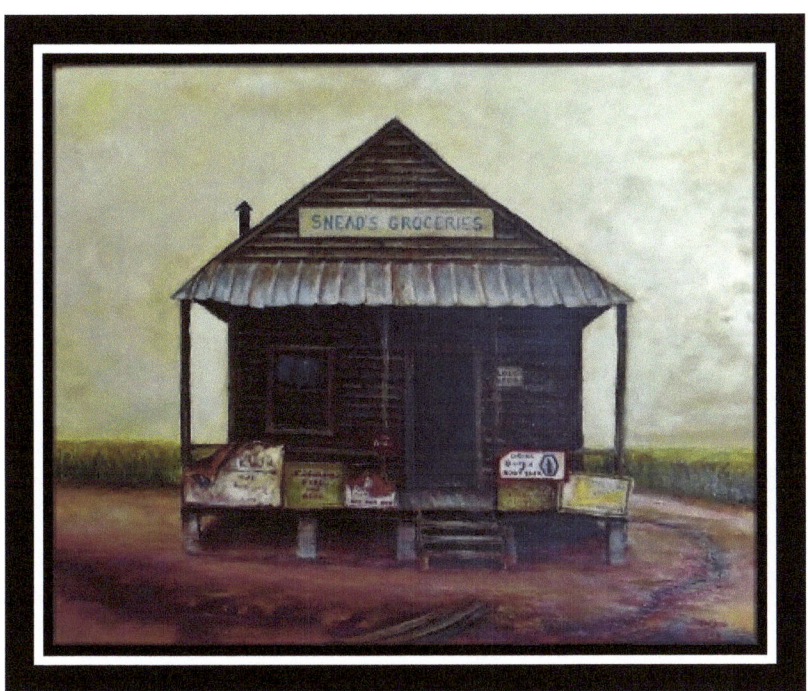

Title Snead's Groceries
Size: 20x24 inches
Medium: Oil on canvas board
Copyright by Dan Wetta 1968

When I used to drive from Virginia to Louisiana, I passed by an old run-down country store that I thought would make a good painting, so using "memory" plus imagination, I did the above painting. Notice that it is called Snead's Groceries. Does that sound familiar? Years later, I thought it was the name of the store where Mississippi's Only Alligator Farm existed!

Since then, friends and family members from North Carolina, Virginia and Louisiana have told me that they remember this store from when they used to live in the country.

But how could they remember something that is at least half imaginary? Did I send a telepathic message of Snead's Groceries into their minds?

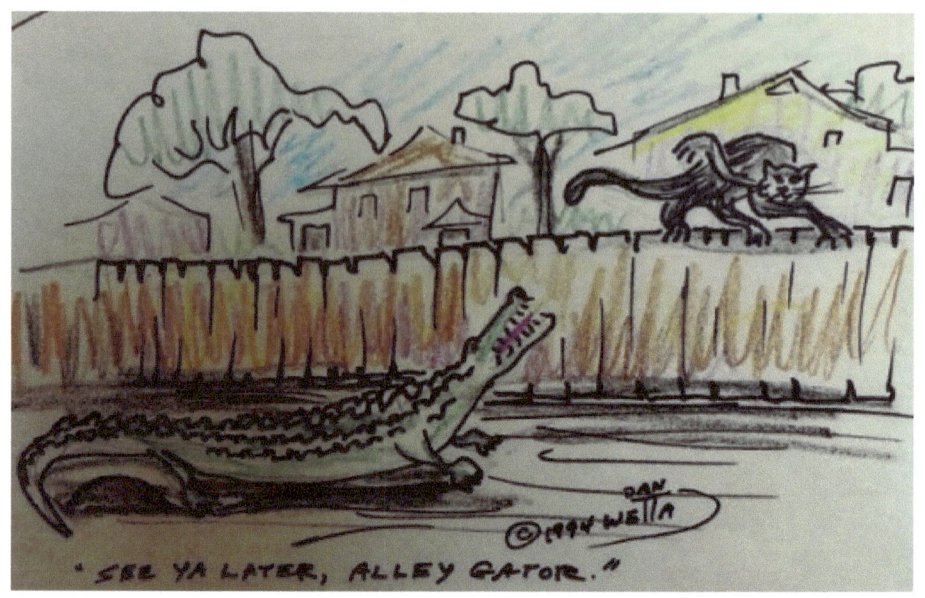

"SEE YA LATER, ALLEY GATOR."

Title: cartoon See 'Ya Later, Gator
Copyright by Dan Wetta, 1994

Goodbye to the memory chapter!

Chapter 3: My Memories and Stories

Beginning with my childhood home on Washington Avenue in New Orleans, Louisiana

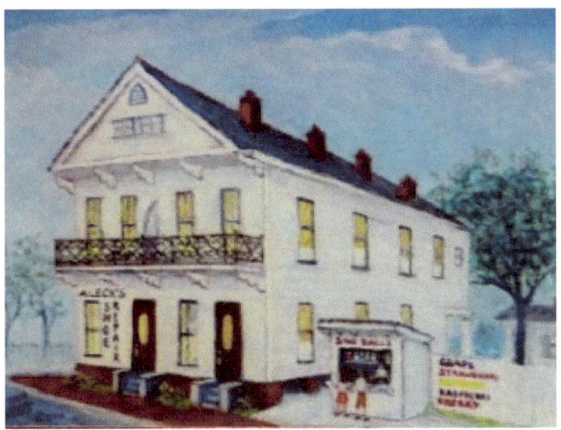

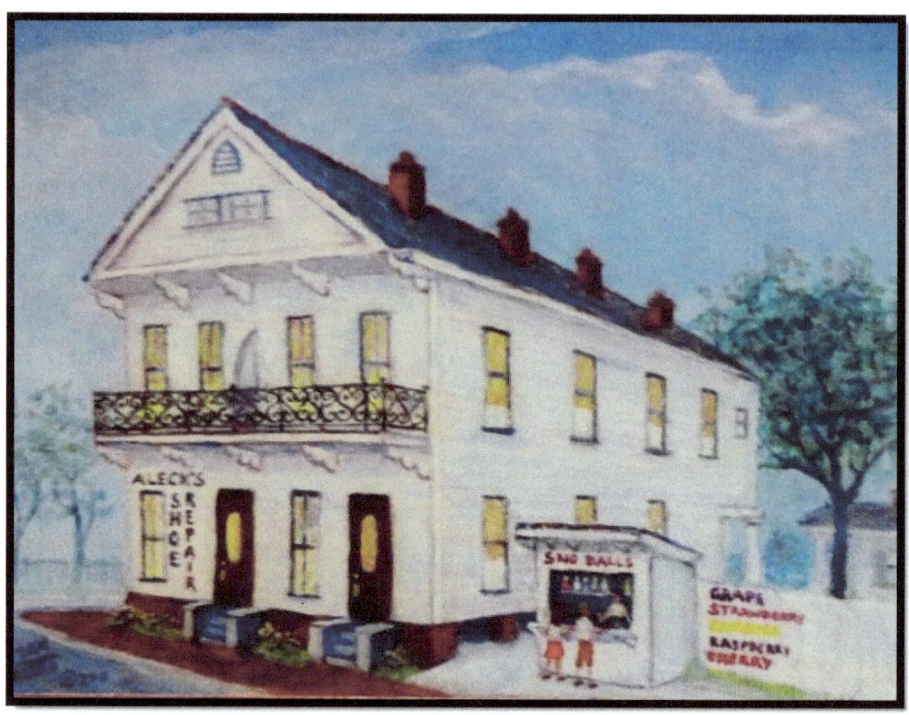

Title: Washington Avenue
Size: 16x20 inches
Medium: Acrylic on canvas
Copyright by Dan Wetta 2006

I painted my childhood house and Snow-Ball Stand from memory. All houses in New Orleans used to have shutters on them, so when I took a second look at the painting, I wondered why I didn't put shutters on the windows. I asked my brother, Raymond, what he remembered.

He laughed and said that our house was probably the only one in New Orleans that didn't have shutters. I guess my memory was pretty good, except for the fact that Raymond said I had painted too many chimneys on the house.

I was ten years old in the summer of 1938 when Uncle Ritchie helped my daddy build that snowball stand for me. Uncle Ritchie was a carpenter, but he had to live with his sister because there was not much work for anybody during the Great Depression of the 1930s.

I had to hand-scrape the ice to make the chips for the snowballs, and my daddy made the different flavored syrups. I worked the stand until the end of summer vacation, when I had to go back to school.

And talking about ice, there was no air-conditioning in those hot summer days. I think there were some primitive electrical refrigerators, but everybody in our neighborhood had an old-fashioned icebox. You had to put a new block of ice in your ice-box every day, because yesterday's always melted away. The ice-man made deliveries daily, and he used to park his truck across the street from our house. What a temptation that was for kids on a hot day in New Orleans! While the ice-man was making deliveries to his customers, my three younger brothers would run over to the truck and swipe a piece of ice.

One time my brother, Raymond, got hit by a car as he ran across the street to the ice truck. His head broke a headlight on the car. They took him to the hospital, and, of course, we were all upset, but he wasn't seriously injured and came home the next day. That's how Raymond got a reputation for being a hard-head.

Those two long windows on the upstairs porch that came all the way down to the floor were very handy on hot summer nights, when it was too hot to sleep in a bed. We kids would grab a pillow and sleep by those windows, where it was just a wee bit cooler.

Our house was on the corner of Annunciation Street and Washington Avenue in the "Irish Channel" of New Orleans. We lived on one side of the house, and a shoemaker and his family lived on the other side. Although we were only a few blocks from the ship-docks along the Mississippi River on Tchopitoulas Street, I had never been aboard any of the banana boats that were always docked there. But one day the shoemaker asked me to deliver a pair of shoes to a merchant sailor on one of those small freighters. Was I ever thrilled! I walked a few blocks down Washington Avenue to the dock, and I climbed a rickety ladder onto the banana boat and delivered the pair of shoes

Several years later, my sister, Anna Marie, married a merchant marine who was an electrician on those little banana boats that sail back and forth from New Orleans to Central and South America. She made him quit the job because he was away from home too often.

SIDE YARD STORY:

Raymond reminded me of the two tough brothers who lived across the street from us. They were good street fighters, and they set up a boxing ring in our side yard for the neighborhood kids. I was a skinny little kid, but they tried to make a boxer out of me. It didn't work out too well. However, I did turn out to become a pretty good distance runner in high school. Raymond says that the older brother from across the street knocked out my friend, Wilmer, but I think it was a kid named Wimpy who got knocked out.

Our side yard was great for kids. One time, Wilmer and I built a clubhouse there. I wouldn't let my three younger brothers join our club. They got mad and began throwing brick-bats at us in the club house. When it began to fall apart from the bombardment, they let Wilmer escape because he wanted to let them join our club. The bombardment began anew, and the clubhouse fell apart, leaving me holding a piece of sheet metal in front of me for protection. I surrendered, and that was the end of my club.

Wilmer and I needed something to keep us busy and cool in the summer, so we used to walk over to the Garden District where there were mansions shaded by Live Oak trees, and we would ring a door bell, and then we would run and hide behind a bush. A maid would open the door and look around puzzled because nobody was there. We got a kick out of that.

ANOTHER SIDE YARD STORY: I had fabricated a small airplane out of balsam wood and tissue paper. A rubber band ran from the tail end to the propeller. When the propeller was wound and released, it would spin as the rubber band would unwind. I set fire to the airplane and sailed it out of a second story window. It flew across the side yard and crashed into our coal shed. Mom happened to look out a downstairs window and was horrified to see it land in the coal shed, which was only a few feet away from a neighbor's house. She got all excited and ran to the shed with a broom and swatted out the fire. Then she came running upstairs and wanted to know, "What were you thinking? You almost set the neighbor's house on fire!" I got bawled out good for that episode.

AND ANOTHER: One evening, my sisters, Joan and Anna Marie, went to a movie at the Garden Theatre on Magazine Street. After the movie, prizes were raffled for the movie-goers. Anna Marie came home with a baby pig she had won! She penned it up in our side yard. During the night, Daddy woke up when he heard the piglet squealing. Somebody was stealing it! Daddy chased the thief for fourteen blocks, but had to quit when he ran out of breath. The next morning, he bawled out Anna Marie for choosing the piglet instead of an option to receive money.

The girls in my family lived in a separate milieu from the boys. Anna Marie said that they used to spy on two teen-age girls who lived next door and were dating. She says the girls used to play the song, "Roll out the Barrels" on a Victrola record player a lot. Prohibition was from 1920 thru 1933, so the song was about beer barrels: "Roll out the barrels, and we'll have a barrel of fun!"

Anna Marie also reminded me about a mentally ill boy who used to steal. One time, he stole shoes from Wilmer's uncle and tried to sell them to mama.

We used to raise Pullets in the side yard. These were small, egg-laying chickens that became pets to us. One day, Daddy decided that we would have a couple of them for Sunday dinner. He wrung their necks, de-feathered them in hot water and cooked them. None of us kids could eat them. Those chickens were our pets!

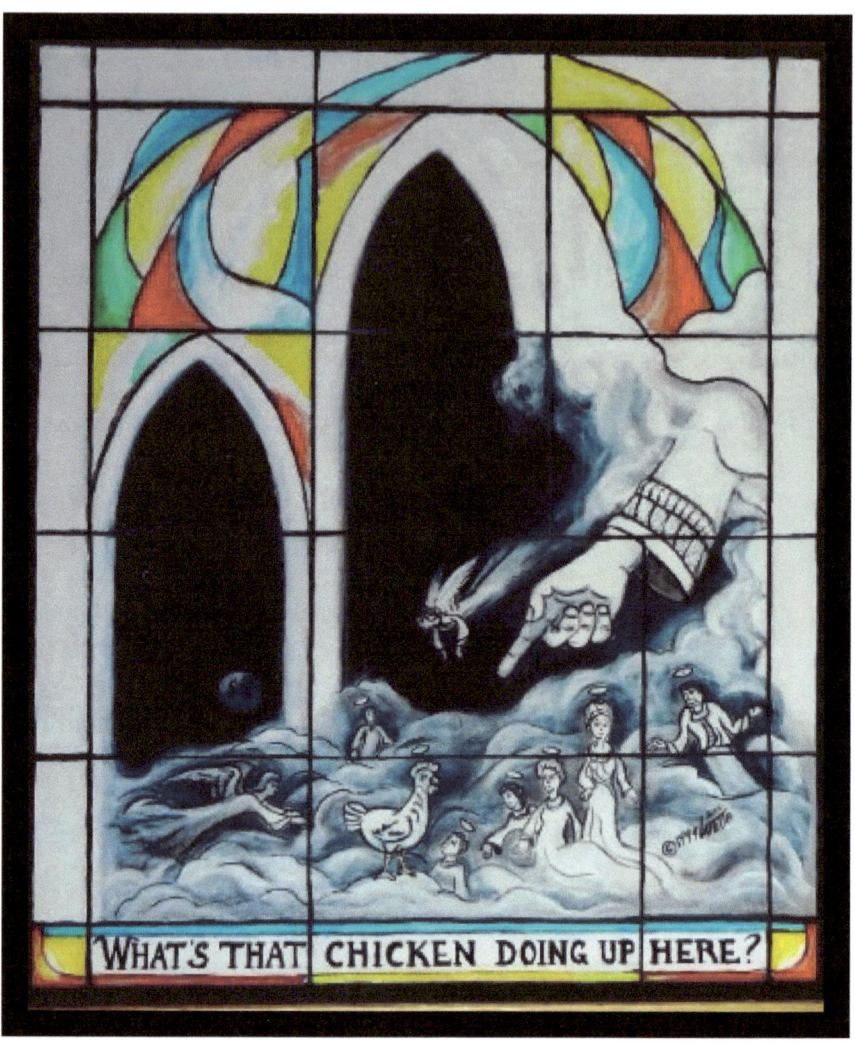

WHAT'S THAT CHICKEN DOING UP HERE?

That side yard was a big part of our lives. We even had a mirliton vine growing on the fence. It produced a squash-like fruit, and, of course, mama used to cook them every once in a while. Delicious! But don't ask me how to pronounce "mirliton." We used to call them "melatones." We mispronounce a lot of words in Louisiana.

Finally, I think the reason this house was such an important part of my life is because I was thirteen in June, 1941, when my mom sent me to St. Joseph's Seminary. So that house was my last childhood home. Six months later, the Japanese attacked Pearl Harbor. When I returned for summer vacation in 1942, things had changed. The family had moved to a house on St. Andrew Street. On top of that, it seemed that the U.S. was going to lose the war to Germany and Japan during that summer.

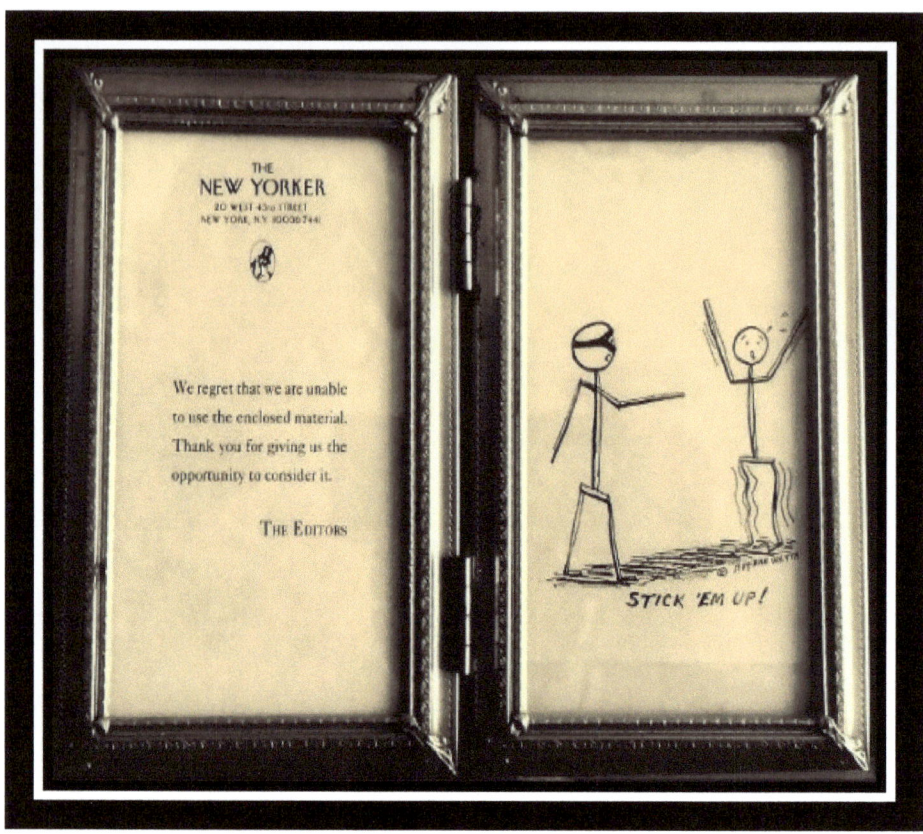

Title: Cartoon Award!

Now you can't say that I didn't warn you about my cartoons! In this double framed holder, there is the rejection notice from The New Yorker Magazine saying that my stick-man cartoon, depicting a stick-man robbery, had been rejected.

This cartoon notice has been posted in all my books.

Warning: A cartoon follows!

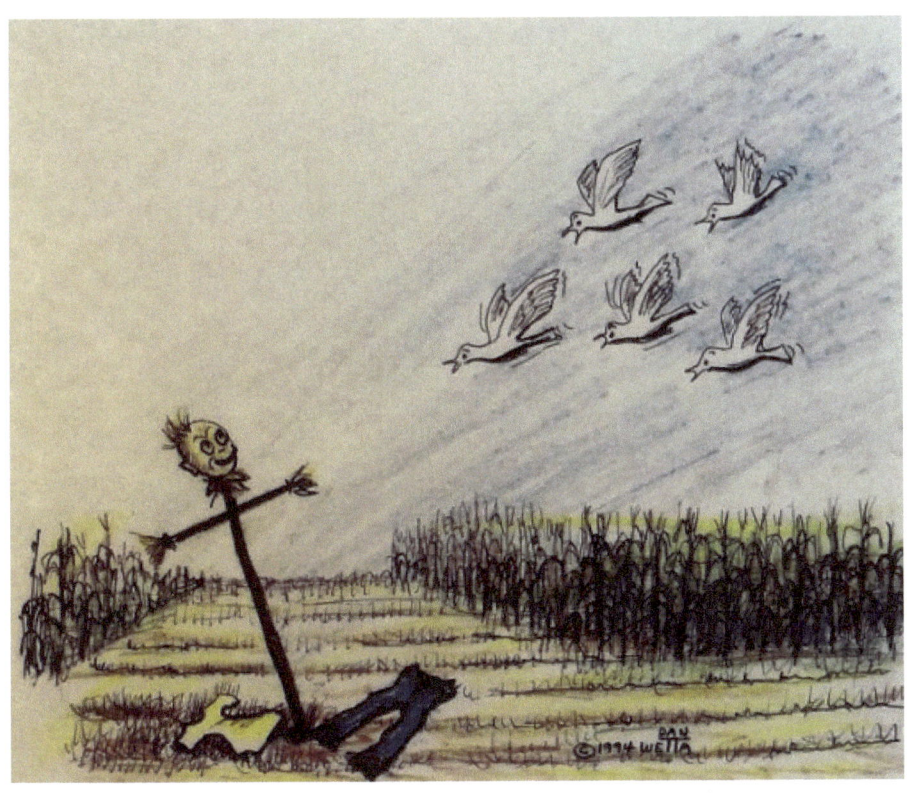

Title: Flashing Scare Crow (cartoon)
Copyright by Dan Wetta 1994

No big deal! Suppose you were a scare crow in a corn field? After two or three months, you would get bored and do the same thing!

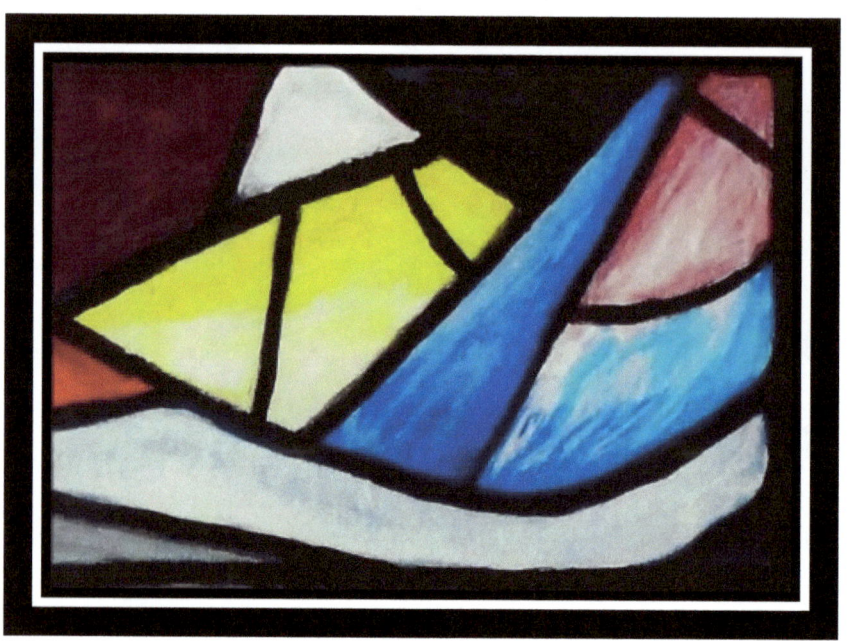

Title: Abstract Seventeen, Daniel in the Lion's Den
Copyright by Dan Wetta 1998

A detail from my painting, "Daniel in the Lion's Den."

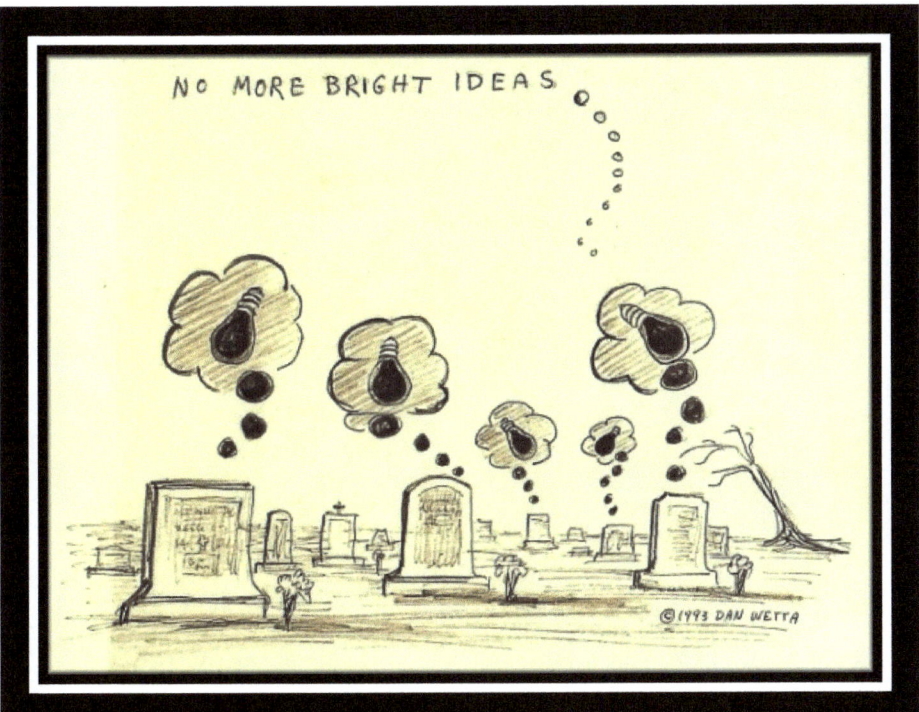

Title: No More Bright Ideas (cartoon)
Copyright by Dan Wetta

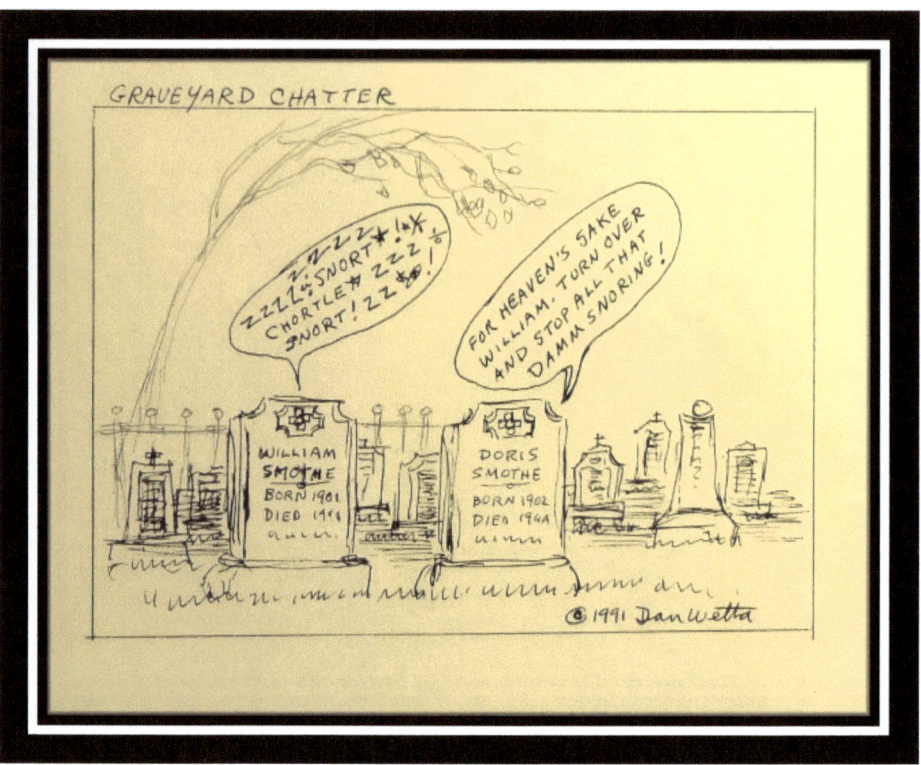

Title: Snoring (cartoon)
Copyright by Dan Wetta, 1991

In the snoring cartoon, Doris tells her husband from the grave, "For heaven's sake, William! Turn over and stop all that damn snoring!"

But what else can you do when you're six feet under...for eternity?

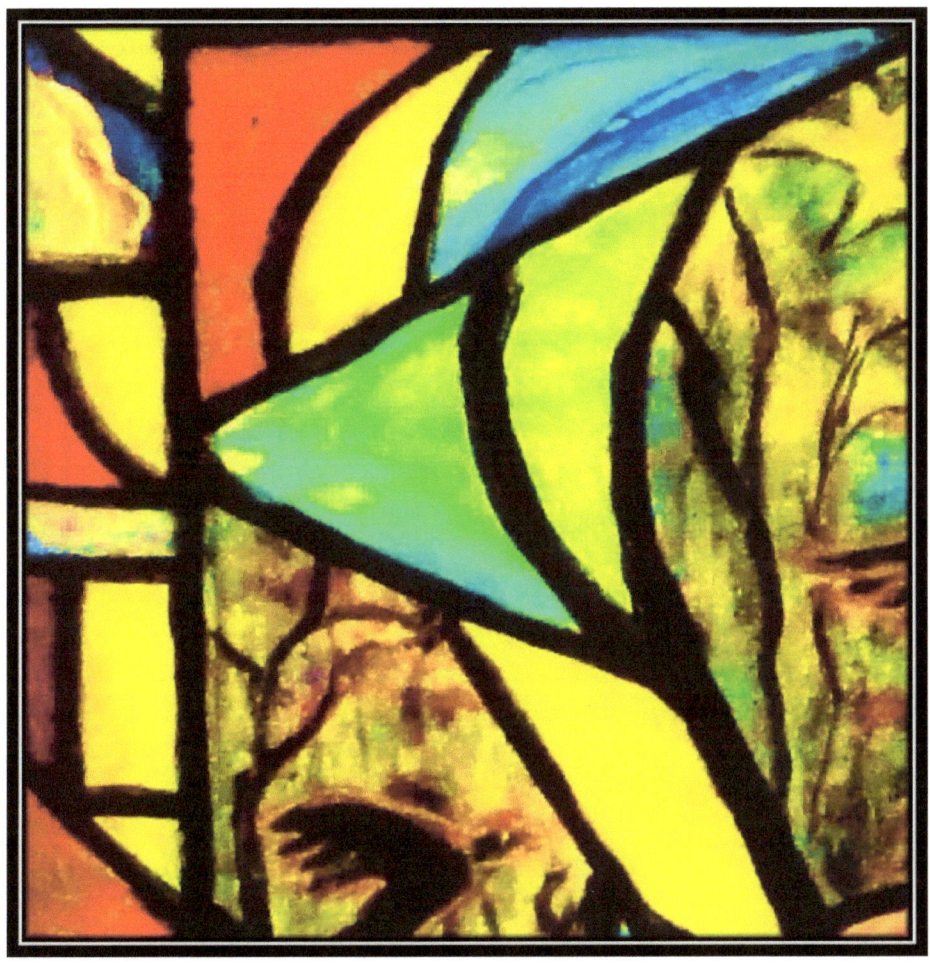

Title: Abstract Eleven, Stained Glass Birds
Copyright by Dan Wetta, 2001

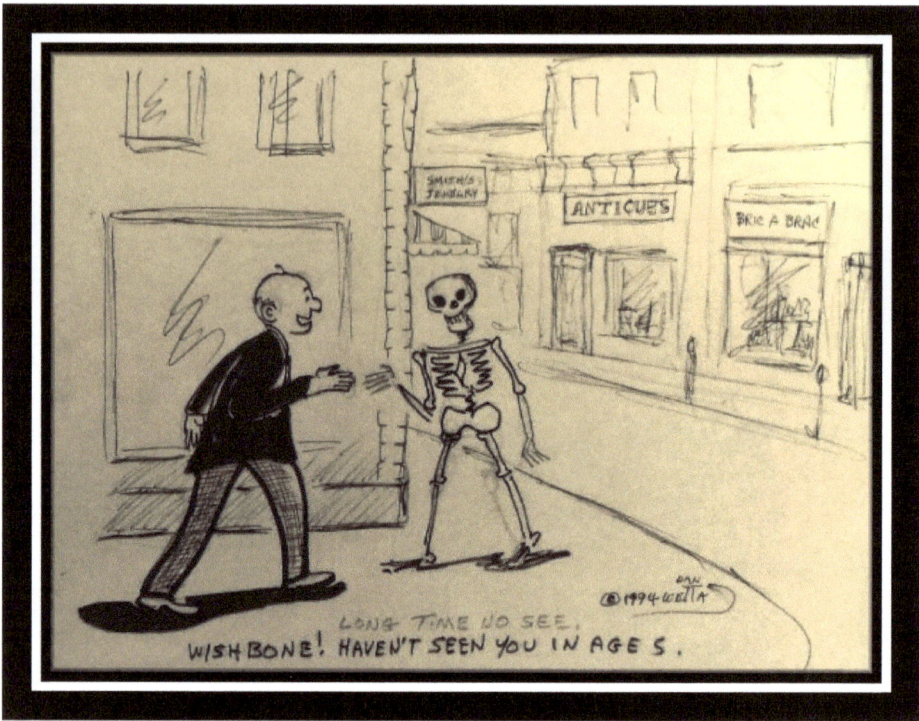

Title: Wish Bone (cartoon)
Copyright by Dan Wetta, 1994

Long time, no see: "Wish Bone! I haven't seen you in ages!"

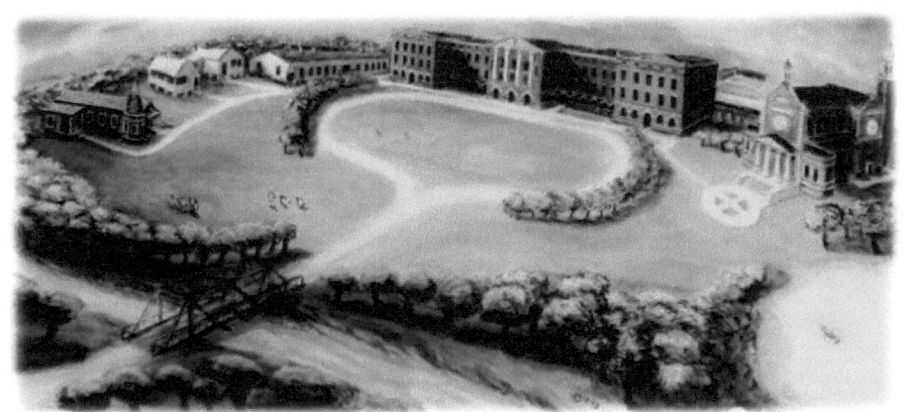

Title: St. Joseph's Seminary
Size: 18x36 inches
Medium: Acrylic on canvas
Copyright by Dan Wetta 1993

    I painted St. Joseph's Seminary in shades of gray to represent time gone by, never to return.

    I was thirteen years old in the summer of 1941, and I was living at our house on Washington Avenue when my mom and Aunt Mae decided that I should become a priest. Aunt Mae's son, Blaise, was already at the seminary. Blaise later became a secular priest in New Orleans. His parishioners were always inviting him to dinner, so he gained weight - too much weight. He died of a heart attack at age 58.

    I didn't really want to be a priest, but in those days, you obeyed your parents. So I said, "If I am going to be a priest, I want to be a Benedictine Monk and teach at the seminary. I filled out the application at the last minute. Then I chickened out and didn't put it in our mail box for the mail man to pick up. Mama came upstairs and asked me if I had mailed the application. I admitted that I had not. She grabbed the application and chased down the mailman. That's how I got into the seminary.

    I was thirteen years old when I entered the seminary, and a couple months later, on December 7th, 1941, I was playing touch football with my classmates, when a student leaned out a window and started ringing a hand bell. That was our signal that recreation was over.

I thought that he was making a mistake because it was too early, but he shouted out to us, "The Japanese just attacked Pearl Harbor!" About that time, I saw two cars speeding away, full of service men who had been visiting their brothers at the seminary. They had to get back to their base immediately.

That river in my painting is the Bogue Falaya River. It is shallow most of the time, just a trickle of water maybe one or two feet deep, but when it rains upstream, it becomes a twelve foot torrent of raging water.

One time, several of us took a heavy wooden skiff from our lake and carried it through the woods to a swollen Bogue Falaya River. The river carried us downstream to a sandy beach where we had a picnic lunch. On the way there, someone lost an oar, and I jumped into the river to retrieve it. It was a dumb thing to do because I am not much of a swimmer, but I was a teenager. That is not all – when I got safely back into the boat, Lloyd Guichet told me that I had been very close to a water moccasin, which was also being carried downstream by the rushing water.

Another dumb thing I did was to challenge my classmate Ivan Arceneaux to a boxing match. He had been a junior-golden-gloves champion in grade school.

In the first round, I got a bloody nose. In the second round, my lip started bleeding. In the third round, one of my classmates asked Father David, the referee, to stop the fight because of all the blood, but Father David said: "No, that's good for him." At least I managed to go all five rounds!

I'm not going to bore you with all the dumb things I did, but smoking was probably the dumbest. I eventually had to have bypass surgery. Then I quit!

Even though smoking was prohibited at the seminary, I used to sneak smokes all the time. One time I thought of a good hiding place. Our swimming pool had a wall around it, but the gate was never locked. One December day, I went to the swimming pool, closed the gate behind me and lit up. A few seconds later I heard footsteps behind me. I turned around, and there was Father Charles. He had been in one of the lockers along the wall saying his prayers.

My punishment for smoking was that I had to kneel in the mess hall with outstretched arms for a week during breakfast, lunch and supper in front of a table of six monks. Whenever my arms got tired and I began to lower them, Father Bede would smile at me and make a gesture with his arms that said: "Oh, no you don't, lift 'em up!" At least I got to eat with the student waiters after the meals were over.

One day, Father David announced that everybody had to sing at church services, so I sang as loudly as I could. The next day, Father David called me aside and said: "Dan, you don't have to sing if you don't want to." Then they formed a "wooden-ear choir" and put some of us in the back of church and told us to keep quiet.

One more memory: You really do go around in a circle when you're lost in the woods! My boxing partner, Ivan, and I were also on the track team, so one day we decided to take a long run through the woods. I told Ivan that we wouldn't get lost as long as we followed the river. It was about twenty yards off to our left. After we had been running for about thirty minutes, I told Ivan that I was going to make sure we were still following the river. I went looking for it, but it was not to be found. We ran another mile or so, came to a cow pasture, and paused to get our bearings. I had no idea where we were, when Ivan said: "I think I've been here before." We ran another mile or so and came upon the cemetery, which was about a quarter mile behind the Seminary. We had gone around in a circle.

When I was eighteen years old, it was time for me to go into the monastery, where I would live in a tiny room for the rest of my life, but I said "Oh no!" - I joined the Army instead!

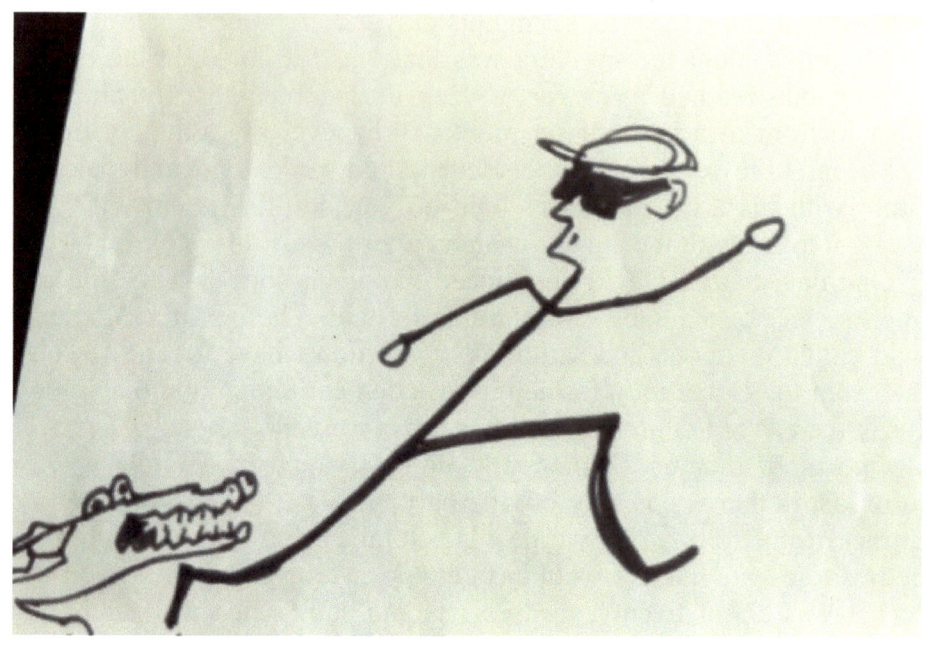

Time to make a break for it! Goodbye, seminary! Hello, world! See 'ya later, alligator!

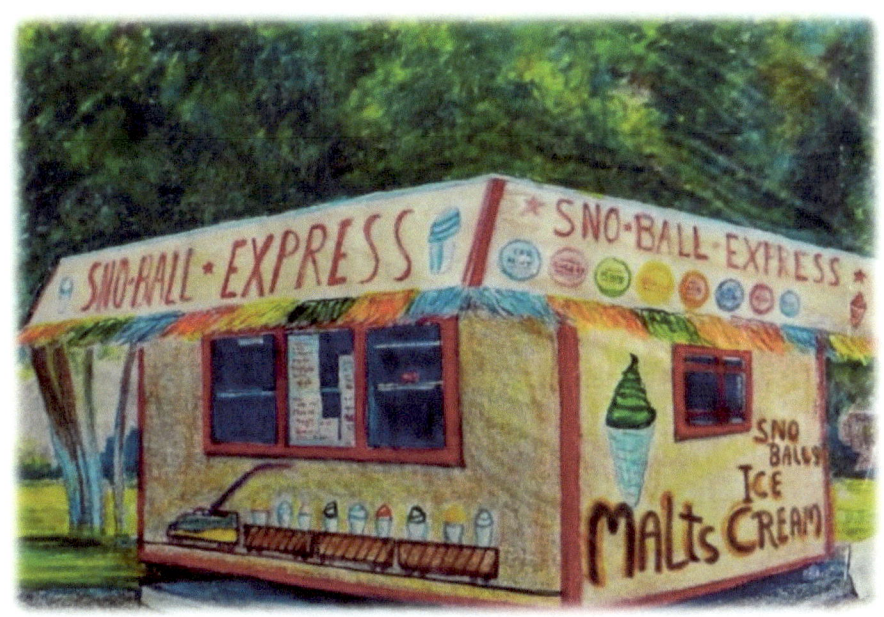

Sno-Ball Express
Size: 11x14 inches
Medium: Mixed media on paper
Copyright by Dan Wetta 1986

It rarely snows in New Orleans, but they know what a sno-ball stand should look like. This one is much more decorative and elaborative than the one I had when I was a kid. But who knows? Maybe in the 1930s I was ahead of my time! In the New Orleans heat and humidity, the sno-balls were an in-demand item.

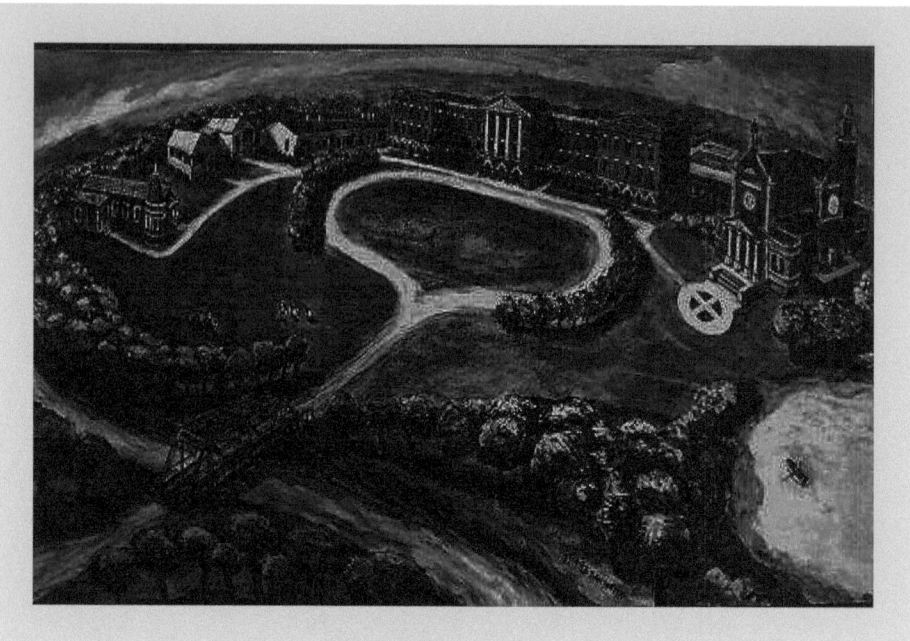

Title: St. Joseph's Seminary at Night

This is a computer enhanced version of my painting of St. Joseph's Seminary. It simulates night. I used to be amazed at the multitude of stars in the sky when I was attending the seminary during World War II, when there was a black-out every night. The black-out eliminated light pollution, which enabled you to see all of the stars.

It reminded me of the days when people had to rely upon the stars to travel across the ocean and even to travel across the desert.

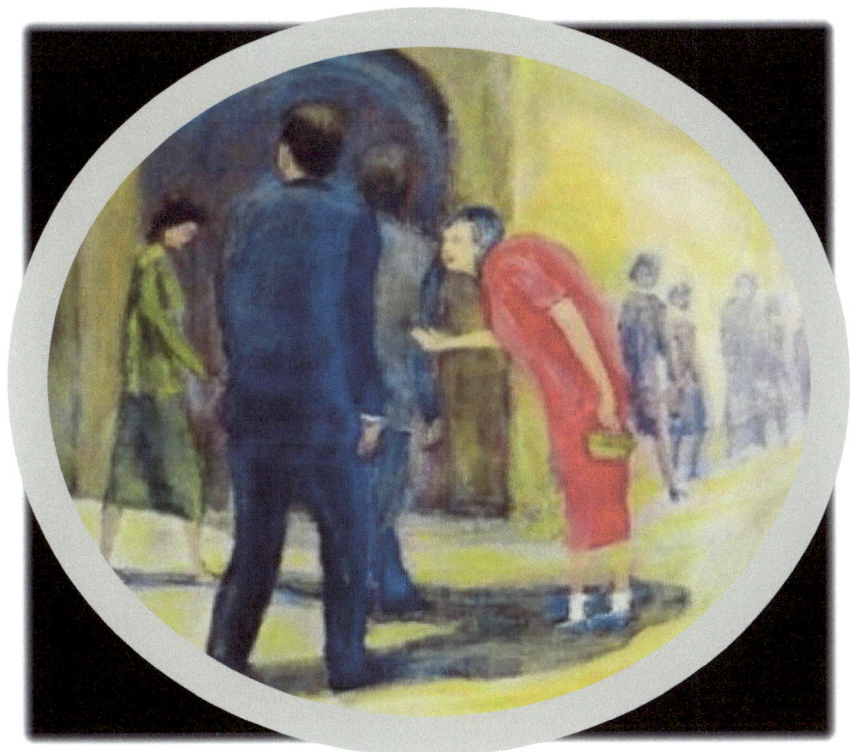

Title: Sally
Size: 12x16 inches
Medium: Acrylic on canvas
Copyright by Dan Wetta

When I used to work in downtown Richmond, Virginia, I would go to lunch at Miller & Rhoads basement cafeteria. M&R was a premier department store in those days, and the basement cafeteria was very popular. On the way there, I would pass several panhandlers, and I would always give a quarter or half-dollar to one woman who was badly hunched over.

I don't know her name, but I called her Sally. Sally was probably homeless, and if she has died by now, I hope she found a comfortable home in heaven.

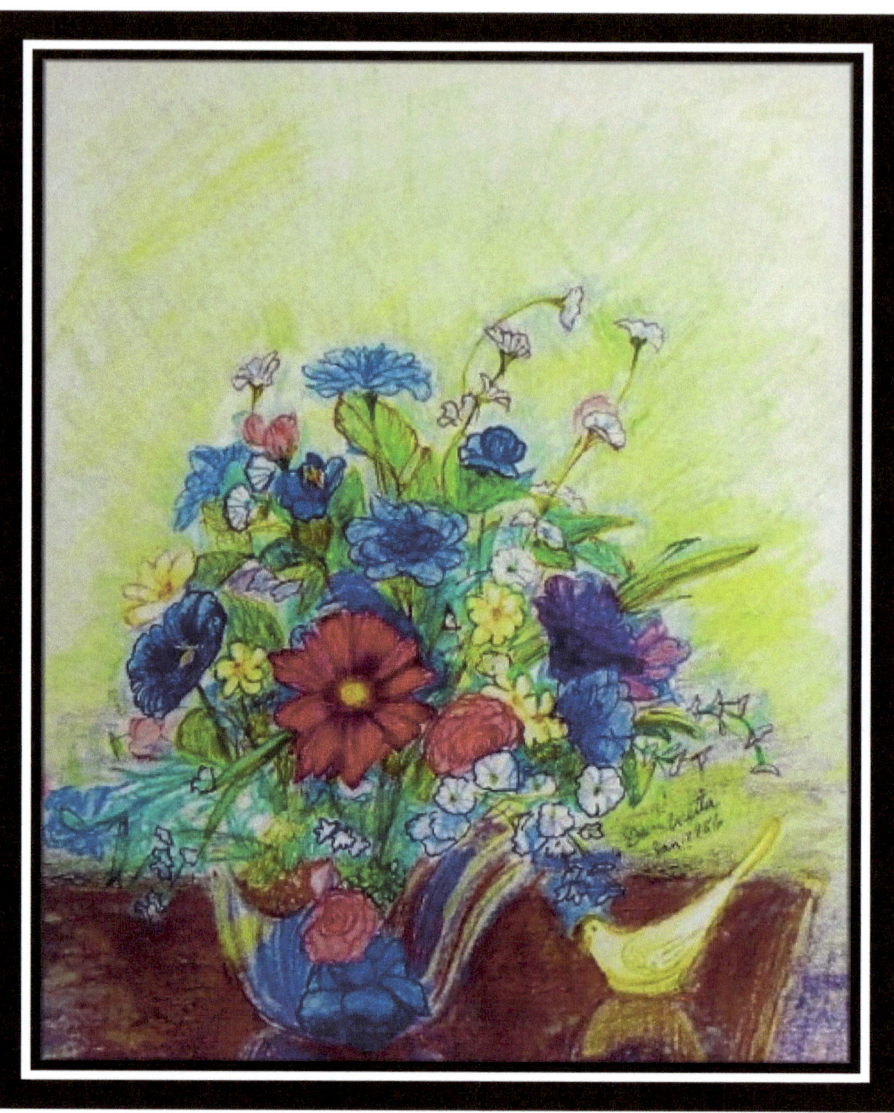

Title: Flowers for Sally (doodle)
Copyright by Dan Wetta, 1986

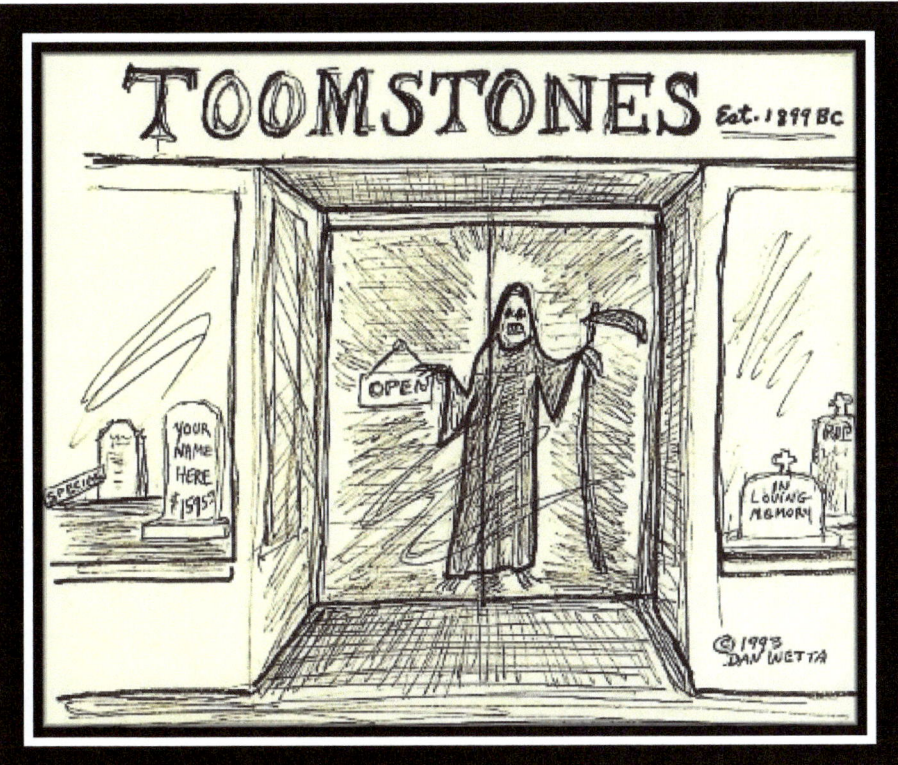

Title: Toomstones (cartoon)
Copyright by Dan Wetta, 1993

Somebody's always trying to make a buck.

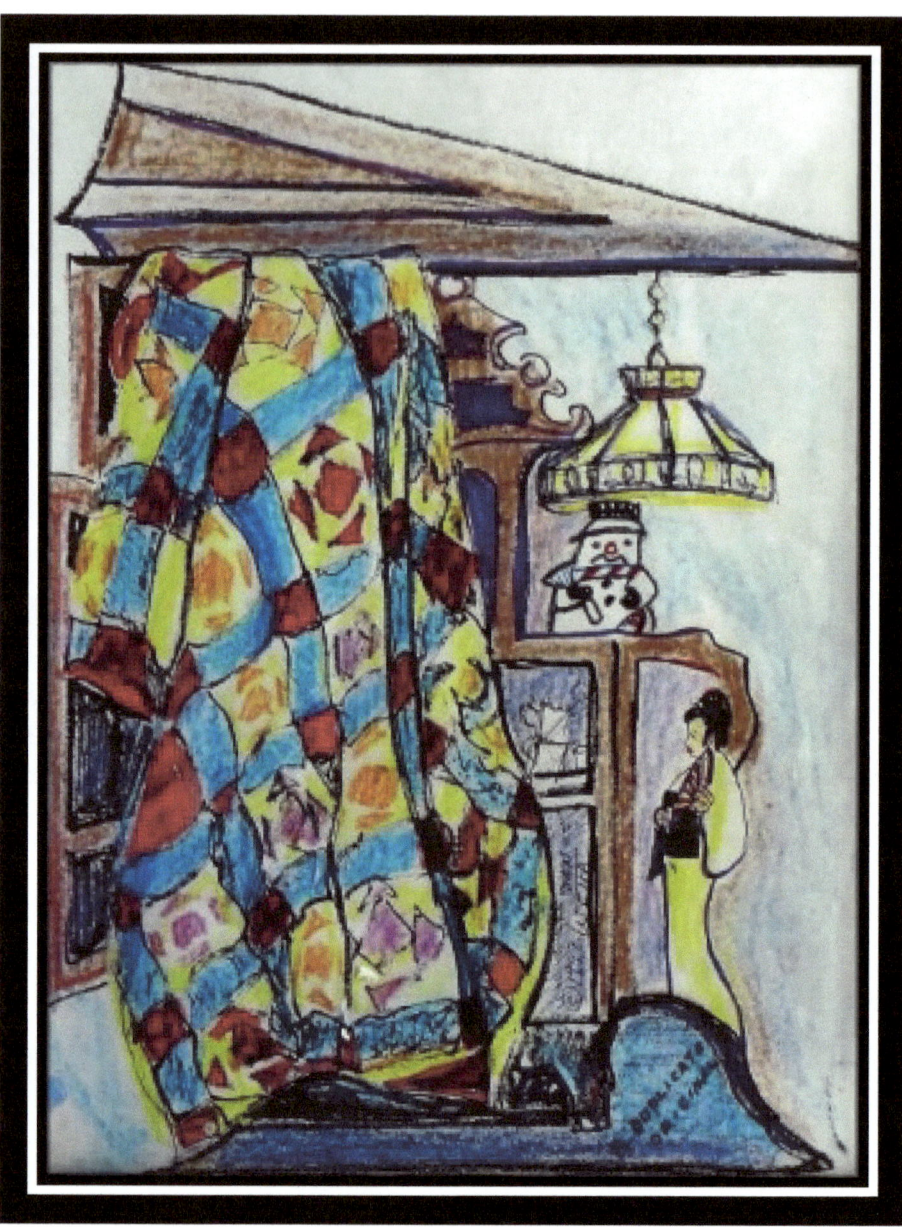

Title: Blanket with Antique Lady (doodle)
Copyright by Dan Wetta, 1997

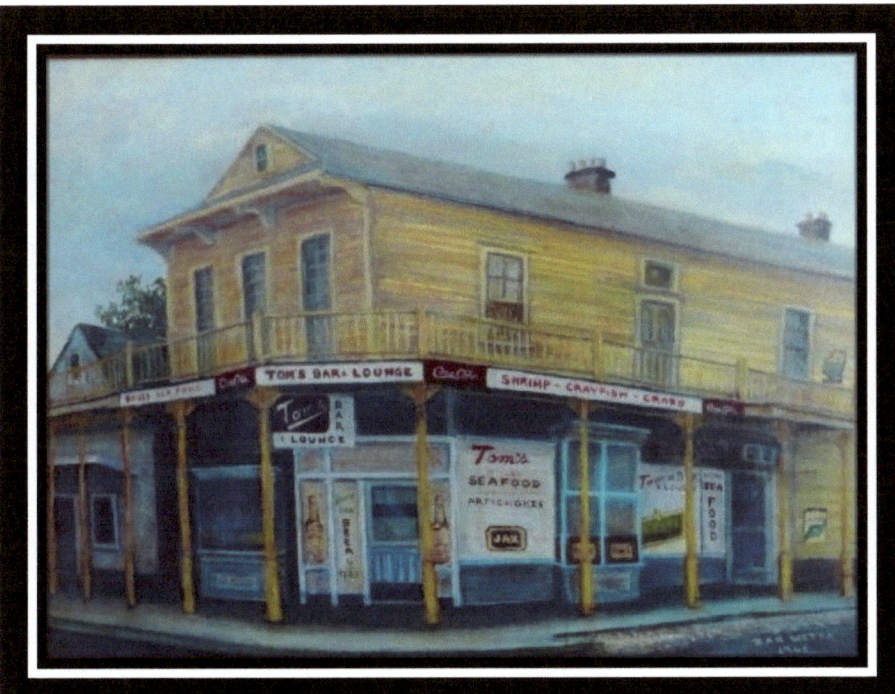

Title: Tom's Bar and Lounge
Size: 18x24 inches
Medium: Oil on canvas board
Copyright by Dan Wetta 1968

Tom's Bar is located at 5538 Magazine Street in New Orleans. The place changes names and owners frequently. It changed to Tyler's Bar in 1968, and in 1985 it was called Sidney's. The president of a neighborhood association said: "A neighborhood bar used to be a quiet cozy place where you could drop in for a drink on your way home. Now they have expanded into regional entertainment centers, packed until 3 and 4 am. The resultant disruption, violence and crime have greatly affected the surrounding areas."

When I was living in our Washington Avenue house during the 1930s, my daddy would hand me two nickels and a pewter pitcher and send me to a bar in the next block, where I would give the pitcher to

Mr. Harry and say: "My daddy wants ten cents worth of beer." Then I would go home with a pitcher full of draught beer. I didn't like beer back then when I was about ten years old, but daddy would pour a little bit into my glass. We would sit at the kitchen table and talk while eating Klotz crackers and cheese. I sure do miss those talks with my daddy.

Later on, in 1995, I was riding along Magazine Street with my brother-in-law, Charlie, and I was surprised to see a crowd of young people outside of Tom's old place. Charlie said it had become a popular hangout for Tulane and Loyola college students.

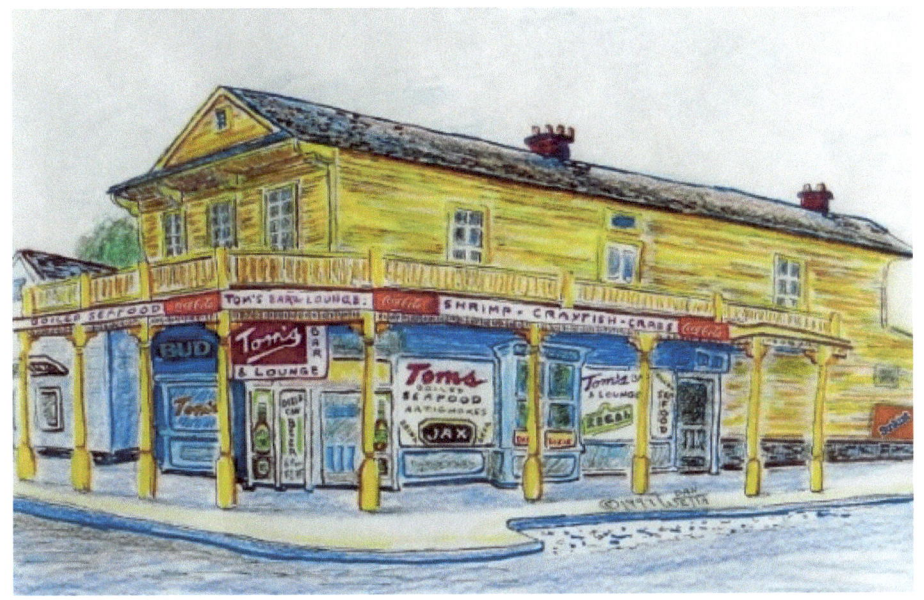

Title: Tom's Bar
Size: 11x14 inches
Medium: Mixed media on paper
Copyright by Dan Wetta 1997

This is just another version of Tom's Bar.

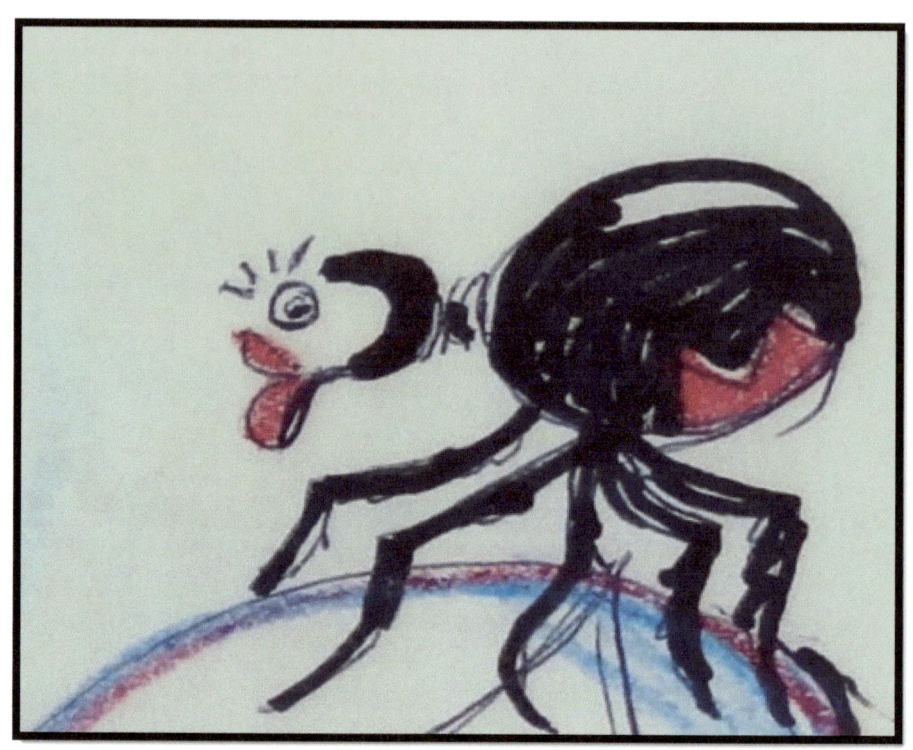

Title: Do You Wanna Kiss? (cartoon)
Copyright by Dan Wetta

How about this for a creepy Valentine card?

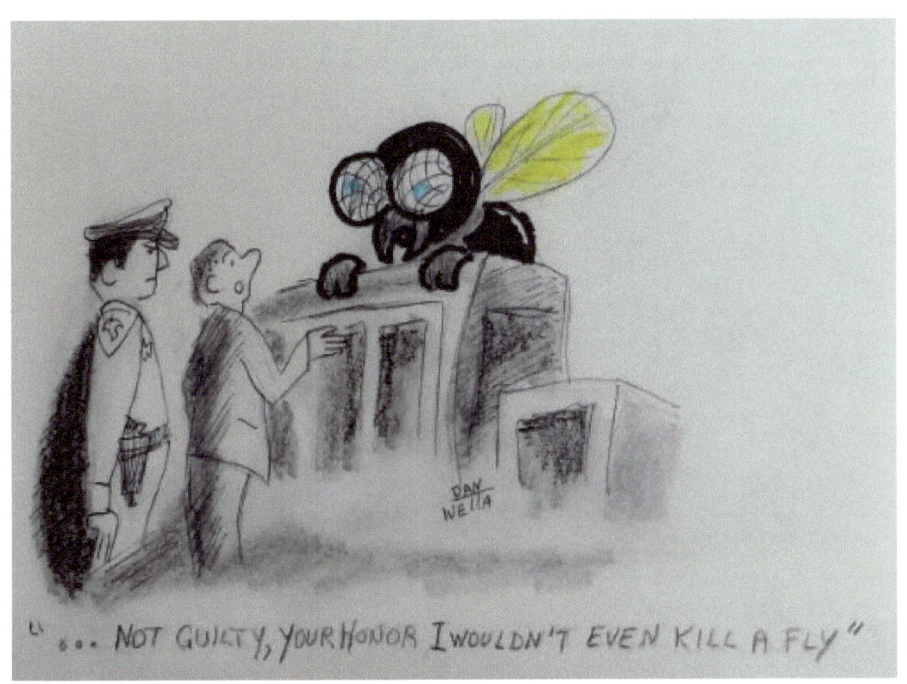

Title: Judge Fly (cartoon)
Copyright by Dan Wetta, 1997

"Not guilty, Your Honor! I wouldn't even kill a fly!"

This is an excerpt from the documentary called, "When Flies Ruled the Earth."

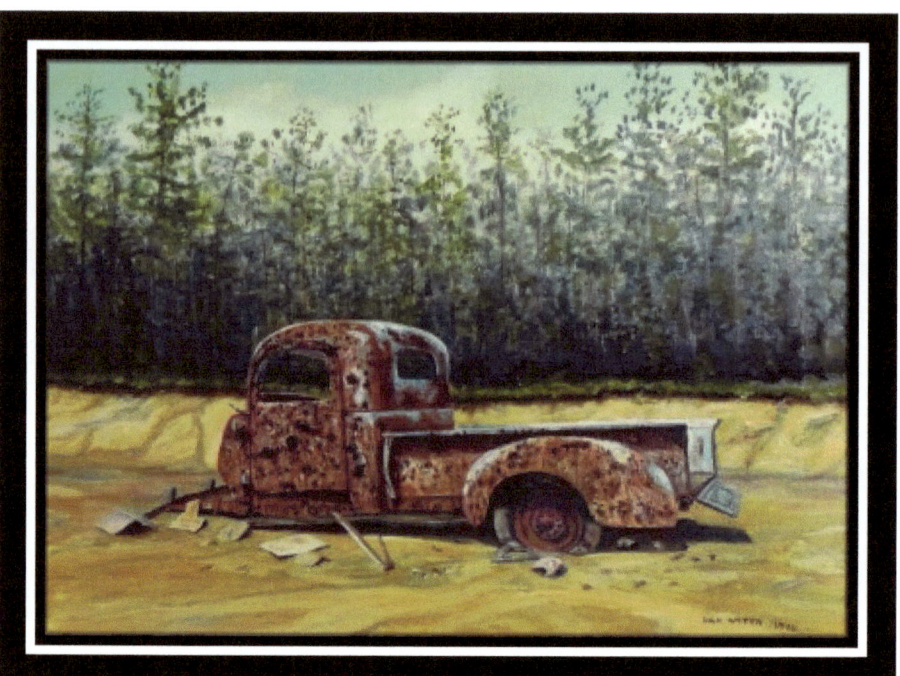

Title: Rusty Truck
Size: 20x24 inches
Medium: Acrylic on canvas
Copyright by Dan Wetta, 1976

I decided to paint this old truck which was full of bullet holes, so I grabbed my camp seat and sketching bag and began drawing. But before I could finish the sketch, a couple of hornets began buzzing around my head. That caused me to realize that the truck was full of hornets.

I moved back a few feet, and the hornets returned to the truck, but not for long. They came back and began buzzing me a second time, so I moved back a few more yards. But this time, several hornets came at me.

I took the hint. They wanted me away from there, so I took a couple snap shots and hurried back to my car. I finished the painting in the safety of my home.

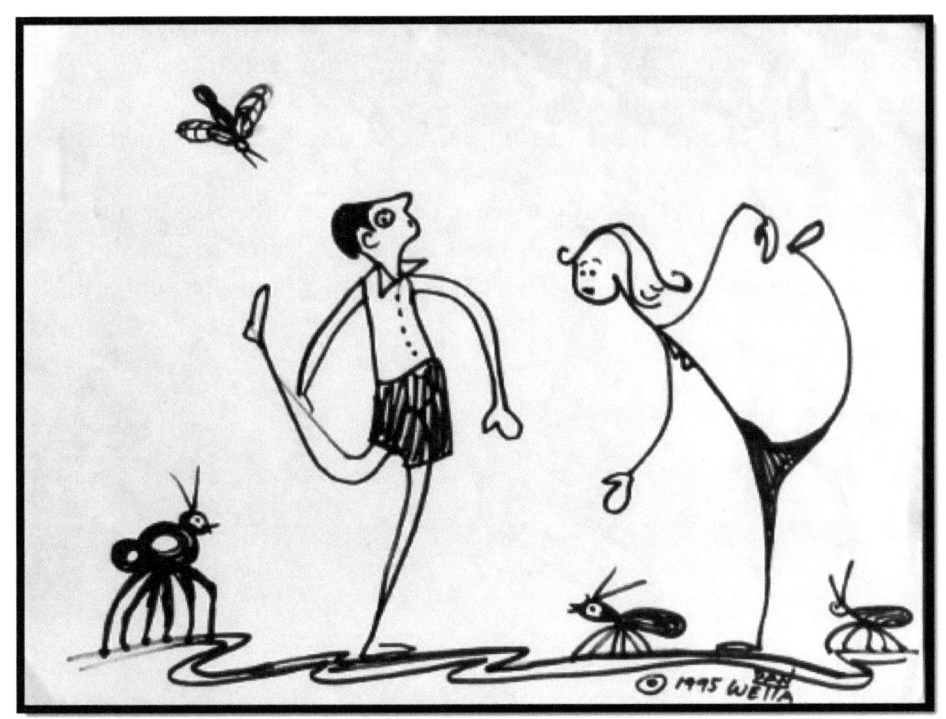

Title: Dancing with Bugs (cartoon)
Copyright by Dan Wetta 1995

That looks like a wasp above the man's head.

I stirred up a hornet's nest one summer when I was cutting the grass. They came out of the ground and began stinging my legs. I instinctively slapped at them until I realized how many were attacking me. I ran into my house and slammed the screen door behind me, but some of them got inside too, so I ran into the bathroom and closed the door. They got in there also. I finished the last ones off by swinging at them with a towel.

I looked out the front door and saw a cone shaped swarm of hornets spinning around their entrance hole above my lawn, so I went out my back door to my neighbor's house, and asked Junie to take me to the emergency room.

On the way there, Junie was telling me about his farmer friend who had been stung by a bee. They found him dead in a field. That story scared the heck out of me, and when we stopped at a traffic signal, I said, "Junie, there are no cars around, let's go thru that red light."

Fortunately I was not allergic to bee stings, so the doctor gave me a shot and told me to go to bed, but I couldn't sleep because the pain from the stings would throb very strong, ease off, and then come back strong –for several hours.

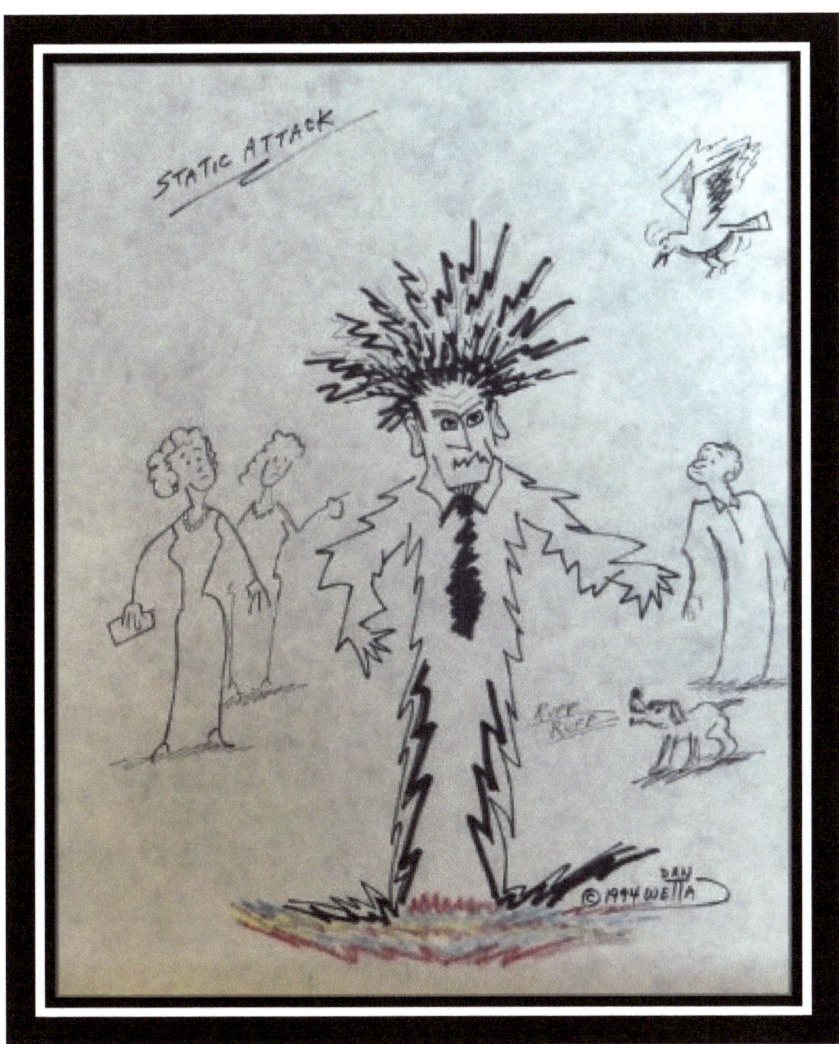

Title: Static Attack (cartoon)
Copyright by Dan Wetta, 1994

When I was about two or three years old, the old houses in New Orleans were not originally wired for electricity, so later they were hastily updated to accommodate electric lights and radios.

In my house there was an electric cord hanging from a ceiling socket over the wall by the sofa, and then down to a nearby radio. I was jumping up and down on the sofa like all toddlers, and I reached up and caught hold of the electric cord.

Electricity started shocking me and I couldn't let go of the cord. My daddy grabbed a long round pillow off the sofa and knocked the wire down from the ceiling socket. He said if he had grabbed me, we both would have been electrocuted.

I get a static attack every time I think about it.

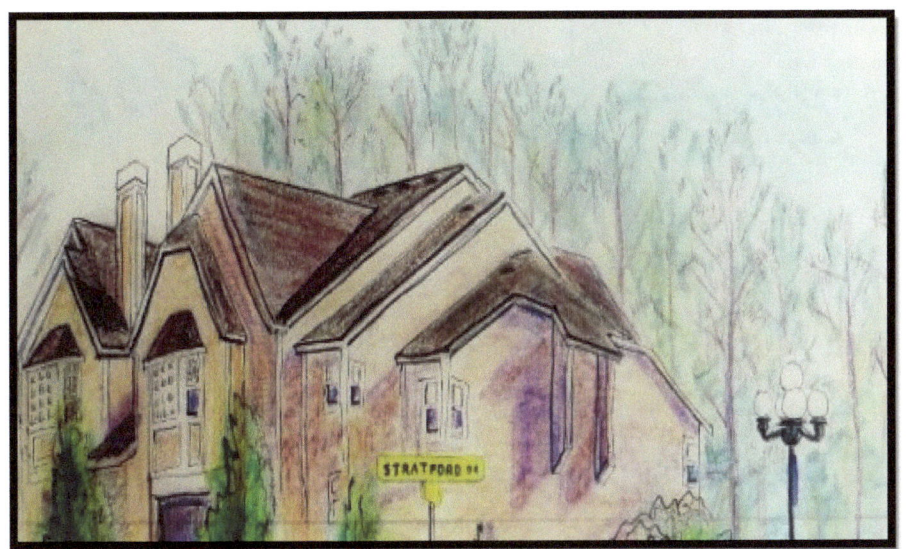

Title: Stratford Drive
Size: 8x20 inches
Copyright by Dan Wetta
Medium: mixed media on paper

Whether you live or die can depend on the name of a street!

That Stratford Drive sign is a few feet away from my condo in York County, Virginia. Unfortunately for my next door neighbor, there is a *Stratford Road* about a mile away from here in James City County, Virginia.

Bud collapsed one day while trying to make a phone call, and he pulled the phone jack out of the wall. His wife came home shortly thereafter and found him on the floor. He mumbled something about being thirsty. Helen could not get the phone hooked back up, so she asked me to call 911.

I emphasized to the operator that we lived in Williamsburg Commons. A few minutes later, we heard the sirens, but the noise faded away, and the ambulance did not come. We waited and waited.

Then the operator called back and said nobody was sick at the address I gave her. I said: "You sent them to Stratford Road! We live on Stratford Drive, near the Golden Corral!" She said: "Oh, that's in York County."

By the time the ambulance got here, Bud was dead.

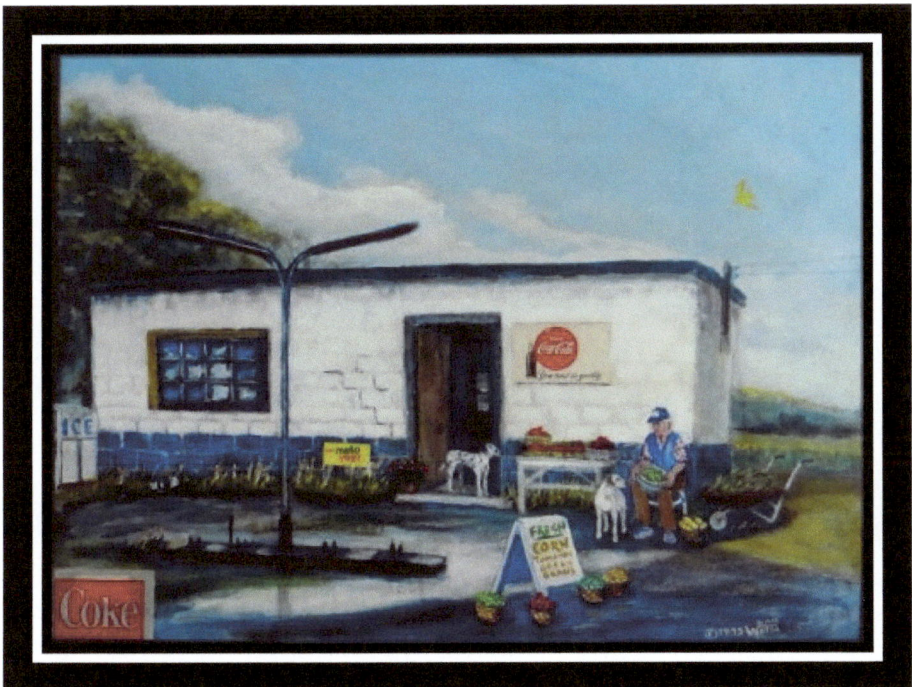

Title: Retirement Villa
Size: 14x18 inches
Medium: Acrylic on artists' Masonite
Copyright by Dan Wetta 1995

I used to ride past this place on my way to work at the Federal Building in Richmond when I was living in Aylett, Virginia.

It looks like the old gentleman grows corn and other vegetables behind the old service station.

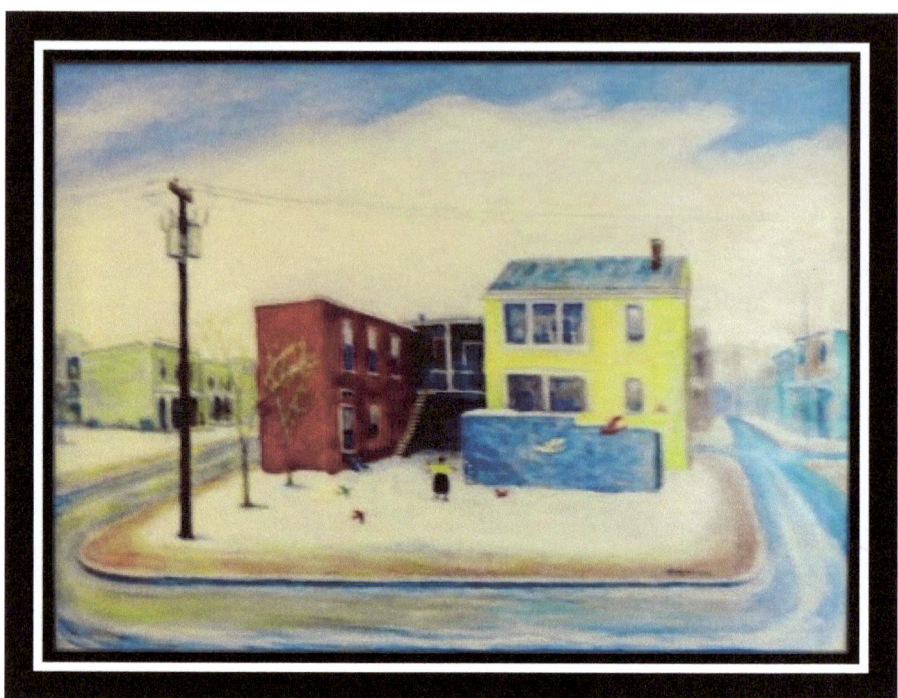

Title: Old Richmond Houses
Size: 30x40 inches
Medium: Acrylic on canvas
Copyright by Dan Wetta, 1993

That elderly lady feeding the birds is probably feeding the birds in heaven now – if birds are allowed in heaven.

I think the side street on the right is East Leigh Street in downtown Richmond, but those old houses have been demolished to make way for office buildings.

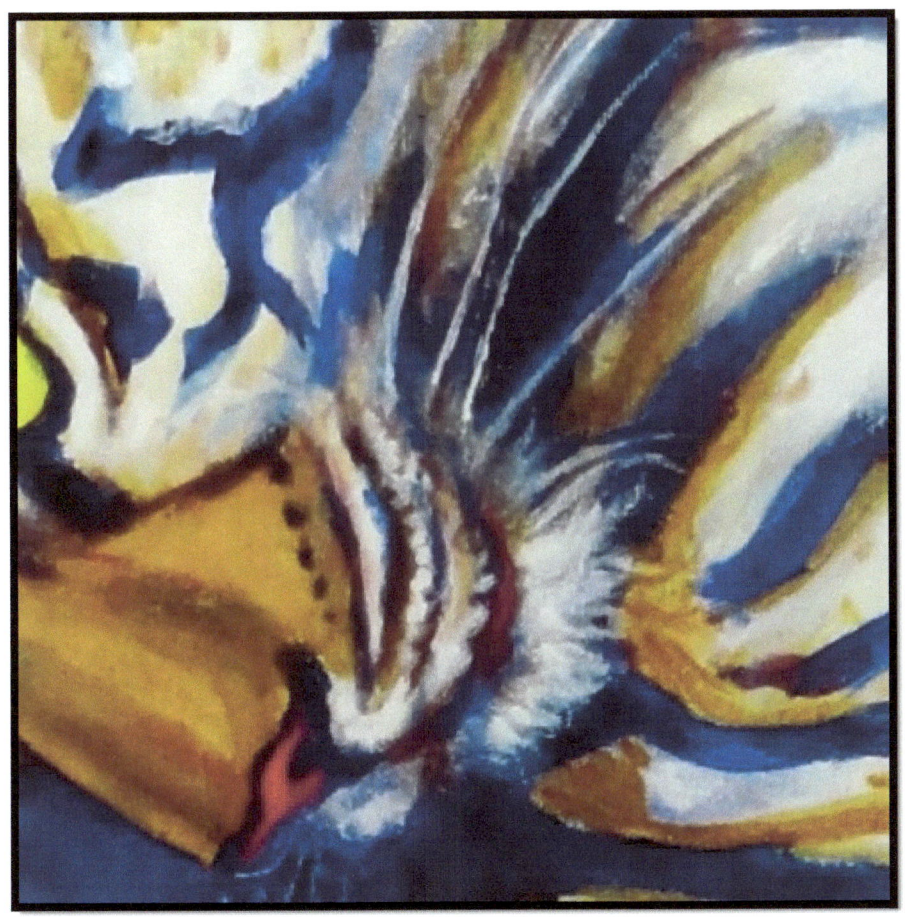

Title: Abstract: Holy T
Copyright by Dan Wetta

A detail from my Holy T painting.

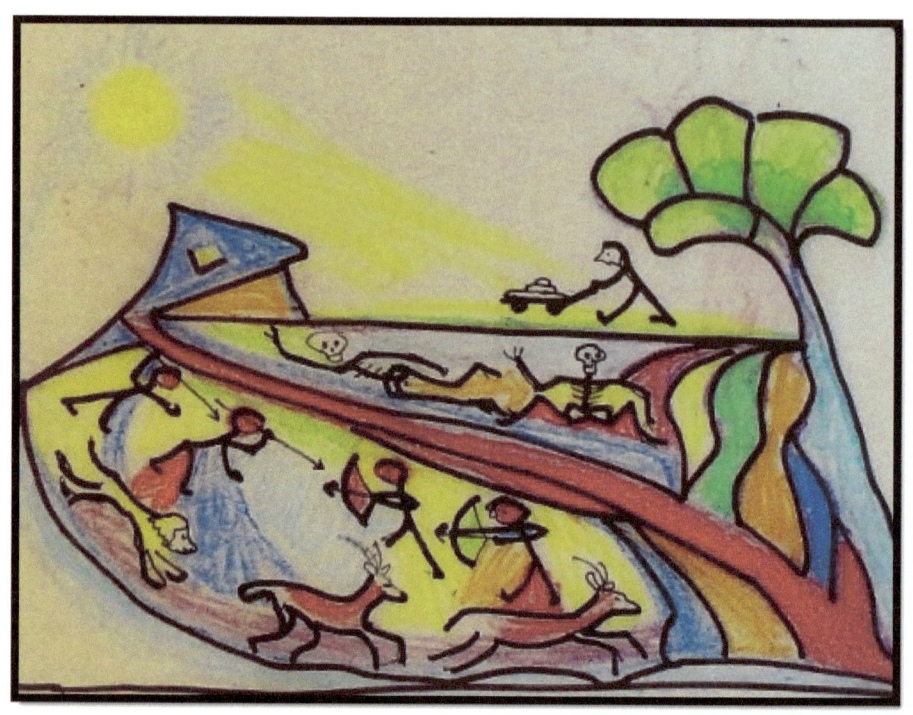

Title: Stained Glass Window (cartoon)
Copyright by Dan Wetta

I did this design for a stained glass window to remind everybody that you never know what might be going on under ground. You remember my experience with the hornets who lived in my yard! This is why I don't like to cut the grass.

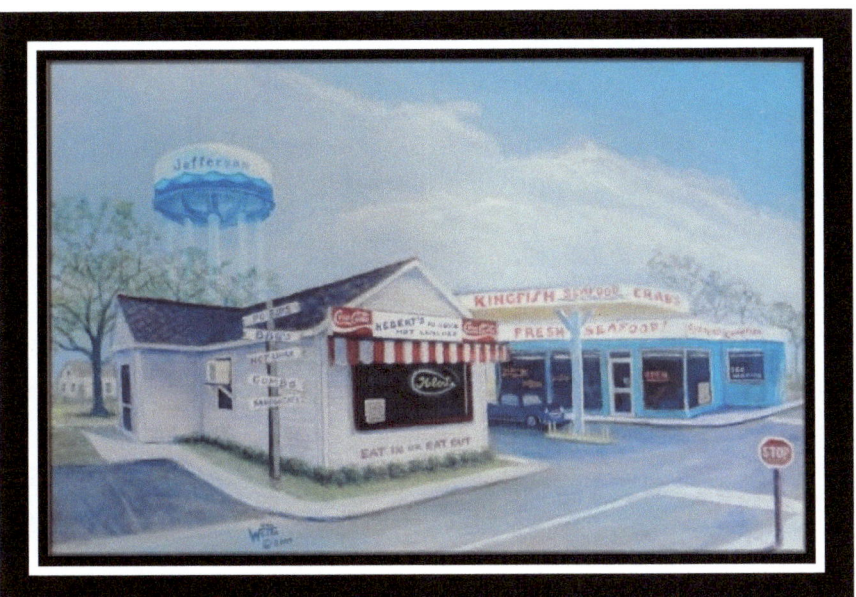

Title: A-Bear's
Size: 24 x 36 inches
Medium: acrylic on canvas
Copyright by Dan Wetta, 2007

Hebert is pronounced "A-bear" in New Orleans and throughout Louisiana.

Hebert's restaurant was in Harahan, Louisiana, where my sister, Anna Marie, lives. Kingfish Seafood was in Slidell, Louisiana, where my brother, Raymond, lives, and Jefferson water tower is in Jefferson Parish, Louisiana, where my sister, Joan, used to live.

When I was at St. Joseph's Seminary, I had three classmates named Hebert: These were Ray Hebert, Whitman Hebert and "Holy Joe" Hebert. They were the smartest guys in our class.

One time, Father Mohr was teaching algebra and got stuck while trying to explain a problem. He called on Ray Hebert to help him with the problem.

I was not very good at algebra, but Ray's explanation was so clear that I thought, "If Ray had been teaching this class, I would be making good grades in algebra."

Ray went on to become a priest in New Orleans.

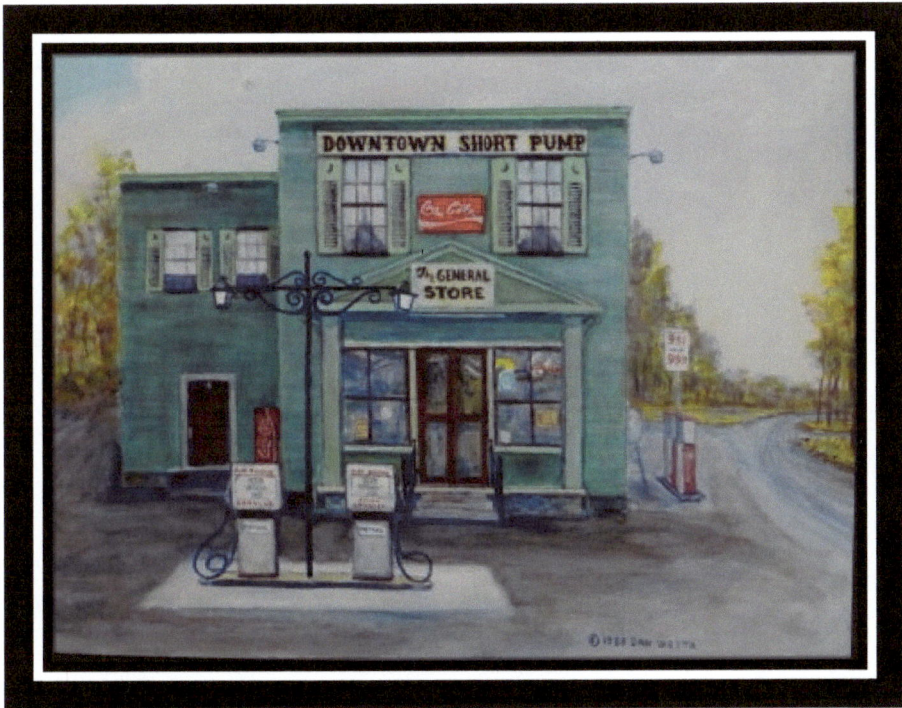

Title: Downtown Short Pump
Size: 16"x20"
Medium: Acrylic on canvas
Copyright by Dan Wetta, 1988

A few years before I did this painting, my next door neighbor said, "Let's go see the fire on West Broad Street." Firemen were planning to stop a forest fire on West Broad Street, about two hundred yards past this store.

As the fire approached, firemen with backpacks were in the woods spraying bushes at the base of pine trees.

As the fire got close to West Broad Street, I couldn't believe my eyes when a burning bush at the base of a pine tree caused the top of the tree to burst into flames like a match stick. But the firemen did their job well. They stopped the fire at West Broad Street.

A few years later, I was near the gas pumps doing a preliminary sketch of Downtown Short Pump when a dump truck almost ran over me. I decided to finish the painting in the safety of my home, so I took a few quick snapshots and got away from there.

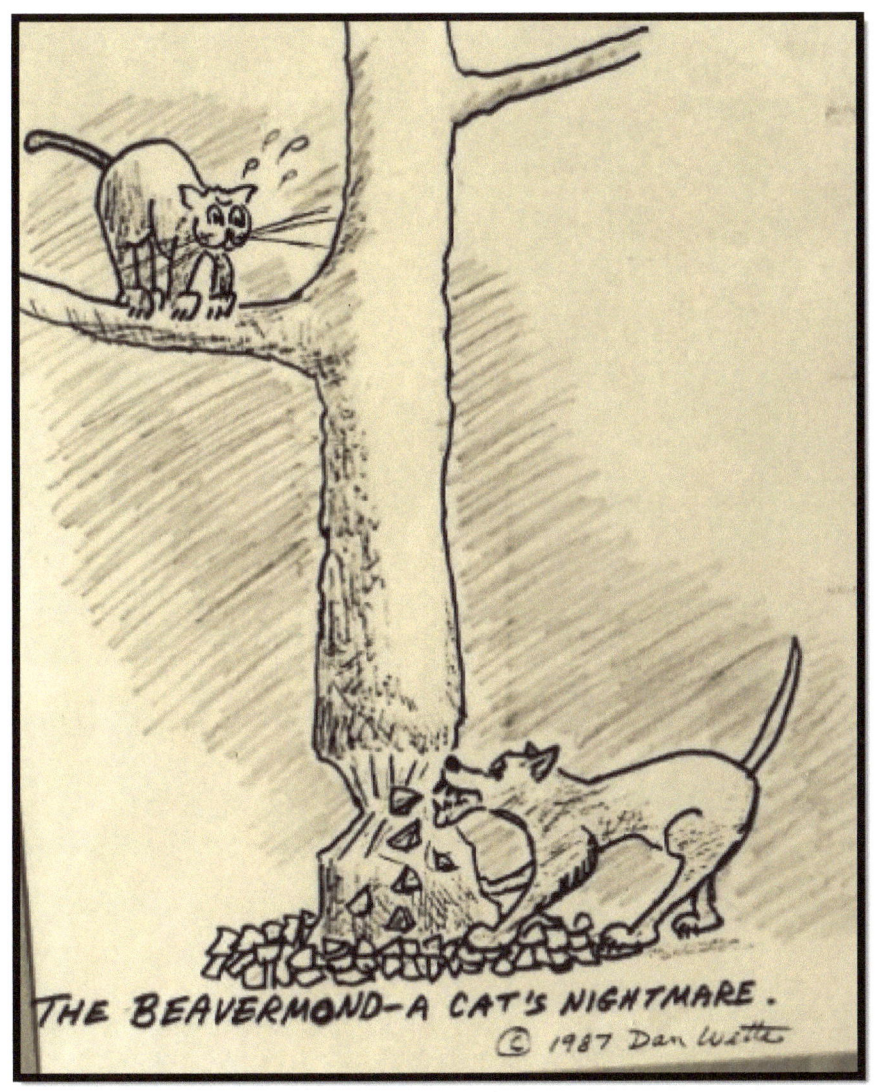

THE BEAVERMOND—A CAT'S NIGHTMARE.

© 1987 Dan Wetta

Title: Beavermond (cartoon)
Copyright by Dan Wetta, 1987

There is no such thing as a Beavermond, so don't worry about the cat up the tree.

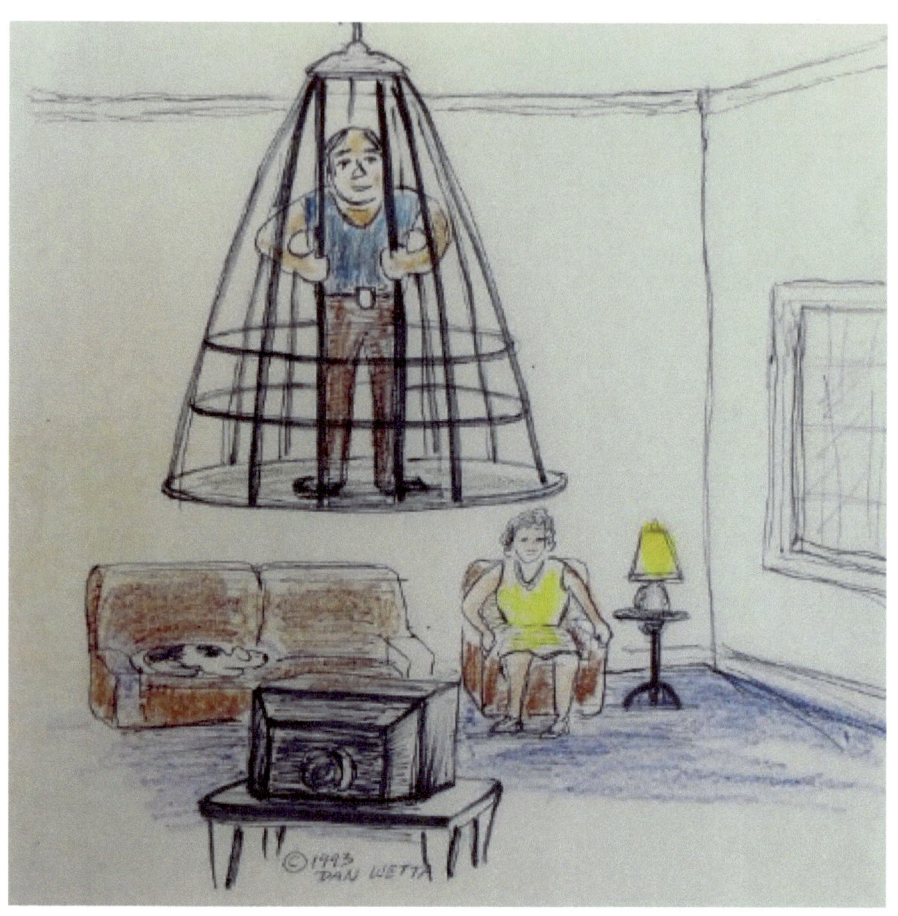

Title: Man in Cage (cartoon)
Copyright by Dan Wetta

Is it OK to put a man in a cage? Ask that lady in the yellow dress
what she thinks.

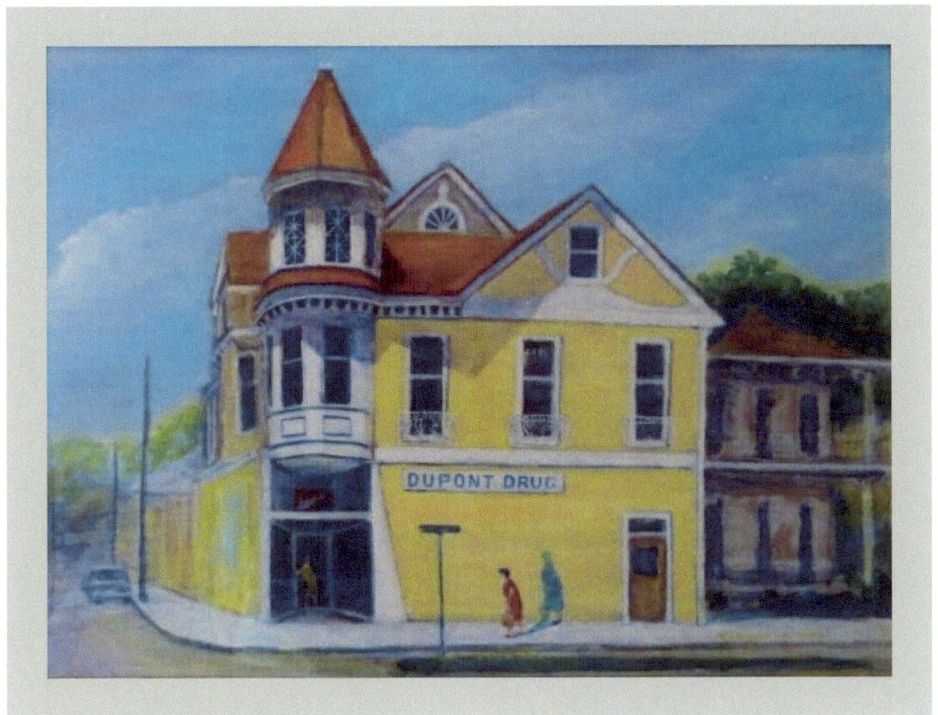

Title: Dupont Drug
Size: 18x24 inches
Medium: Acrylic on hard board
Copyright by Dan Wetta 1988

I used to walk on Magazine Street from Washington Avenue to Audubon Park in New Orleans in the 1930s. I think that Dupont Drug was a white house which stood out from the other houses because of its Victorian architecture – and so much different from the two-story shotgun duplexes of New Orleans.

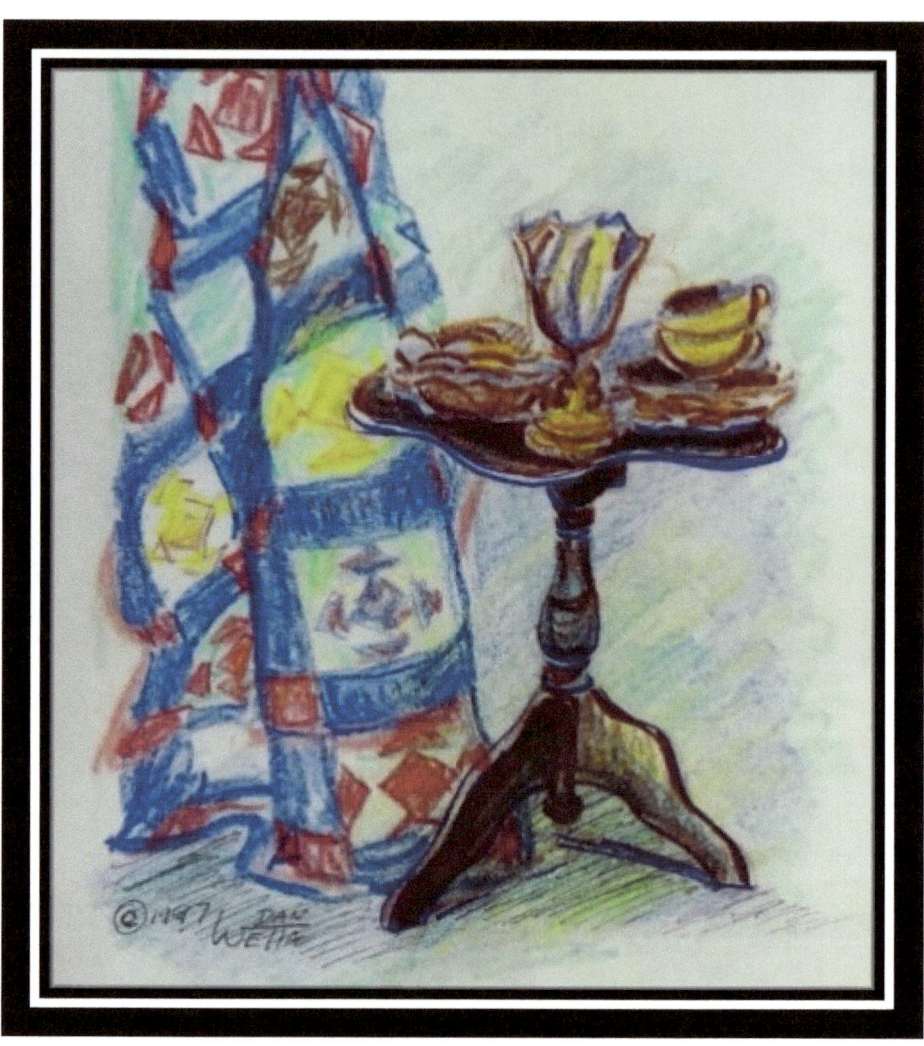

Title: Among the Antiques (doodle)
Copyright by Dan Wetta 1997

This is one of the doodles I did when I was renting a space at an antique store.

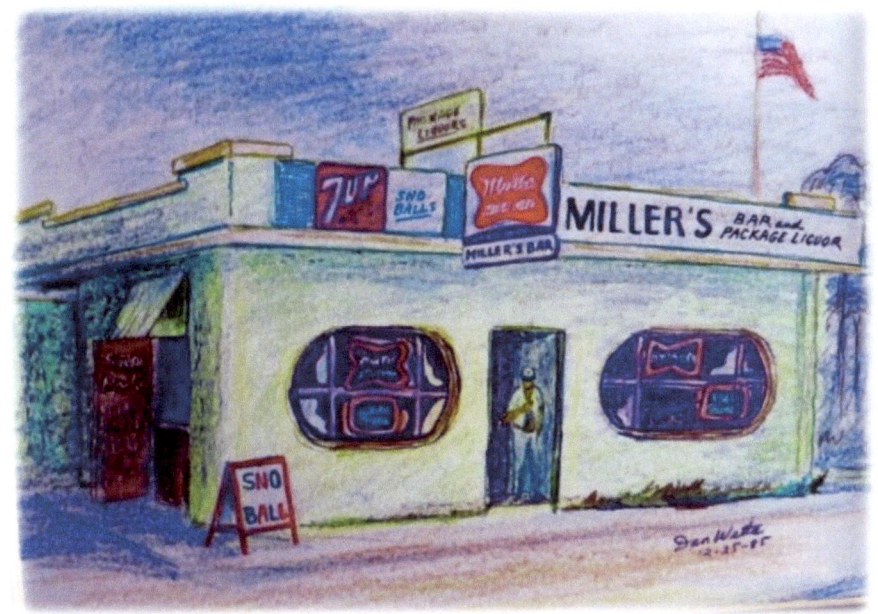

Title: Millers Bar
Size: 11x14 inches
Medium: mixed media on paper
Copyright by Dan Wetta 1987

Miller's bar was on Jefferson Avenue, an area that was under two or three feet of water during Hurricane Katrina. So if that man in the doorway was an alcoholic, his supply of liquor would have been cut off when Miller's went out of service.

PS Notice that Sno-Ball sign – sno balls and package liquors?

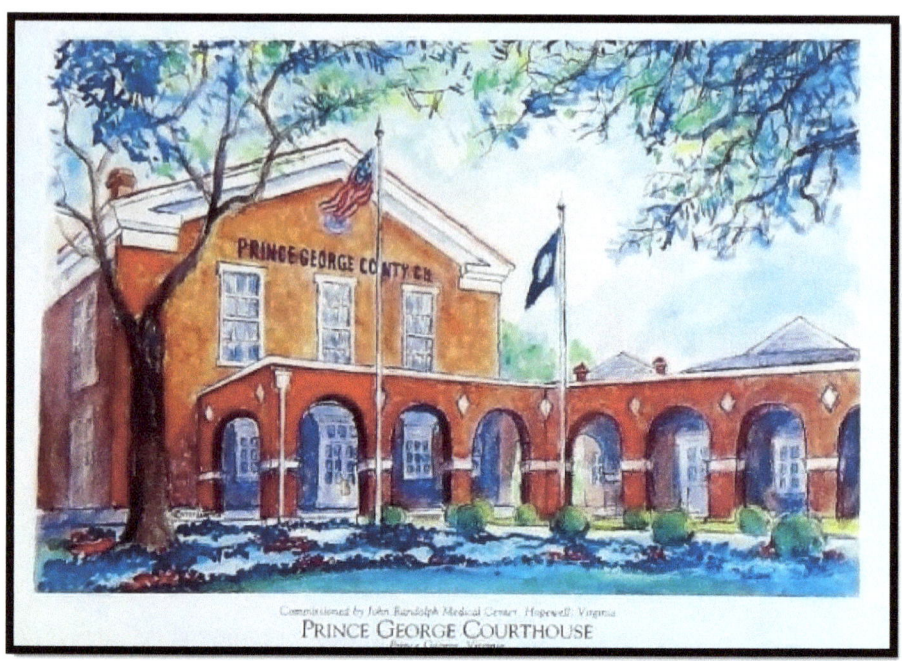

Commissioned by John Randolph Medical Center Hopewell, Virginia
PRINCE GEORGE COURTHOUSE
Prince George, Virginia

Title: Prince George Courthouse
Size: 16x20 inches
Medium: Acrylic on paper
Copyright by Dan Wetta

 I painted this for the John Randolph Medical Center in Hopewell, Virginia. The hospital was commemorating 75 years of operation in the community by issuing limited edition prints of historic sites in the area. This painting was also used on the cover of stationery cards sold in the hospital gift shop.

 This courthouse was built around 1884 to replace the old court house, which had been damaged during the Civil War.

Chapter 4: Wistful Times

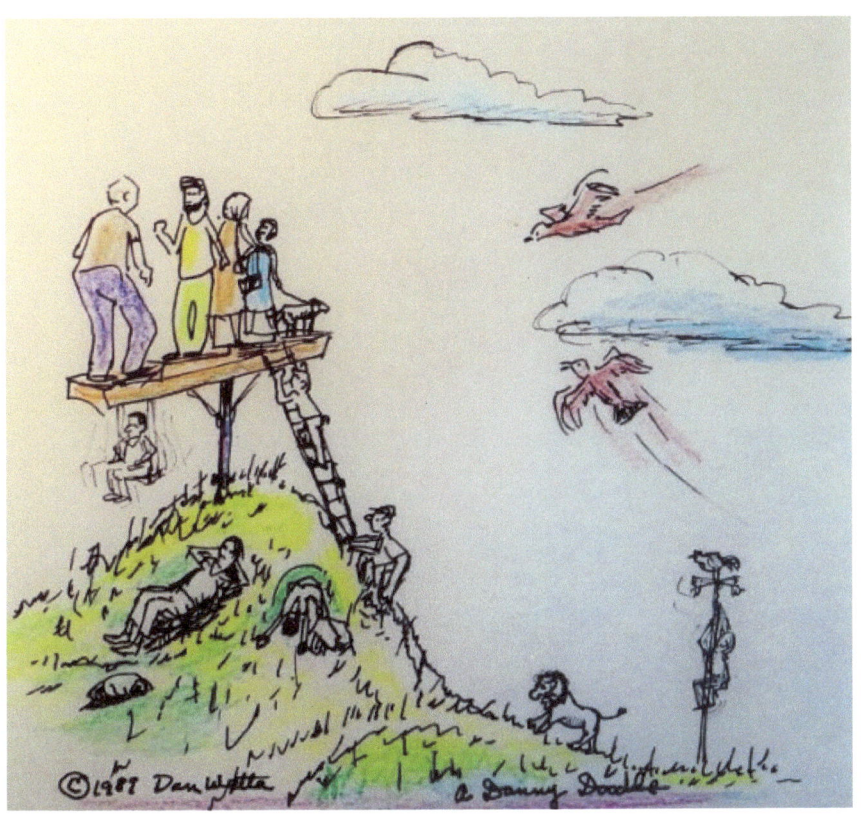

Title: Monkey Hill (cartoon)
Copyright by Dan Wetta, 1989

The only hill in the flat land around New Orleans is an artificial one in Audubon Park. When I was a kid, we used to call it, "Monkey Hill." It is about the size depicted above, but as you can see, I took a few liberties when I decided to recreate it in this cartoon.

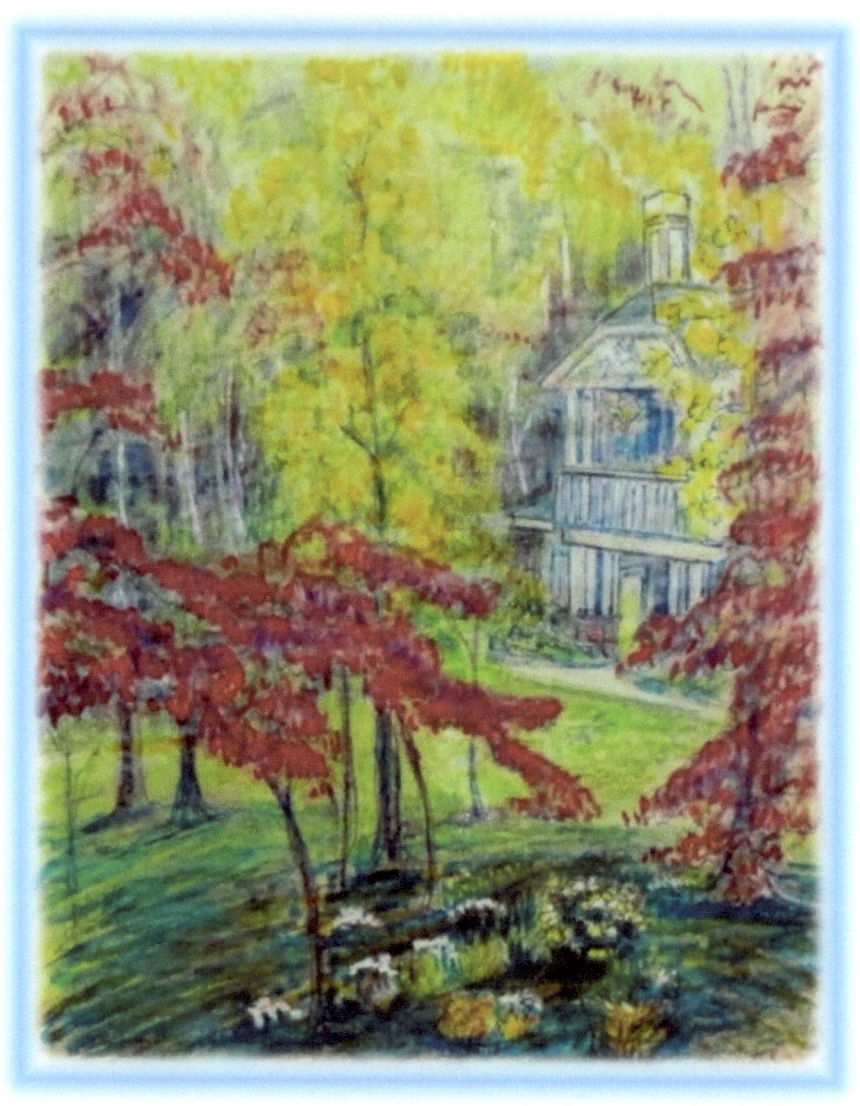

Title: Looking Down Williamsburg Commons
Size: 16x20 inches
Medium: Mixed media on paper
Copyright by Dan Wetta, 1992

"Looking Down Williamsburg Commons": I did this from a second-story, open hallway in Williamsburg Commons, the condominium neighborhood where I live. This is a light drawing, and I used the colors of the trees to pull out the life of the scene.

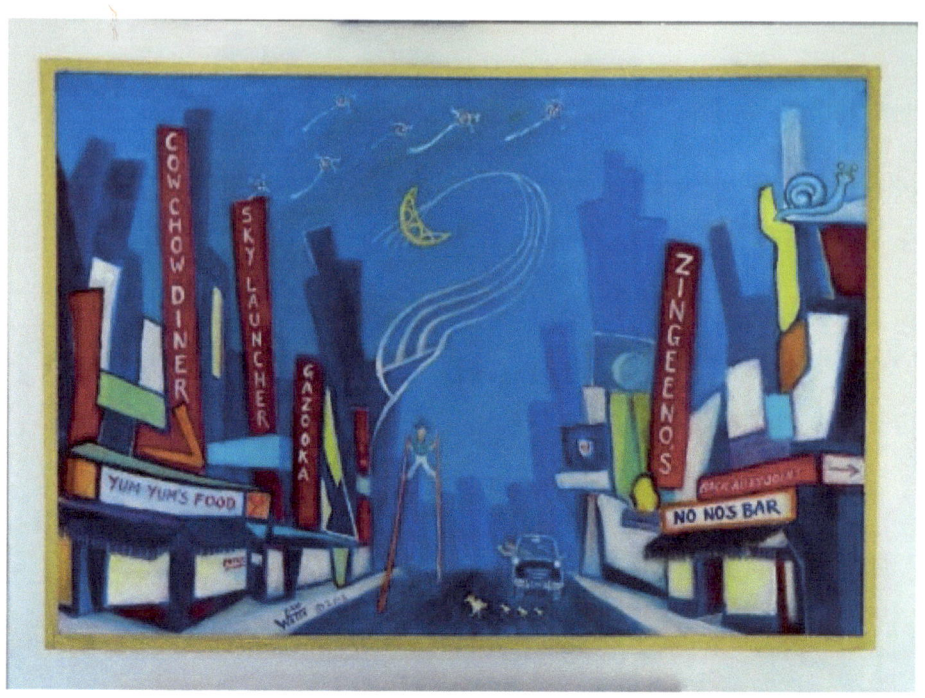

Title: Whimsical Night
Size: 24x36 inches
Medium: Acrylic on canvas
Copyright by Dan Wetta, 2012

The inspiration for this painting was a Tokyo night scene. It is a nonsensical painting experiment.

A friend asked me what that snail was doing on the roof. I said, "I don't know, but I do know what those chickens are doing. They are crossing the road to get to the other side."

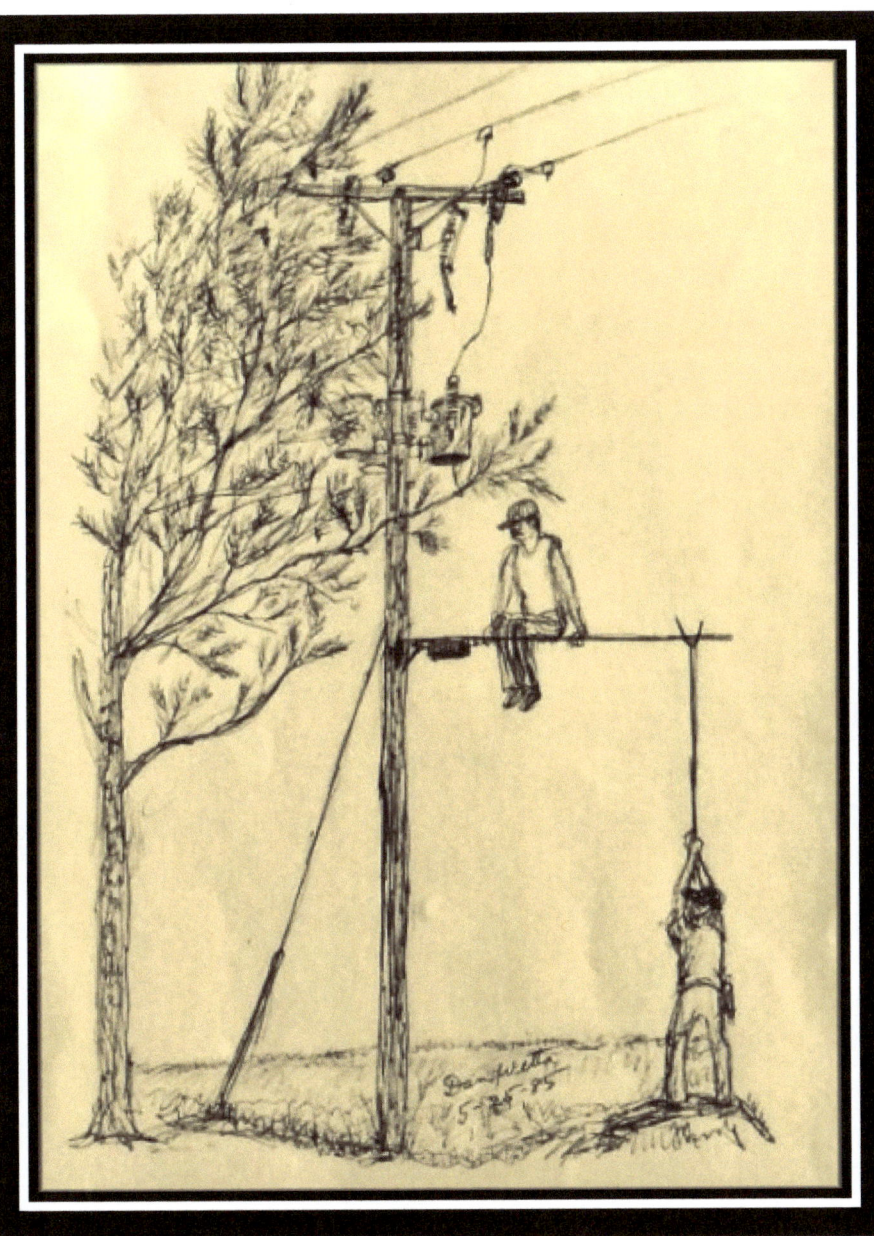

Title: What's This? (drawing)
Copyright by Dan Wetta, 1985

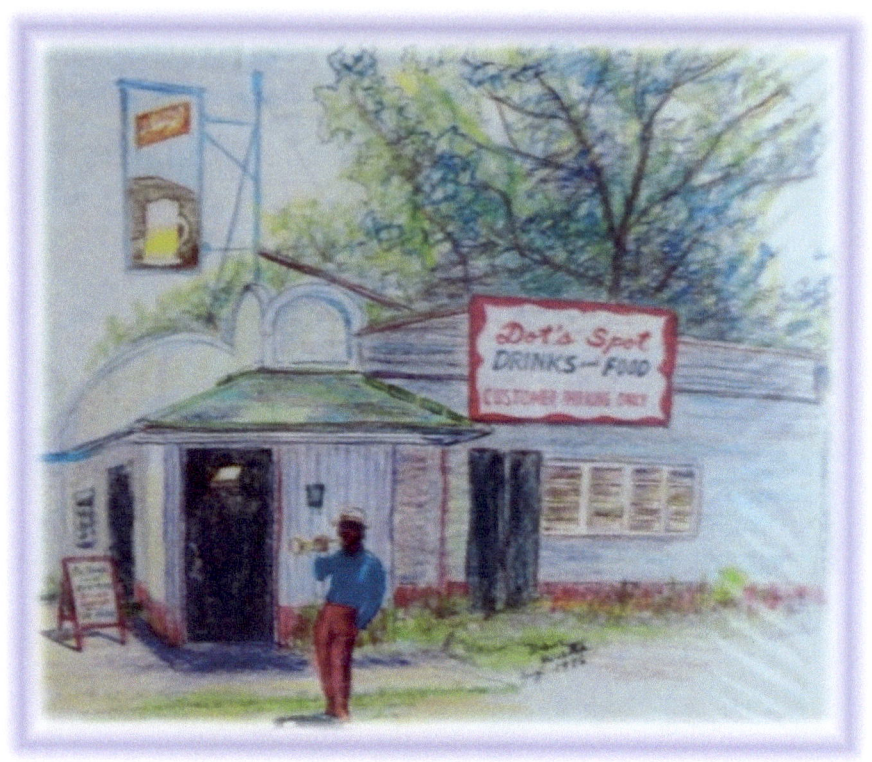

Title: Dot's Spot
Size: 14"x18"
Medium: Mixed media on paper
Copyright by Dan Wetta, 1985

Dot's Spot looks like it has seen better days. I suspect that the bugler is blowing taps for Dot's Spot, as if he had a premonition that it would not survive Hurricane Katrina.

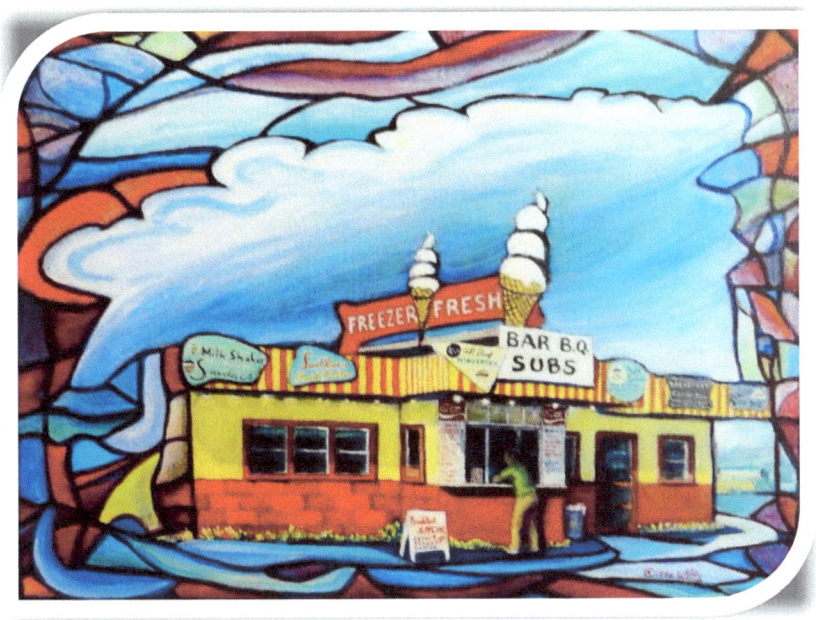

Title: Bar B Q
Size: 18x24 inches
Medium: Acrylic on canvas
Copyright by Dan Wetta, 1996

This colorful place was just outside Richmond, near Ashland, Virginia.

If people still have to eat after they die and go to heaven, I hope the stained glass touch will help to get this BAR-B-Q stand up there.

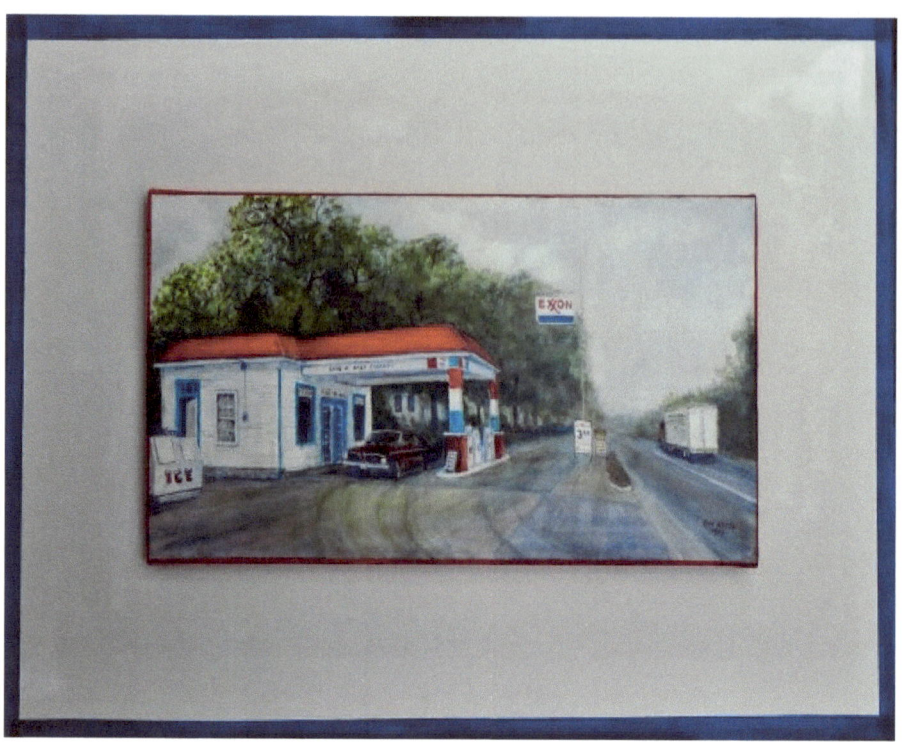

Title: Save a Step
Size: 12x24 inch canvas on 24x36 inch canvas
Medium Acrylic on canvas
Copyright by Dan Wetta, 1987

This place is on Richmond Road in Toano, Virginia, but the gasoline pumps are gone now. This service station has been converted into a barbershop called, "Cut-N-Up."

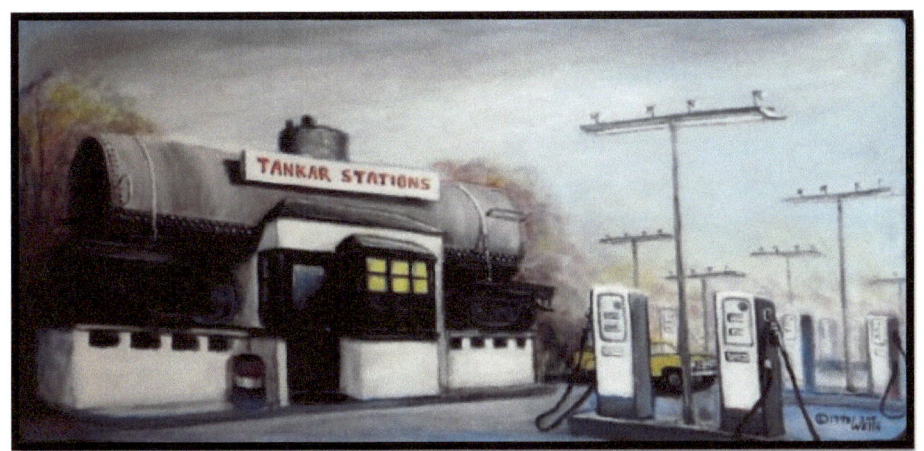

Title: Tankar Stations
Size: 12x24 inches
Medium: Acrylic on canvas
Copyright by Dan Wetta, 1998

This "Tankar Station" was on West Broad Street near Staples Mill Road in west-end Richmond, Virginia, but it is gone now.
I don't know where it went.

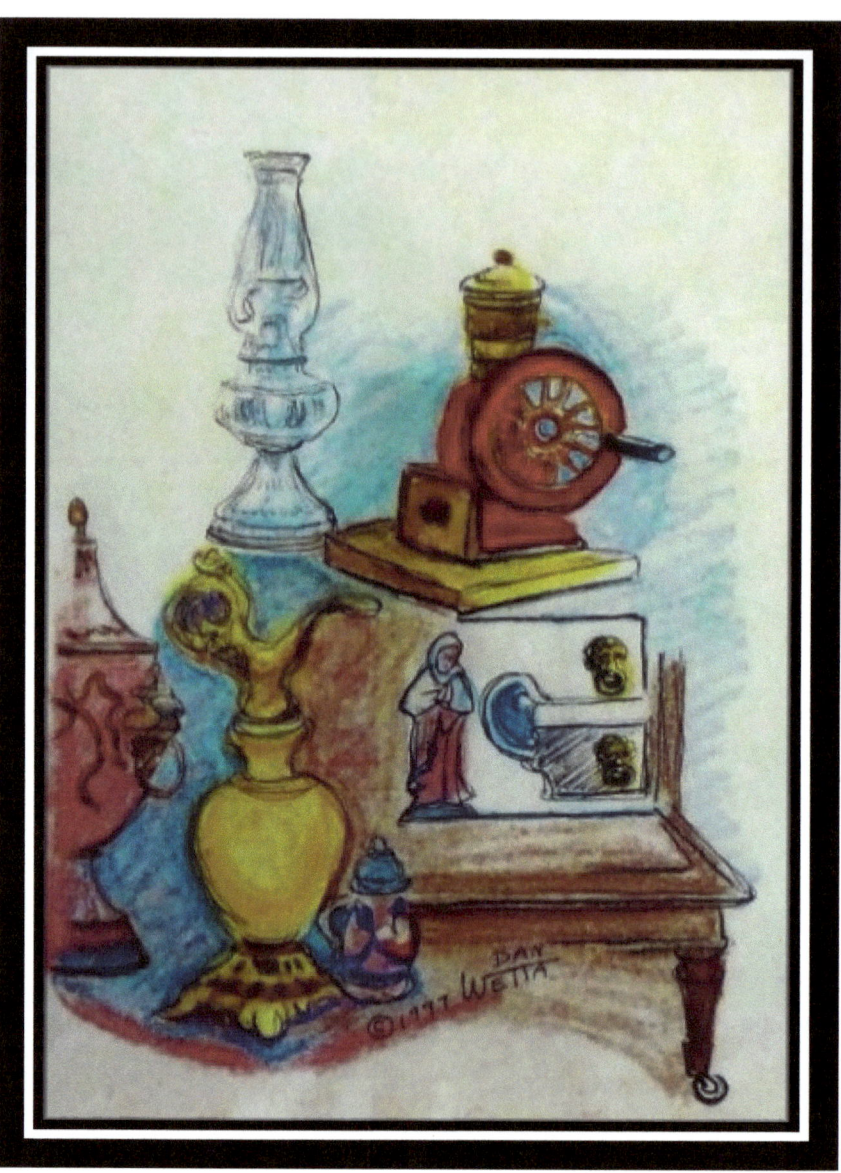

Title: Antique Grinder and Things (doodle)
Copyright by Dan Wetta, 1997

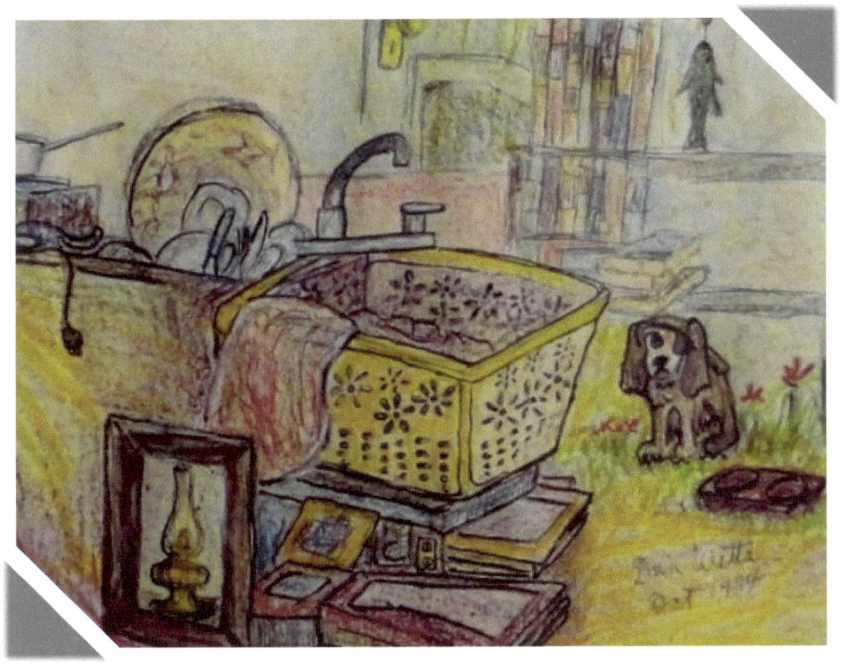

Title: Pepper
Size: 10 x 12 inches
Copyright by Dan Wetta, 1984
Medium: Mixed media on paper

I lived in a remote area of Virginia for a few years, and I used to take care of Pepper for my neighbors every once in a while, when they went away for the weekend. Pepper had only one good eye, because he had been hit by a car.

There was also a mean German Shepherd who ran loose in the area. One time when I was walking Pepper, I noticed the German Shepherd in the woods along the road. I was afraid he was going to come at me, but Pepper suddenly broke loose and ran straight at the larger dog. Pepper stared him down while I continued on my way to my house, which was close by.

That little dog was protecting me!

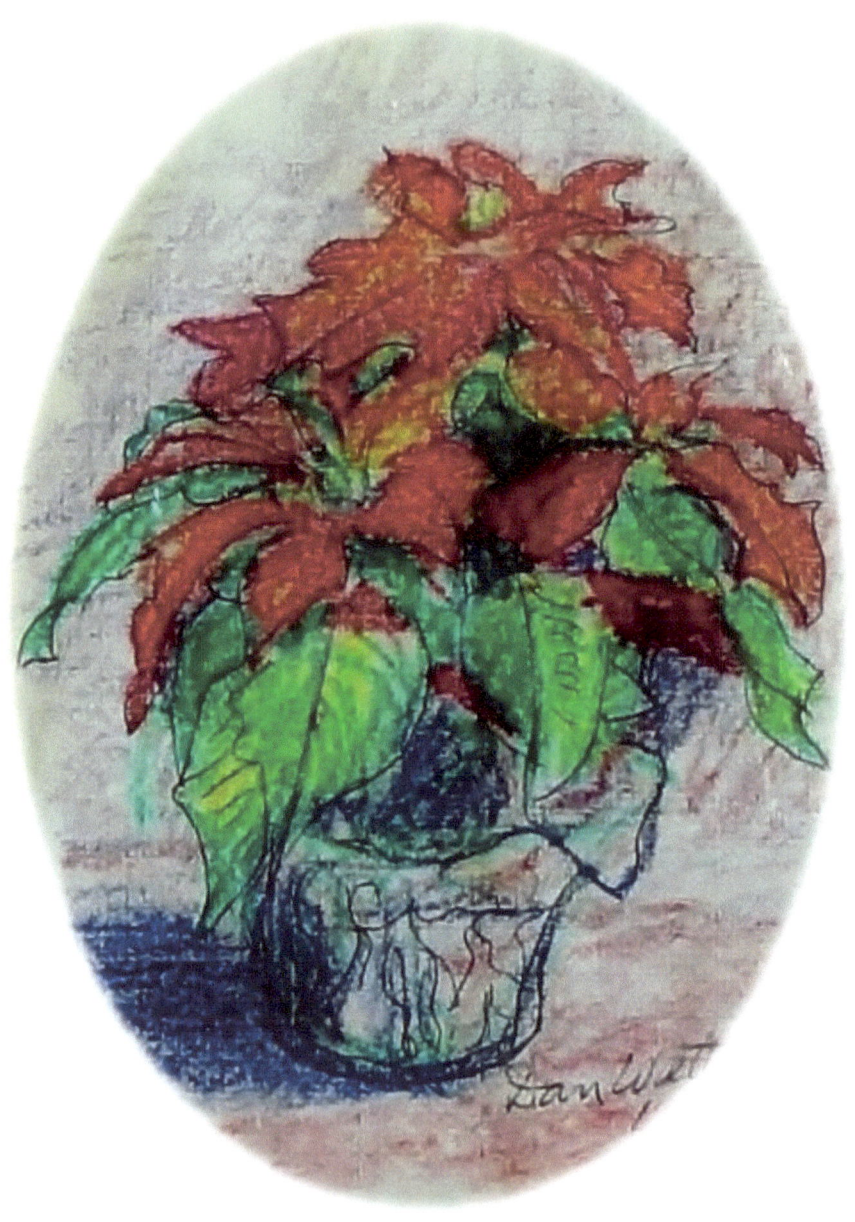

Title: Some Flowers in a Pot (doodle)
Copyright by Dan Wetta, 1985

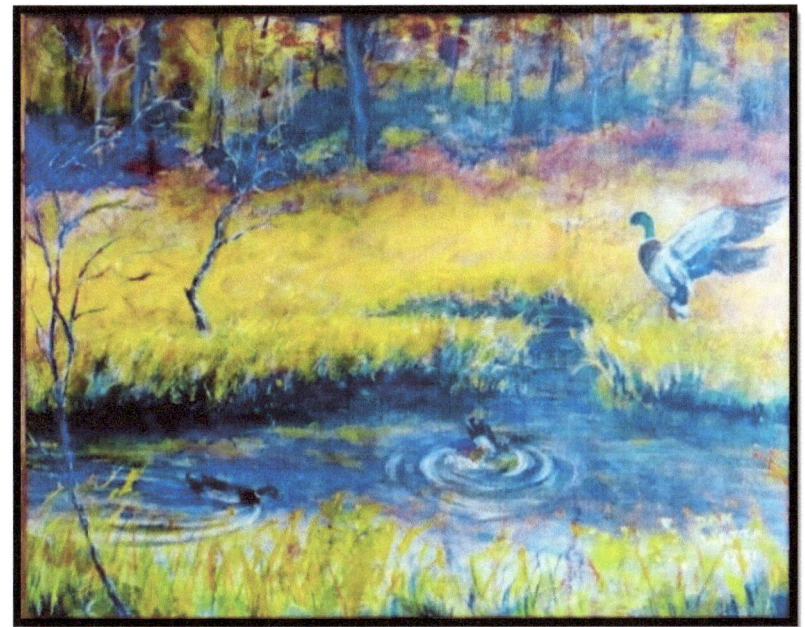

Title: Backyard Marsh
Size: 16x20 inches
Medium: Acrylic on canvas
Copyright by Dan Wetta, 1981

I don't know why I painted such a limited view of my backyard when I lived in Aylett, Virginia.

There was a beaver dam in the marsh, and at night you could hear the water flowing over the dam while the owls were hooting. I used to "hoo hoo" back at them. They probably wondered, "Who is that jackass trying to act like a hoot-owl?"

But where there is a marsh, there are ticks and insects, lots of them.

One day when I was mowing the front lawn, a spider jumped off a tree branch and bit me on the arm. Another time, I was moving a pile of branches, and a bunch of hornets stung me.

In hunting season, you could hear the dogs barking in the woods across the marsh. It was okay living in the country for a few months, but I discovered that I prefer the comforts of city life.

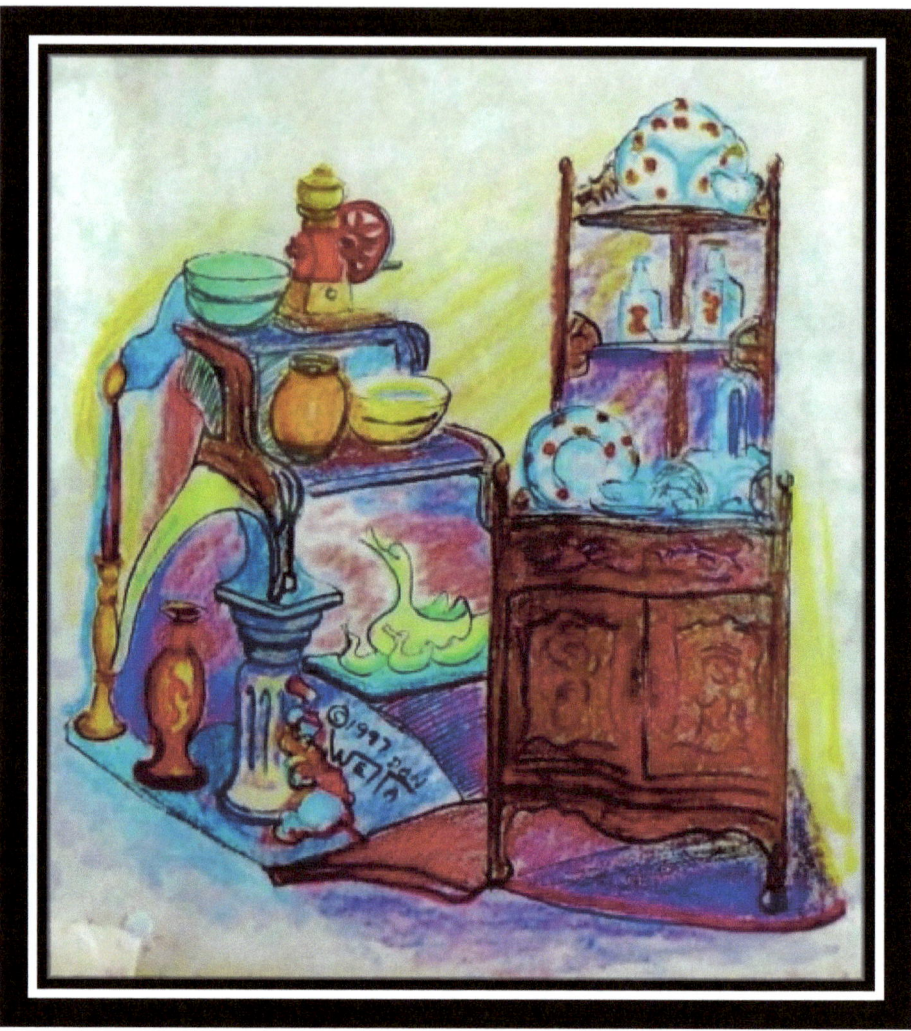

Title: Antique Cabinet with Dishes (doodle)
Copyright by Dan Wetta, 1997

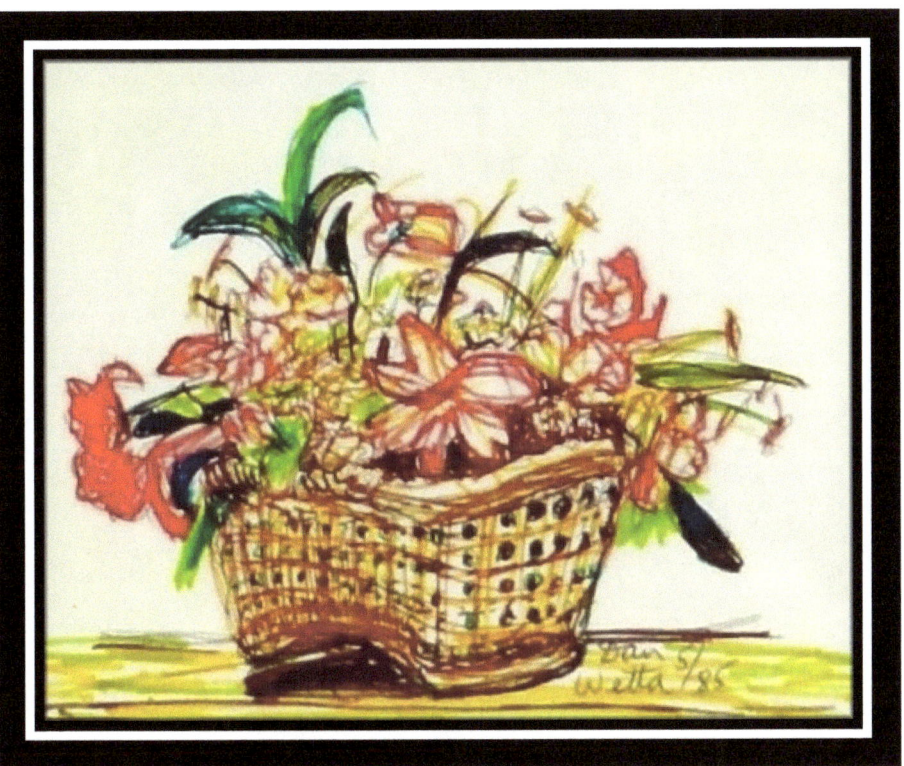

Title: Basket of Flowers (doodle)
Copyright by Dan Wetta, 1985

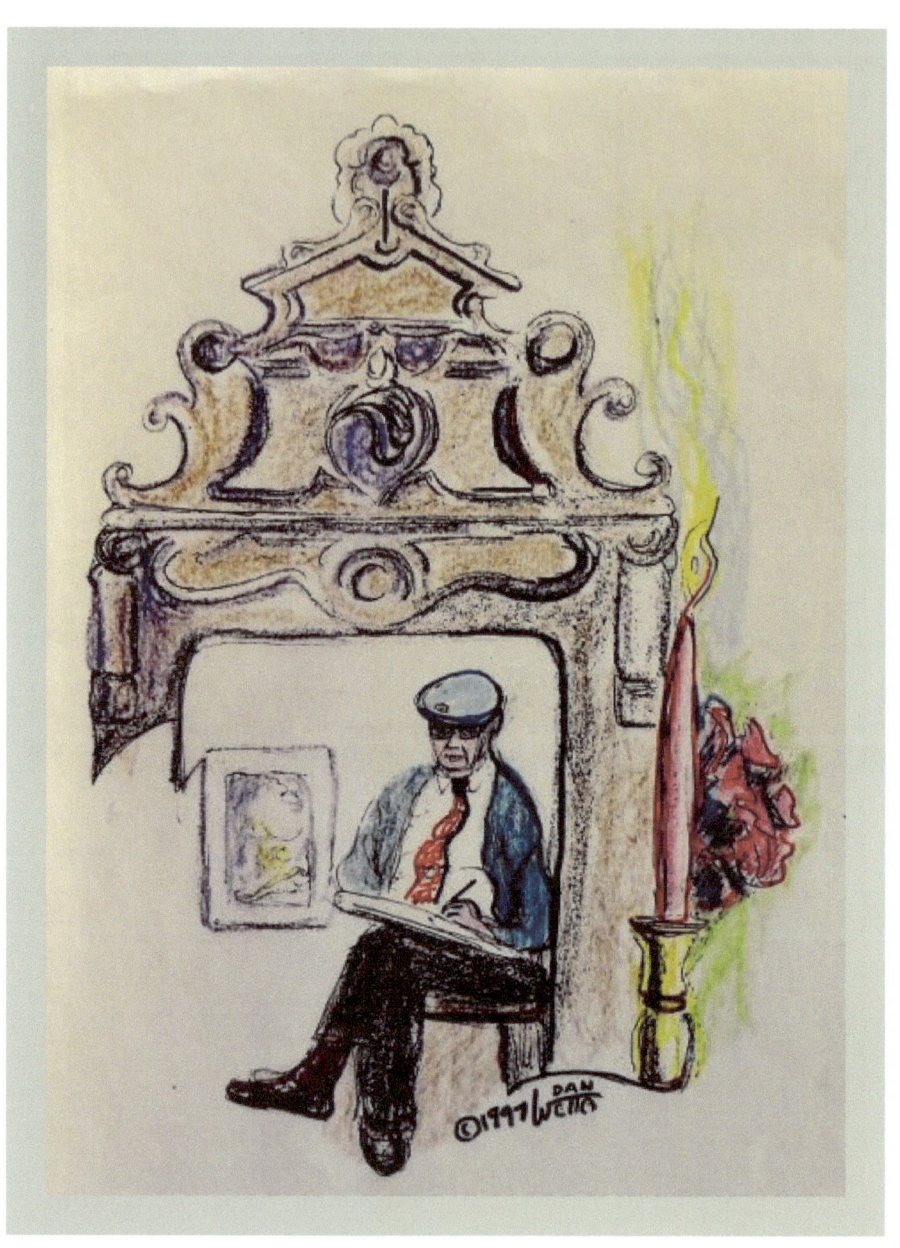

Title: Self Portrait (doodle)
Copyright by Dan Wetta, 1997

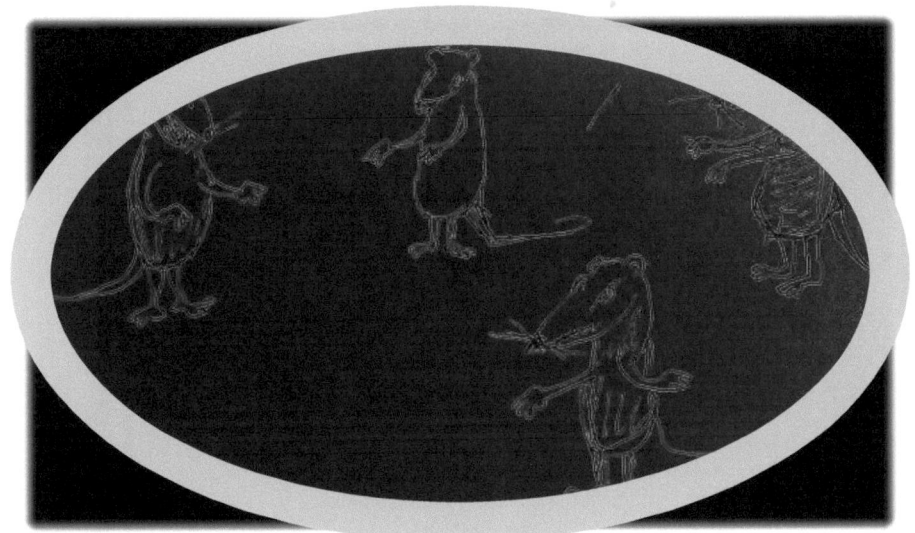

Title: Rats in the Darkness (cartoon)
Copyright by Dan Wetta

You never know what might be lurking under your bed. No wonder we have nightmares!

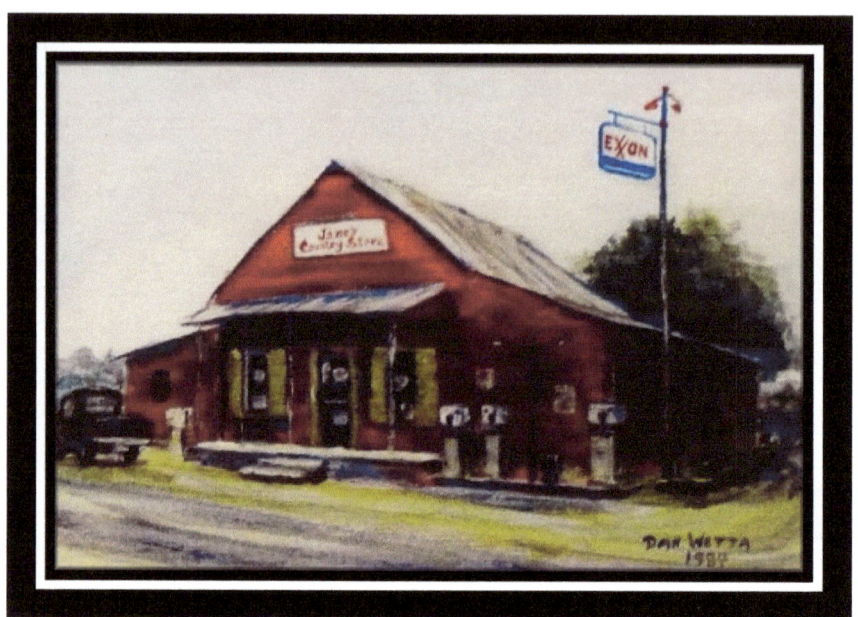

Title: Jane's Country Store
Size: 9x12 inches
Medium: Acrylic on canvas
Copyright by Dan Wetta, 1984

I wish I had painted this on an 18x24 inch canvas.

I took a snapshot of this store near Aylett, Virginia and painted it later.

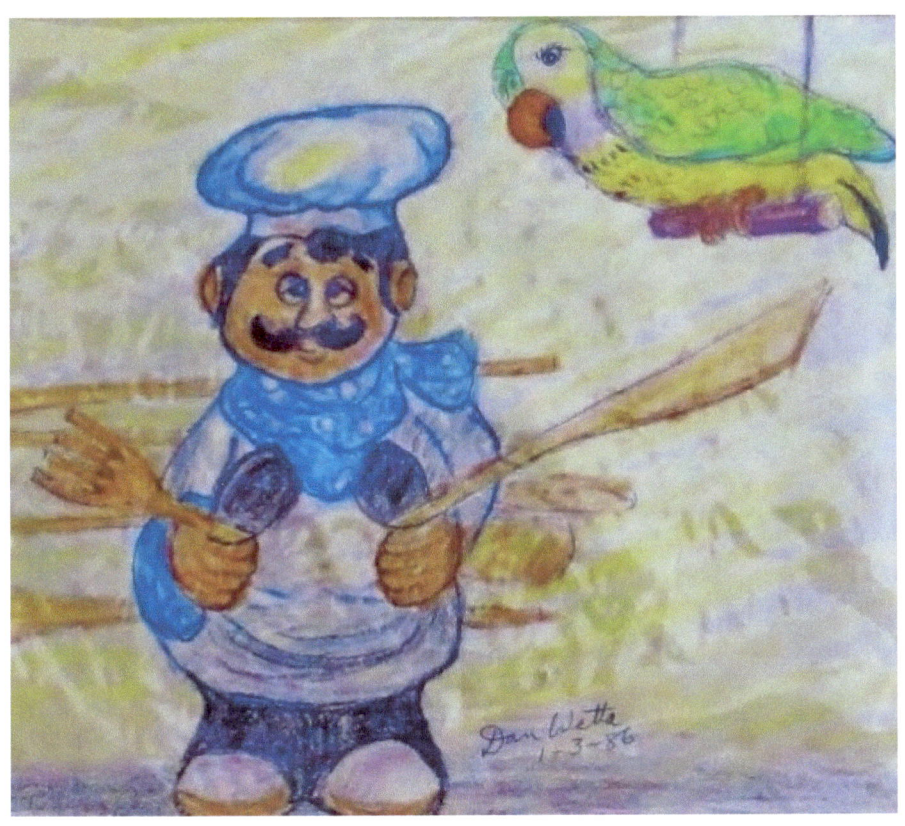

Title: Cook and Parrot (doodle)
Copyright by Dan Wetta, 1986

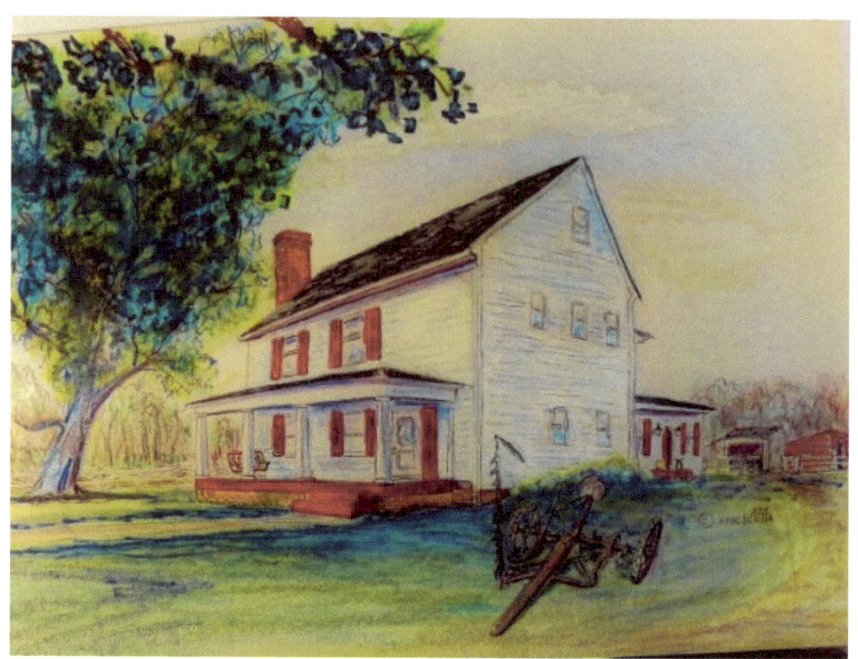

Title: Whitehall Tavern
Sub-title: Geddy House
Size: 12x18 inches
Medium: Mixed media on paper
Copyright by Dan Wetta, 1996

In 1805, William Geddy, Sr. and his son, William, built Whitehall Tavern on a 326 acre farm located at the intersection of Richmond Road and Stage Road in Toano, Virginia, about fifteen miles from Williamsburg.

The tavern was a rest station on the long journey between Richmond and Williamsburg. It survived all the major battles in the local area during the War Between the States.

The house was listed on the National Register in 2007.

This house has continued in the family line for multiple generations, and the current owner, Bertrand Geddy, maintains the property.

My granddaughter, Keira, lived there with the Geddy children for several years, which is how I came to do a painting of it.

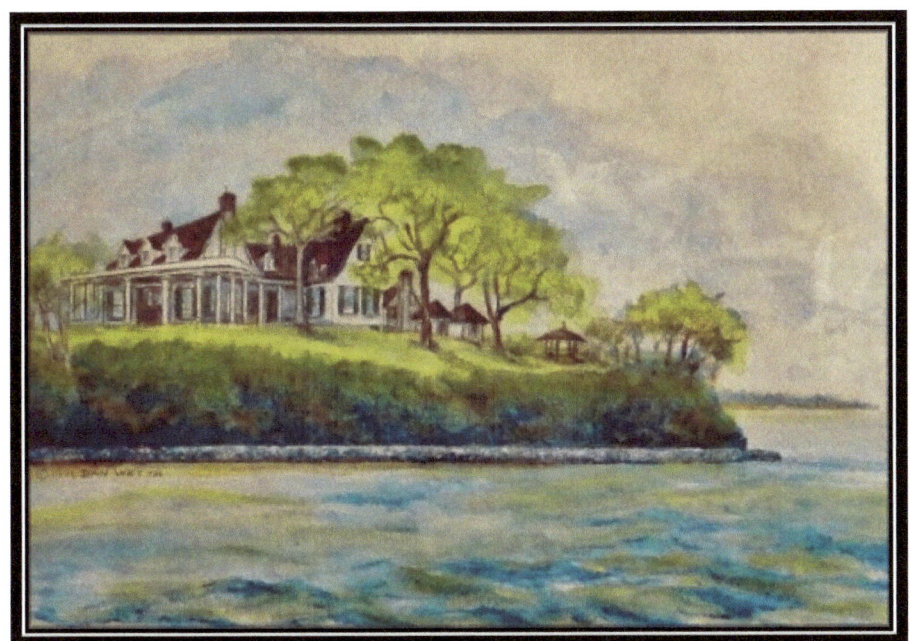

Title Appomattox Manor
Size: 16x20 inches
Medium: print on paper
Copyright by Dan Wetta, 1991

My original painting is on display in the lobby of John Randolph Medical Center in Hopewell, Virginia.

Appomattox Manor is a former plantation in Hopewell. It is best known as the Union Headquarters during the Siege of Petersburg during 1864-65. It is now administered by the National Park Service.

The Eppes family remained on their plantation until the arrival of Union gunboats in 1862, which forced them to flee to Petersburg. Soon thereafter, all their slaves joined the Union Forces. After the surrender, Dr. Eppes returned and found his home and plantation in near ruin. His wife and children did not return until 1866.

P.S. Appomattox Manor is just as hard to spell as Mississippi!

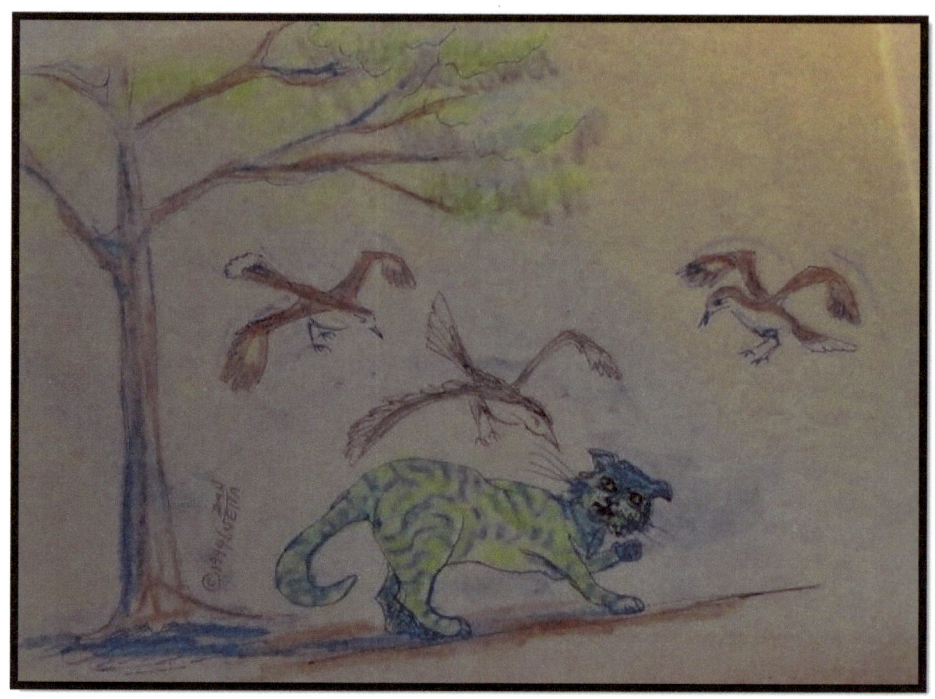

Title: Cat Birds (cartoon)
Copyright by Dan Wetta, 1994

I think Mocking Birds are also called "Cat-Birds." They will attack people if you get too close to their nest in the spring.

Maybe this should be called a "Cat-toon."

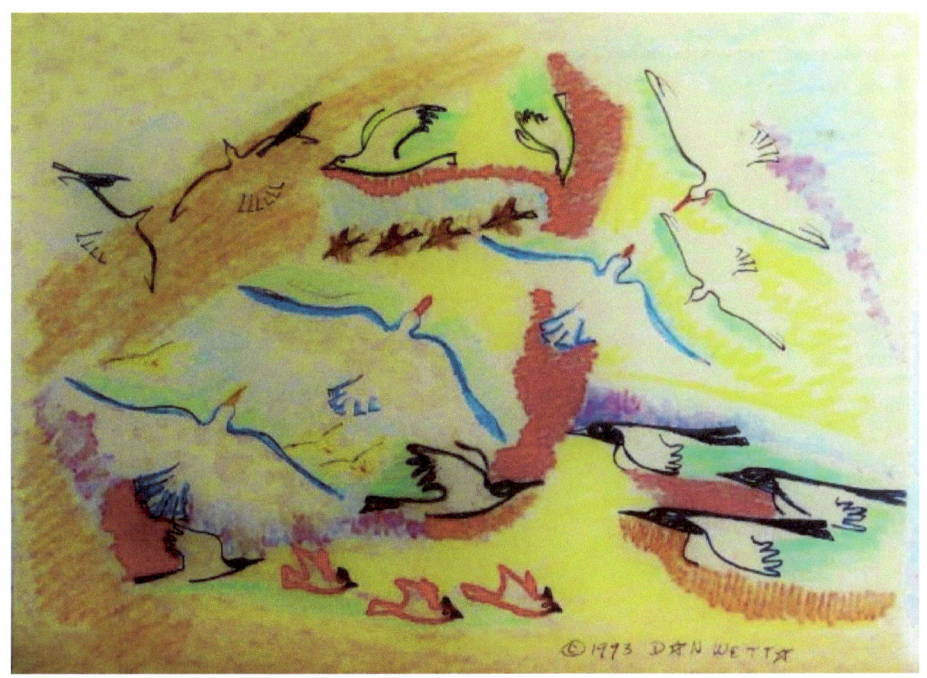

Title: Bird Doodle (cartoon)
Copyright by Dan Wetta, 1993

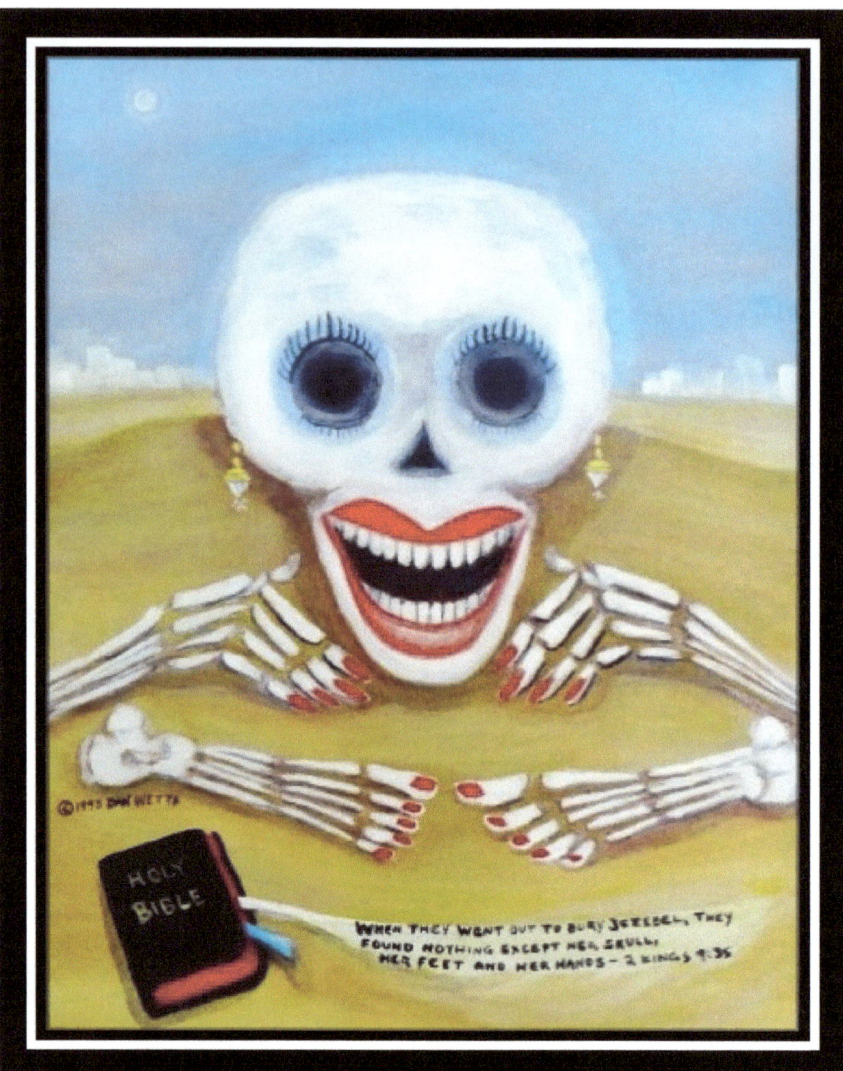

Title: Jezebel the Painted Woman
Size: 18x24 inches
Medium: Acrylic on canvas
Copyright by Dan Wetta, 1993

This is a satirical rendering of the death of Jezebel. I have painted other bible death scenes, but Jezebel's is probably the most gruesome.

After her son Jehoram had been slain, Jezebel painted her eyes and adorned her head. King Jehu accused her of fornication and witch craft and then had her thrown out of a window. King Jehu then ran over her body in his chariot.

When his servants went out to bury her, stray dogs had eaten her, so they found nothing of her but her skull, hands and feet.

P.S. Some people sympathize with Jezebel. Read full story beginning at 2 Kings 9:35.

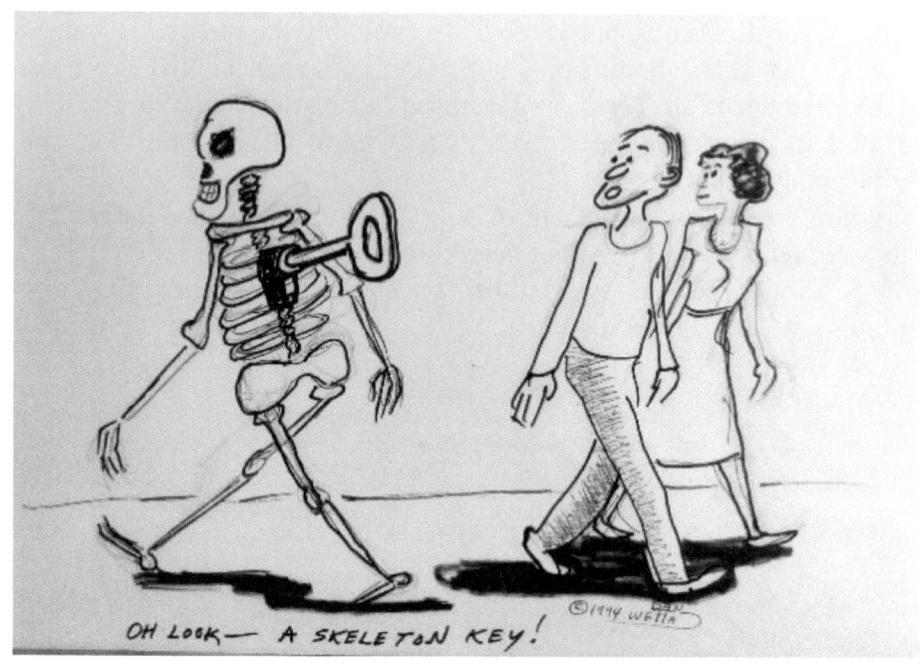

OH LOOK — A SKELETON KEY!

Title: Look, Skeleton Key! (cartoon)
Copyright by Dan Wetta, 1985

    I have always been fascinated by skeletons and bones. I did a series of "Crazy Bones" cartoons.

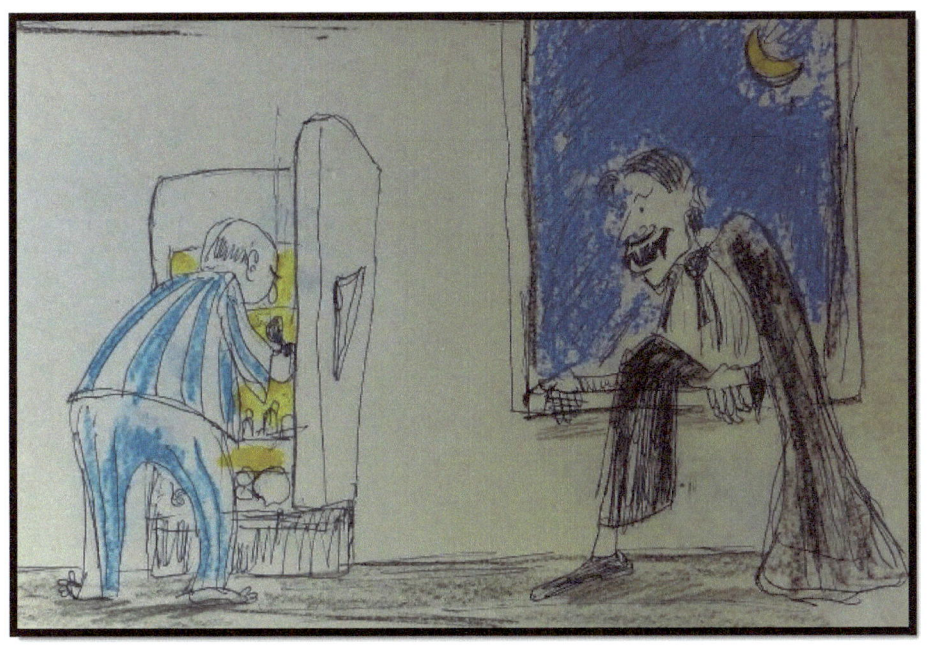

Title: Midnight Snacks, to each his own! (cartoon)
Copyright by Dan Wetta, 1989

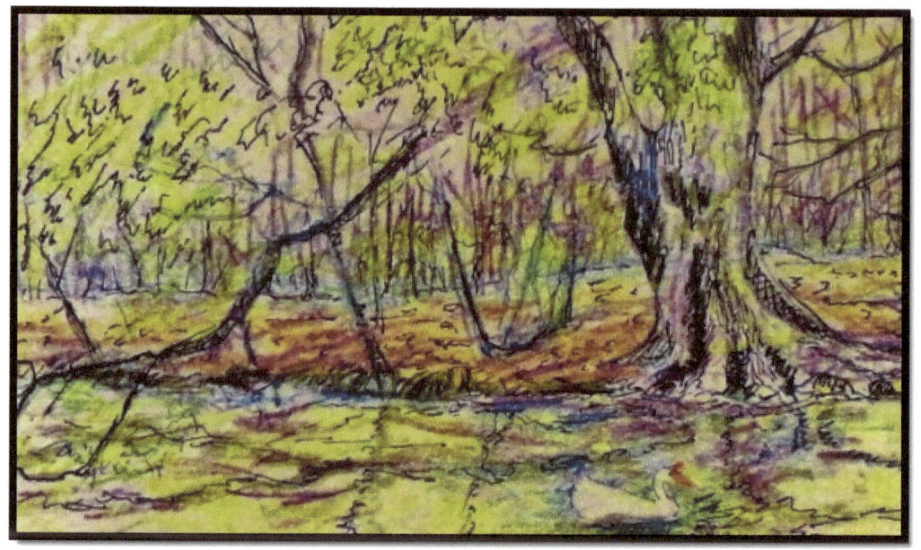

Title: Tree on Lagoon
Size: 9 x 12 inches
Medium: Mixed media on paper
Copyright, Dan Wetta

This is a sketch of a lagoon in Audubon Park, New Orleans, La.

While I was doing this sketch, a swan came out of the water and pecked the toes of a man who was taking a nap in the shade of a Live-Oak tree.

Yikes! Talk about surprised!

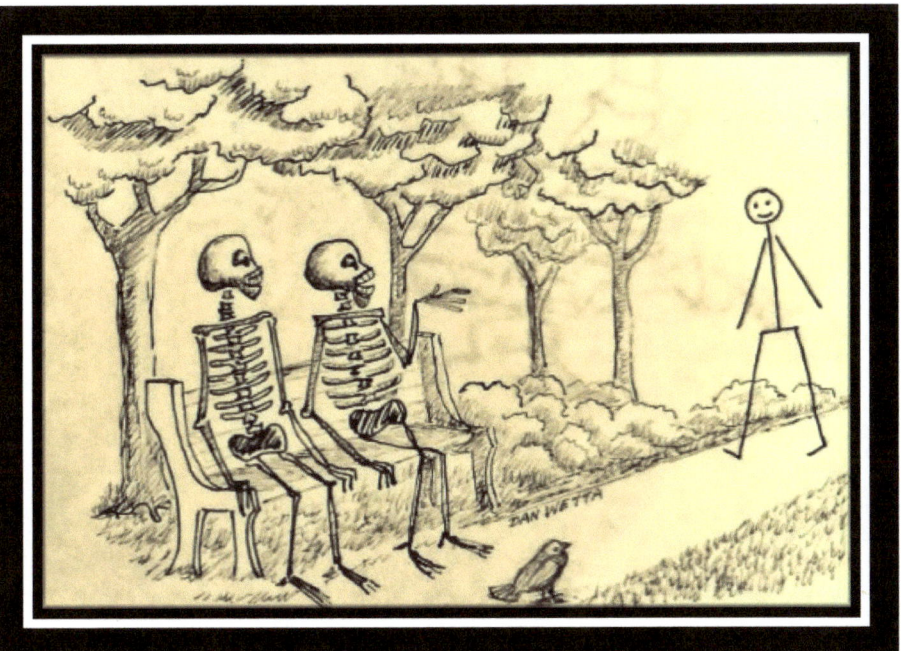

Title: Oh Look, Here Comes Smiley Face (cartoon)
Copyright by Dan Wetta

This is another of my "Crazy Bones" cartoons.

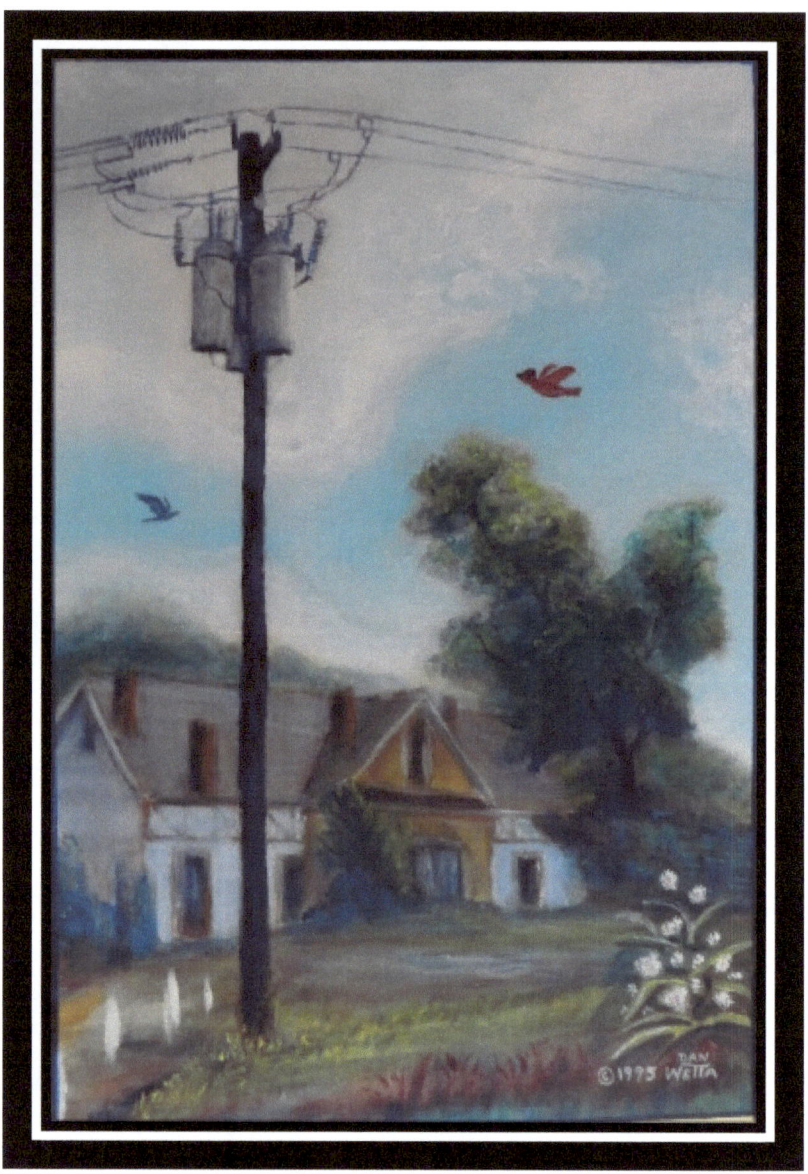

Title: Utility Pole
Size: 14x18 inches
Medium: Acrylic on canvas
Copyright by Dan Wetta, 1995

I painted this when I was taking an art class at J. Sargent Reynolds Community College in Richmond, Virginia. The professor took us to a pond full of lily pads, but I was so fascinated by the top of the utility pole that I painted it instead.

That old house in the background was abandoned.

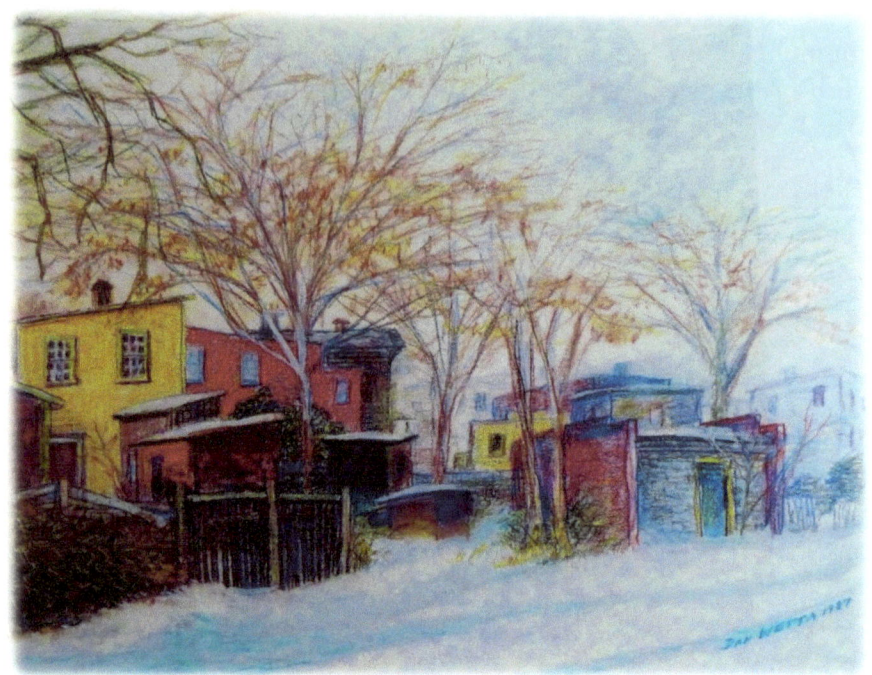

Title: Wood Pile
Size: 11x14 inches
Medium: Mixed media on paper
Copyright by Dan Wetta, 1987

This is my original sketch. Later on, in 2011, I took the wood pile and yellow house and put them in another scene.

People set out their trash cans in alleys like this in old Richmond, and when the trash man comes by twice a week, the dogs go crazy barking at them.

By the looks of the snow in this scene, it's probably too cold for the dogs to come outside, so I guess the trash man appreciates the quiet for a change.

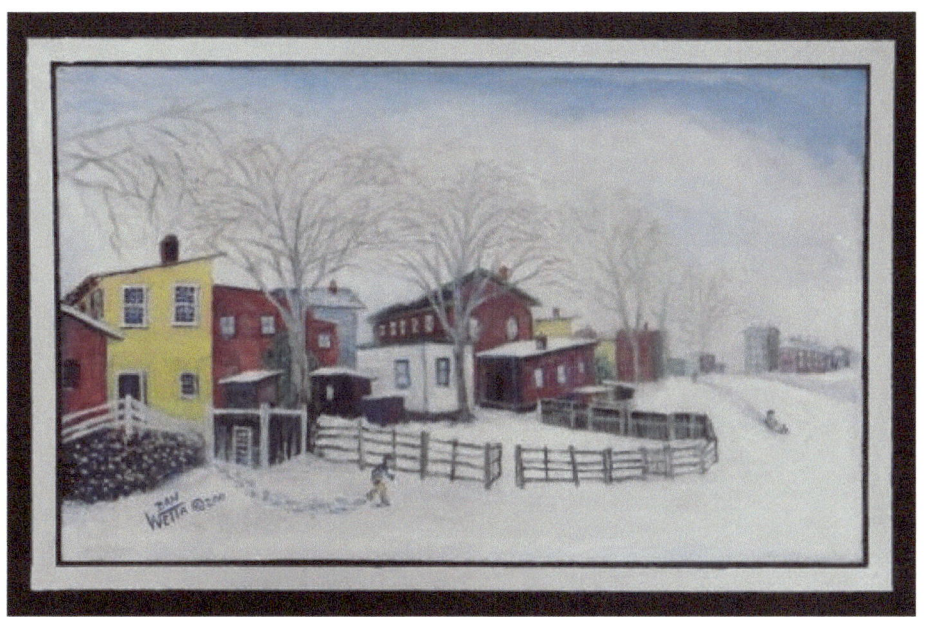

Title: North 4th Street, Richmond VA (final version)
Size: 24x36 inches
Medium: Acrylic on canvas
Copyright by Dan Wetta

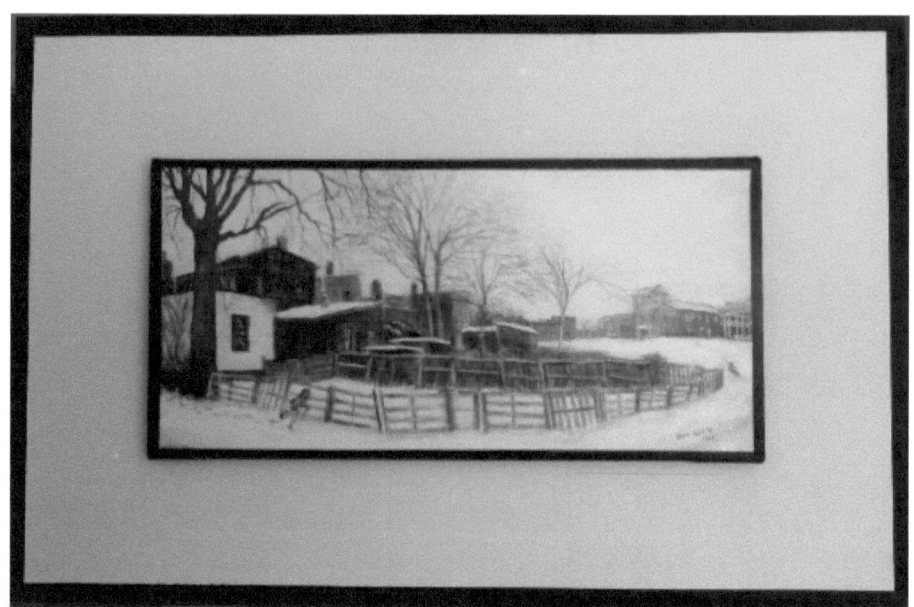

Title: North 4th Street (original version)

I did two versions of this scene because I thought this one was too dull

I think the yellow house in the version of the previous page brightens the scene.

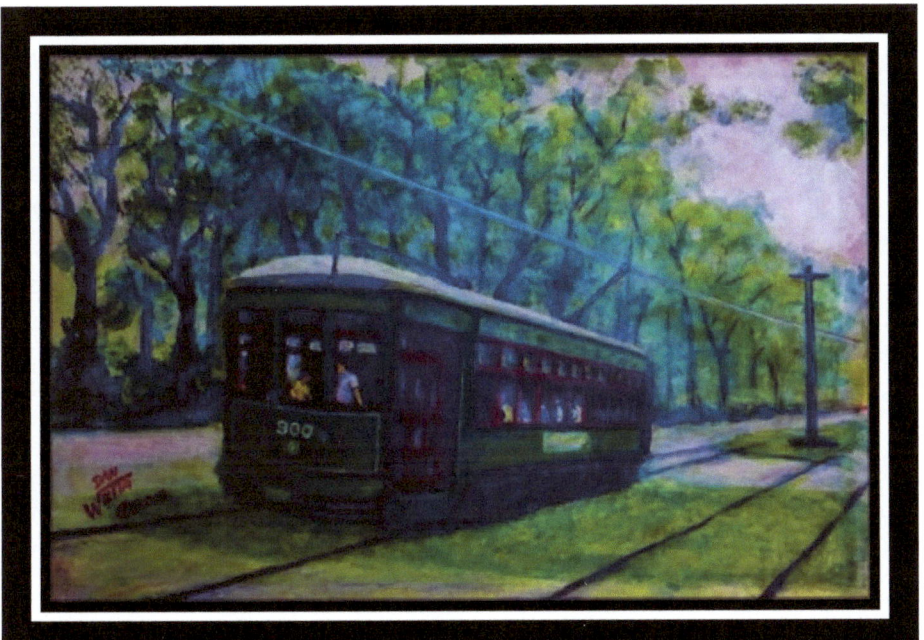

Title: Street Car in New Orleans
Size: 22x30 inches
Medium: Acrylic on canvas
Copyright by Dan Wetta

When I was a teenager, I used to ride the streetcars in New Orleans. I especially remember riding the St. Charles streetcar coming home at night, when there weren't many passengers. The conductor would speed up, the street car would rock from side to side, and the wind blowing through the open windows cooled you off on a hot summer night.

My mom had an uncle who started out as a streetcar conductor in New Orleans; namely, Uncle Joseph. To keep from getting bored when business was slow, he used to add and subtract the house numbers along the route.

This was in the 1920s, before electronic calculators and adding machines. He became such a good mathematician that he got a job calculating the odds at the race tracks. He traveled around the country according to the racing seasons. Every once in a while, he would return to the track in New Orleans and visit my mom and dad. Uncle Joseph made a lot of money, which he invested in real estate. He gave Mom a two story house located on St. Andrew Street.

Then there was his brother, Uncle Willie, who was also a streetcar conductor. He never married. He lived with his niece, Helen. Every once in a while, he would start drinking and Aunt Helen would kick him out. He would then go to a priest and take a pledge not to drink for six months, and Aunt Helen would let him come back. This was in the days before Alcoholics Anonymous.

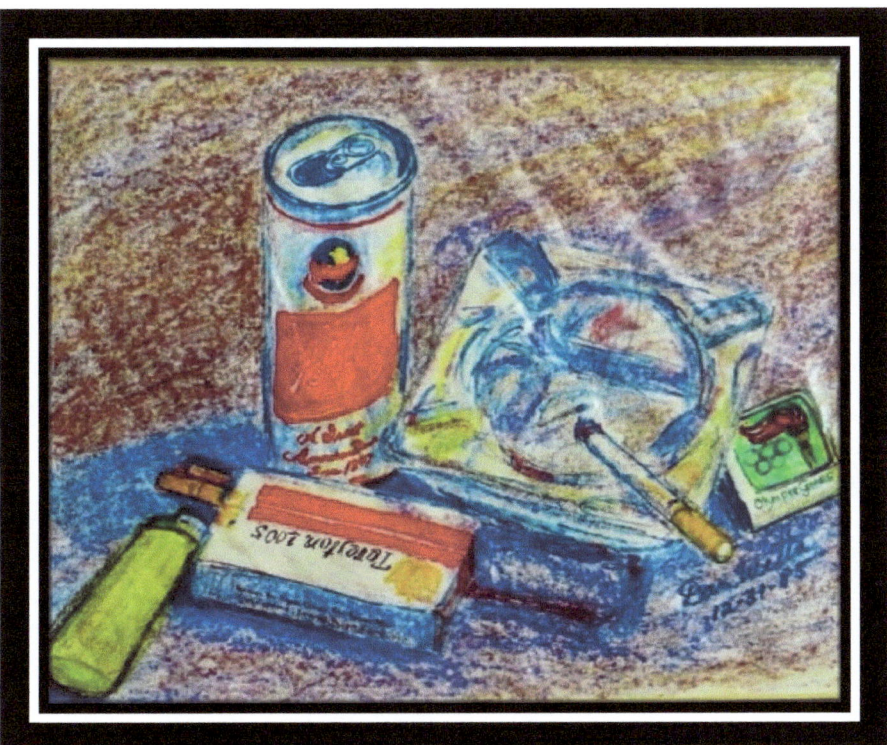

Title: Cigarette Smoke (doodle)
Copyright by Dan Wetta, 1985

I started smoking when I was a teenager and later tried to quit many times without success. I finally quit in 1991, when I had triple bypass surgery. This scared me enough to stop.

If you know somebody who is trying to quit, be patient with them. It took bypass trauma to make me quit.

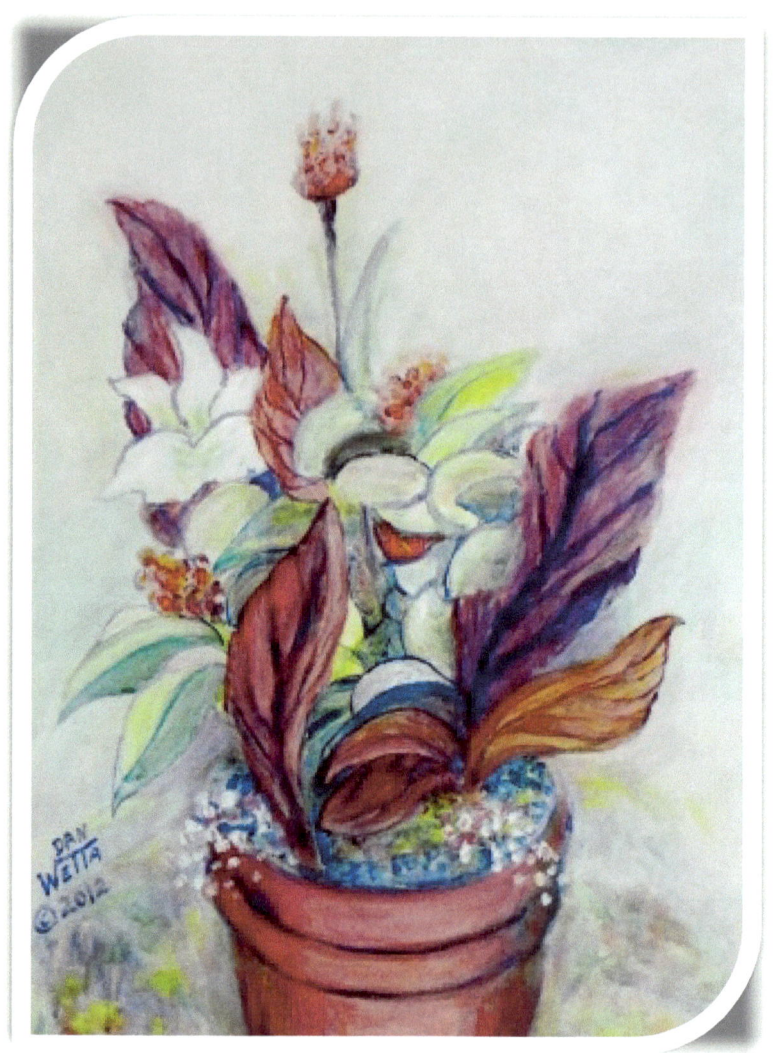

Title: Flowers Near the Swimming Pool
Size: 18x24
Medium: Acrylic on canvas
Copyright by Dan Wetta, 2012

I did the original sketch of this painting of flowers while my great-grandchildren were in the swimming pool at Williamsburg Commons in Williamsburg, Virginia. Often during the summertime, my two granddaughters, Keira and April, would bring their children to my small neighborhood pool for a swim.

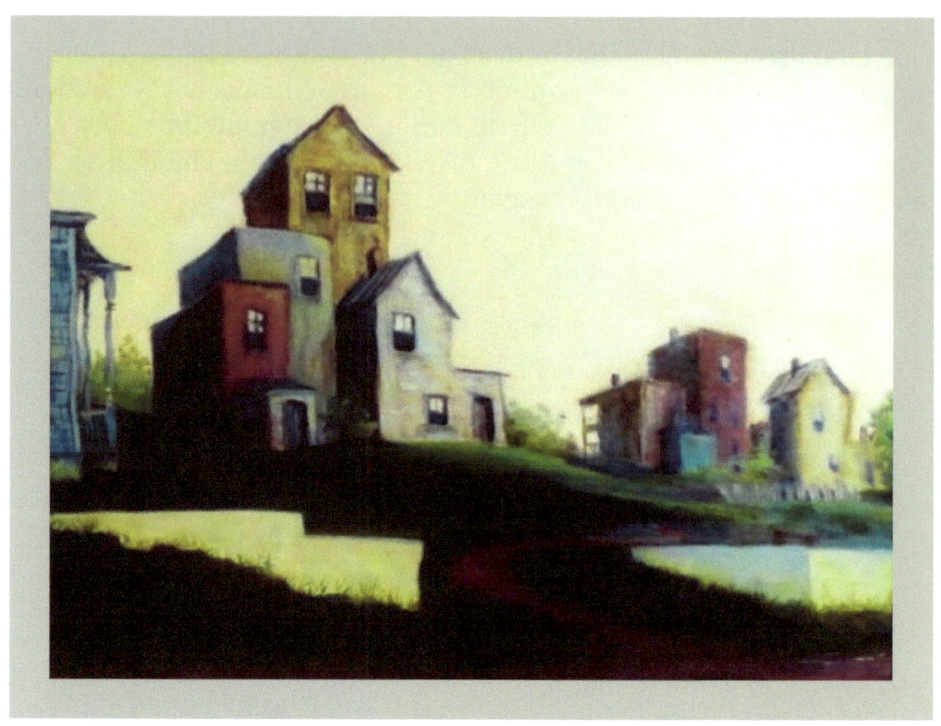

Title: Jamie's Castle
Size: 18x24 inches
Medium: Oil on canvas
Copyright by Dan Wetta, 1962

My son, Stephen, used to have a playmate named Jamie. Jamie lived in a child's world of imagination, and years later, Jamie's imagination seems to have rubbed off on Stephen, because Stephen is now teaching creative writing at Hunter College in New York.

It seems like Jamie's imagination also got to me, because when I saw some houses on Patterson Avenue in Richmond, Virginia, they reminded me of a castle, Jamie's Castle.

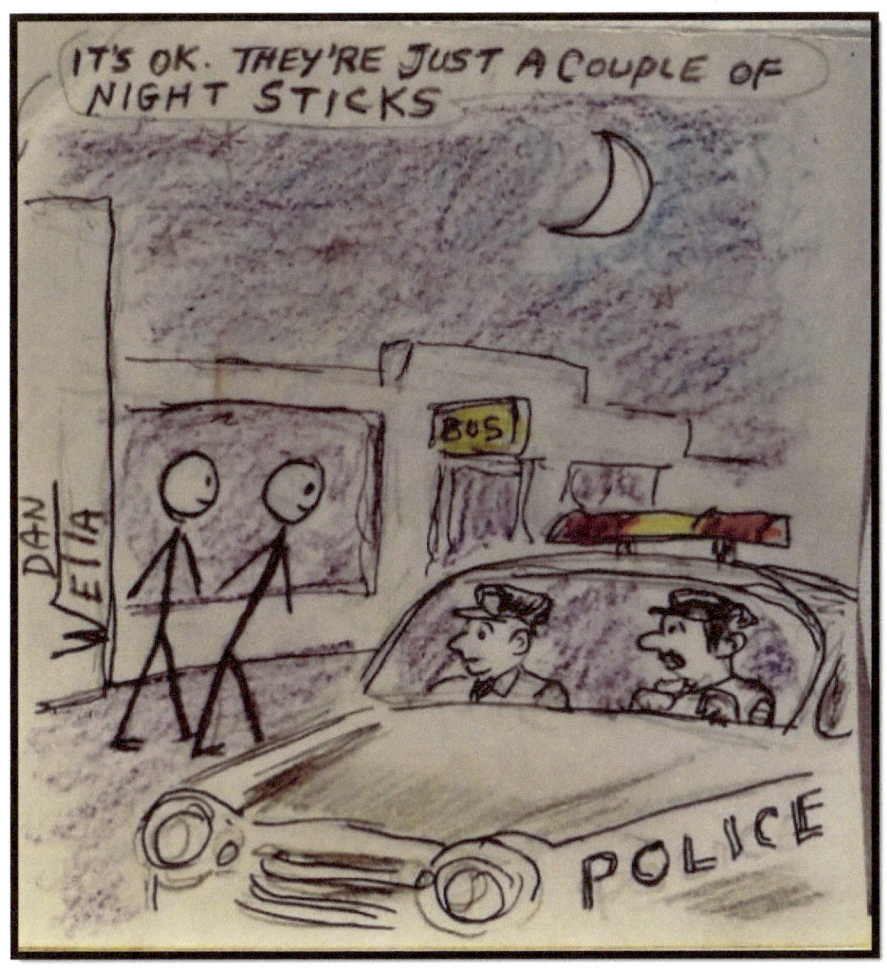

Title: Night Sticks and Police (cartoon)
Copyright by Dan Wetta

"It's ok. They're just a couple of night sticks."

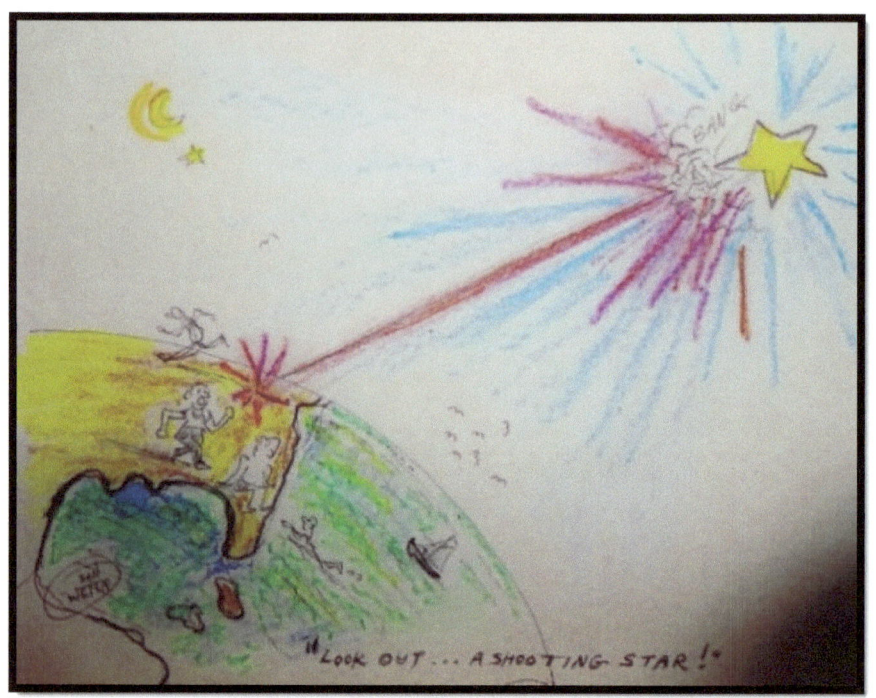

Title: Shooting Star (cartoon)
Size: 12 x 15 inches
Medium: Acrylic on paper
Copyright by Dan Wetta

"Look out! A shooting star!"

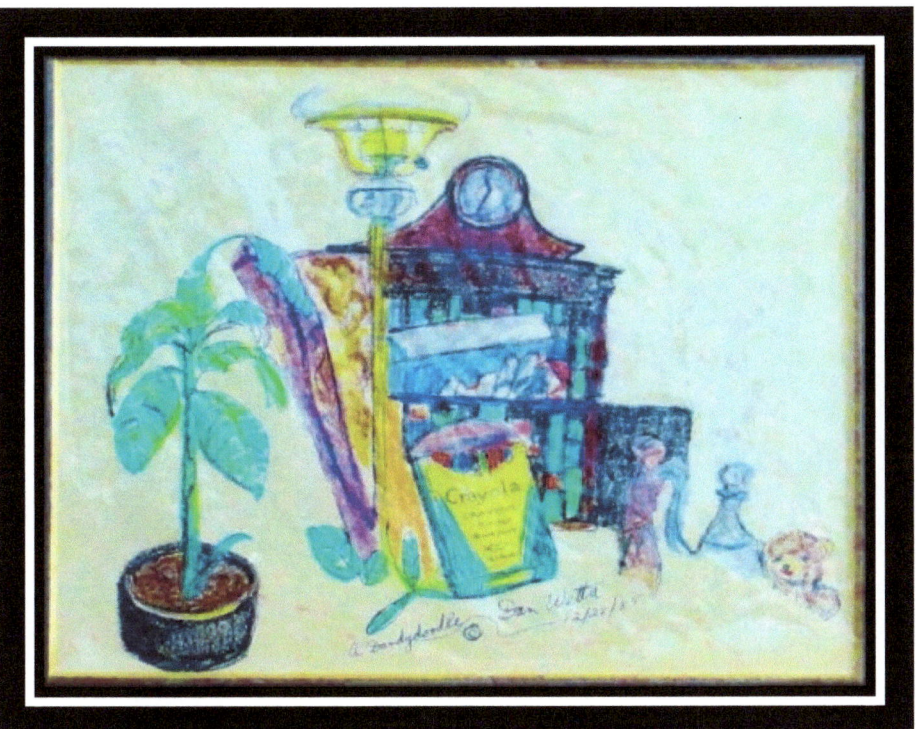

Title: Crayola Doodle
Copyright by Dan Wetta, 1985

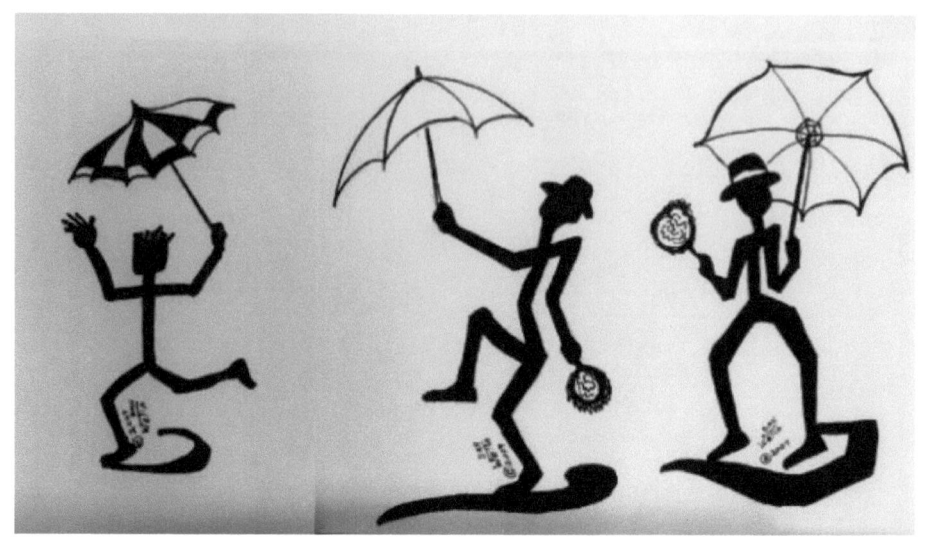

Title: "New Awlins" Street Fun
Copyright by Dan Wetta

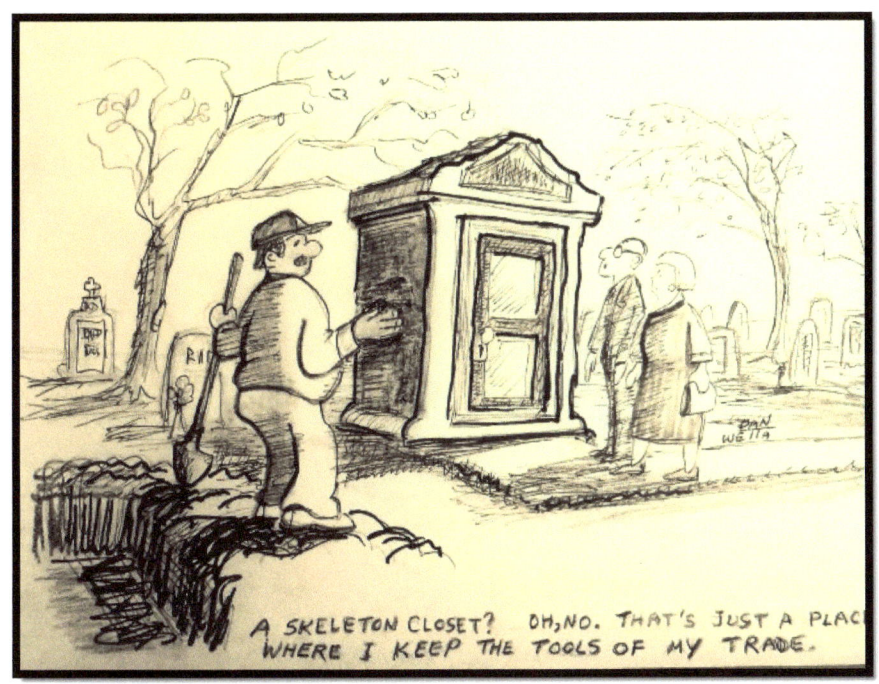

Title: Graveyard Tool Shed (cartoon)
Copyright by Dan Wetta, 1997

"A skeleton closet? Oh, no. That's just a place where I keep the tools of my trade."

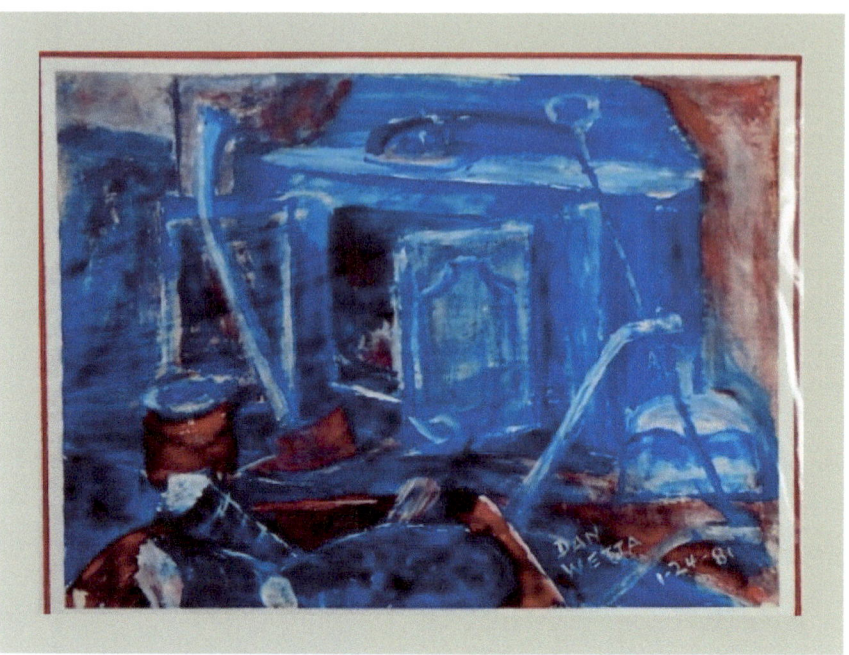

Title: Fireplace Insert
Size: 24x36 inches
Medium: Mixed media on paper
Copyright by Dan Wetta, 1981

This is a practice painting I did when I was taking art lessons at J Sargent Reynolds Community College in Richmond. The fireplace insert was at my house in Aylett, Virginia.

One cold night, I went outside and got some firewood. I placed the frozen wood close to the fire, and after a while, all kinds of bugs began crawling out of the thawed fire wood. Apparently they woke up when the firewood began to thaw.

Another time, when the door to the fireplace insert was closed for the summer, I heard a racket coming from inside it. I opened the door to see what was going on, and a squirrel came running out! I grabbed a broom, opened the front door, and chased him out of the house. I decided that I preferred to live in town.

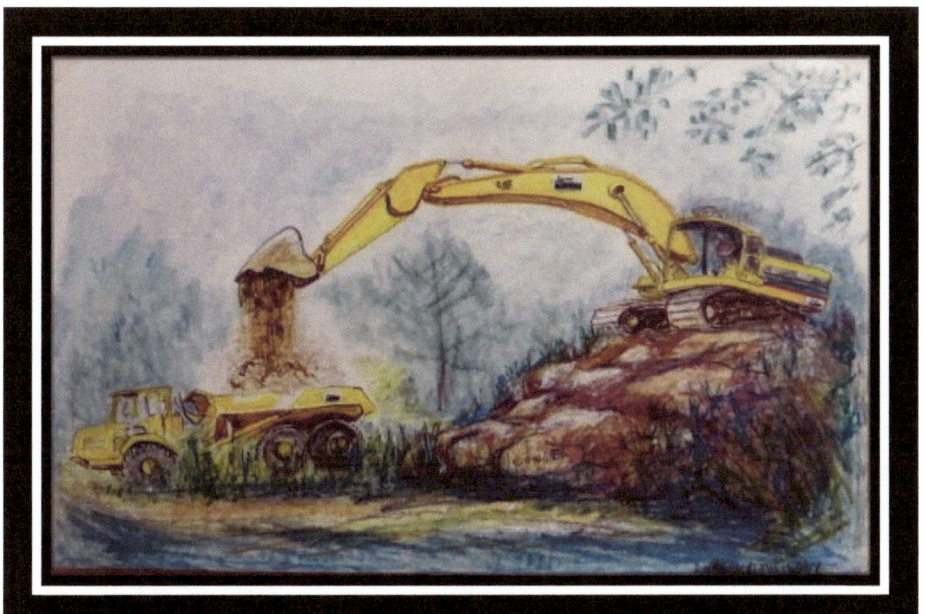

Title: Dirt Digging
Size: 16X20 inches
Medium: Mixed media on paper
Copyright by Dan Wetta

The motto of this company is, "We Move Mountains!"

I am an artist, not a construction worker, so I was a little nervous when I was sketching this, because the operator was digging the dirt out from under himself.

That pile of mud was at the end of Commons Way in Williamsburg Commons. When they finally removed the dirt pile, they extended the road to a farm field where homeless people were living in makeshift huts and growing marijuana plants.

They were evicted to make way for two story houses.

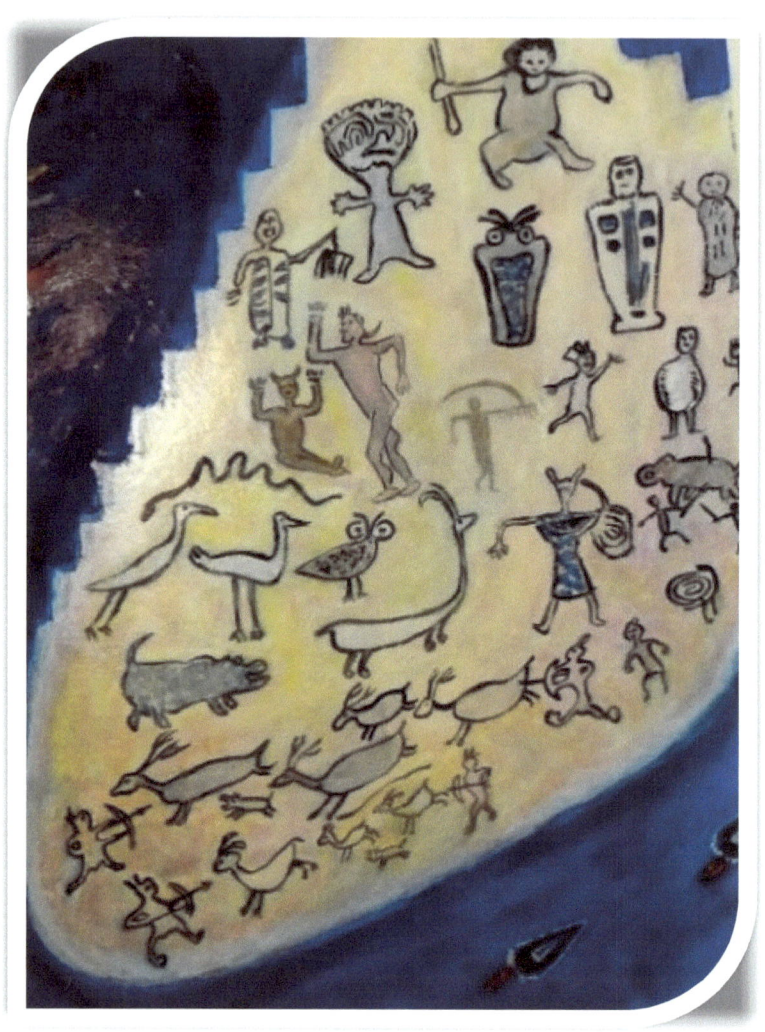

Title: Our Ancestors
Copyright by Dan Wetta

Do you think we used to look like this? If so, does anybody in the above copy of ancient cave art remind you of someone you know?

Chapter 5: Birds, Birds, Birds!

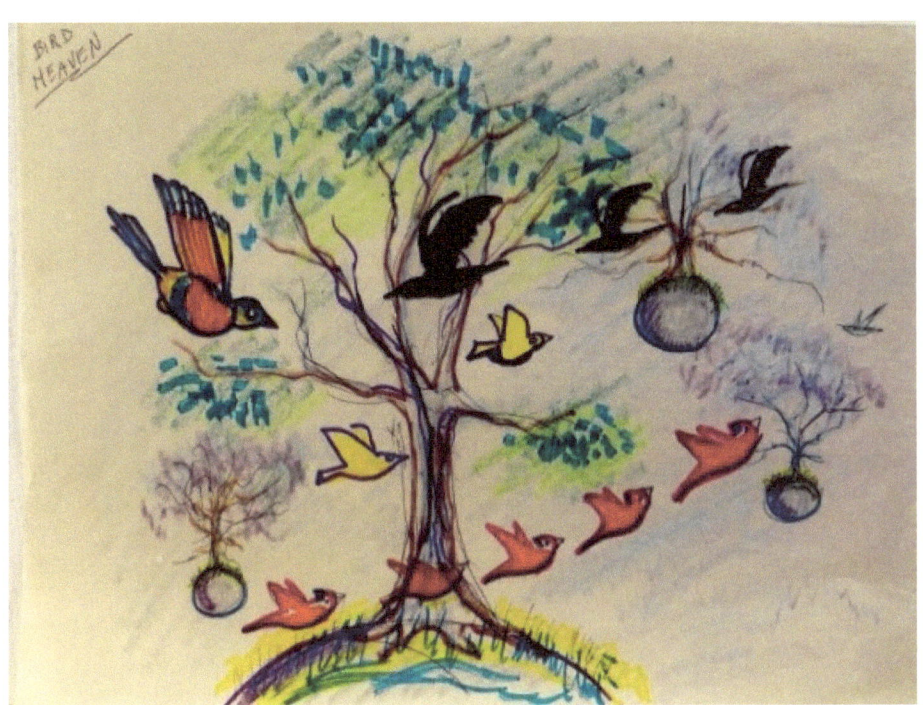

Title: Bird Haven
Copyright by Dan Wetta

I was going to call this drawing "Bird Heaven, but I changed it to "Bird Haven," because I don't think they allow birds in heaven.

However, they might allow trees in heaven, because a couple of the Psalms mention trees in the house of the Lord. See Psalms 52:8 and 93:12. Trees without birds?

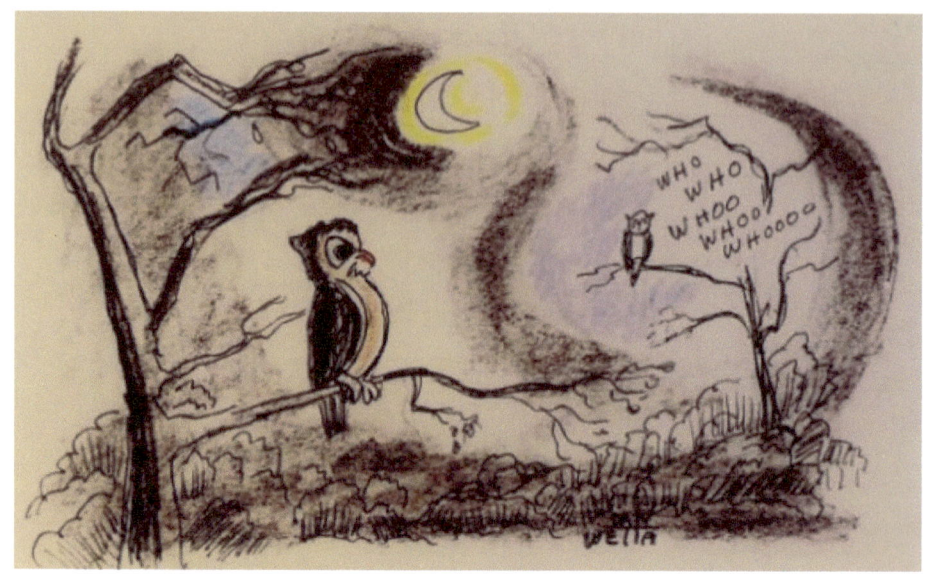

Title: Who Whoo Whooo (drawing)
Copyright by Dan Wetta

If you have ever lived in the woods or in the country, you know that the owls tell the same bedtime story every night:

"Who Whoo Whooo?"

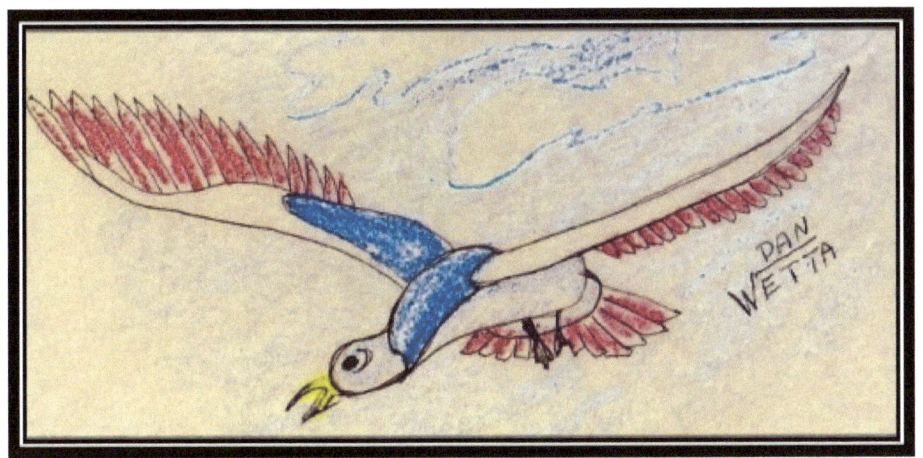

Title: Stupid Bird (cartoon)
Copyright by Dan Wetta

I was trying to design a red, white and blue patriotic bird, but this didn't quite work out. Oh, well, you can't win 'em all! I thought the bird looked stupid; and, hence, the name!

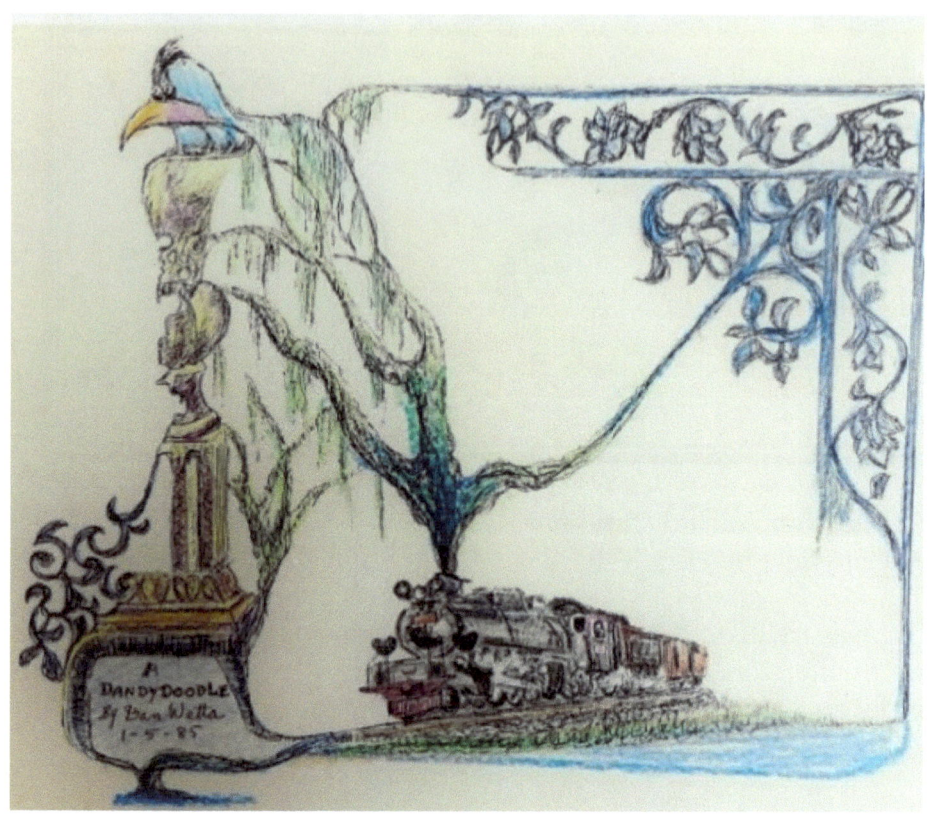

Title: Train and Buzzard (doodle)
Copyright by Dan Wetta, 1985

I also put some Louisiana ironwork and moss into this doodle, but the Louisiana moss is dying out, and they don't put much intricacy into the ironwork anymore.

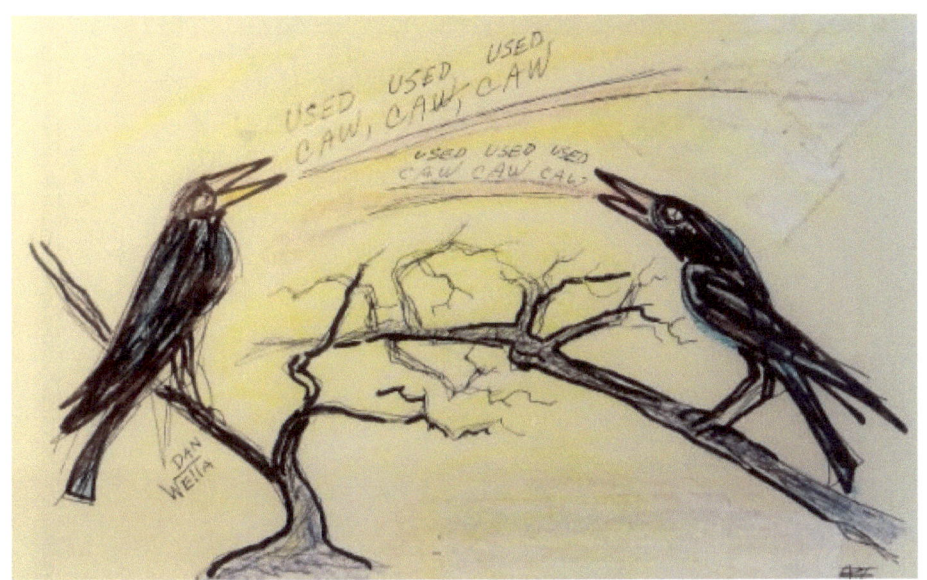

Title: Used Caws (cartoon)
Copyright by Dan Wetta

"Used caw, used caw, used caw!"

When I can't think of a good cartoon gag, I draw stuff like this. But I do think I have heard crows saying this.

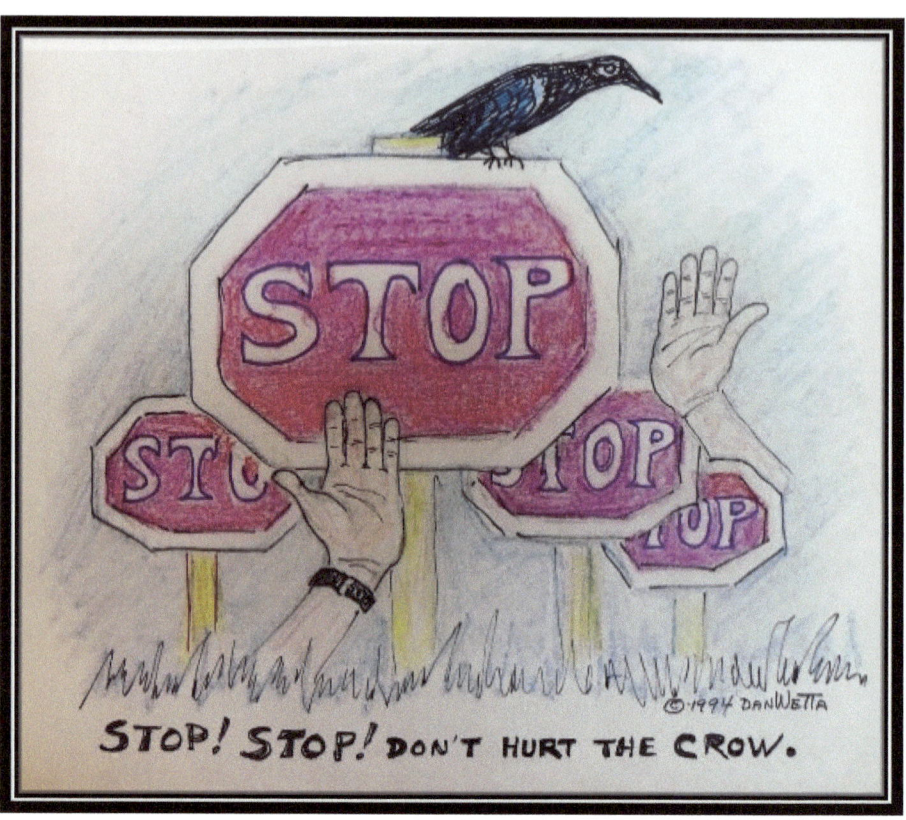

Title: Stop! Don't Hurt the Crow (cartoon)
Copyright by Dan Wetta, 1994

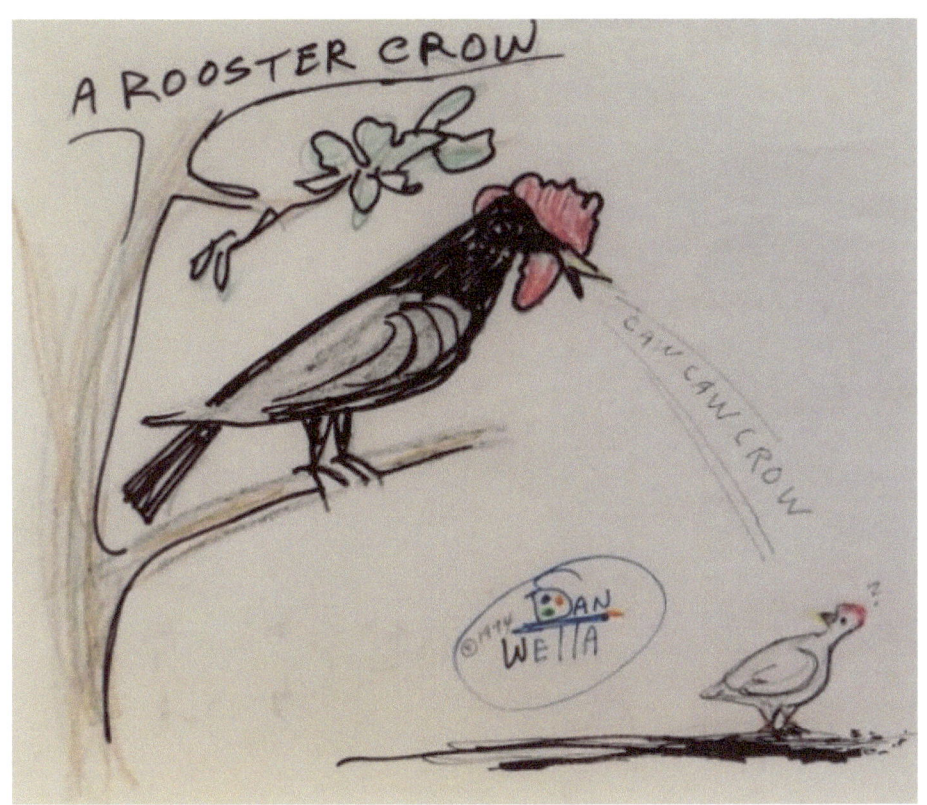

Title: A Rooster Crow (cartoon)
Copyright by Dan Wetta, 1994

"Caw, caw, crow!"
This is what you would call a CAWTOON.

Haw haw!

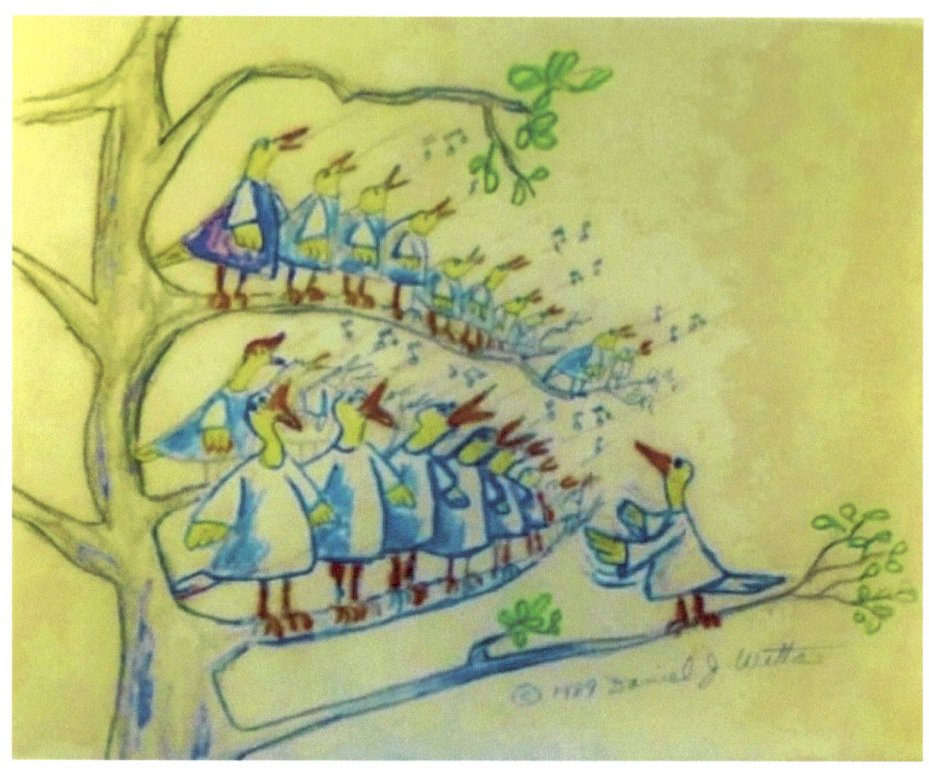

Title: Bird Choir (cartoon)
Copyright by Dan Wetta, 1989

When I was living in the country, I woke up one spring morning to the most beautiful sound I ever heard. I ran outside to see where it was coming from, and this is what I saw.

Chapter 6: Miscellany

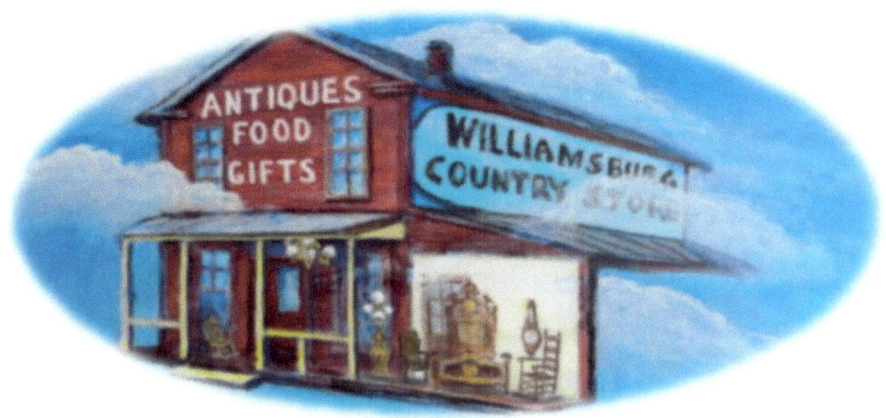

Title: Williamsburg Country Store
Size: 12x24 inches
Medium: Acrylic on canvas
Copyright by Dan Wetta, 1995

This store was located on Richmond Road near Toano, Virginia, but it is not there now.

It was probably demolished, but I wish old buildings like this didn't have to be torn to bits just because they have grown old, so I made it look like it is still alive and floating around in the sky.

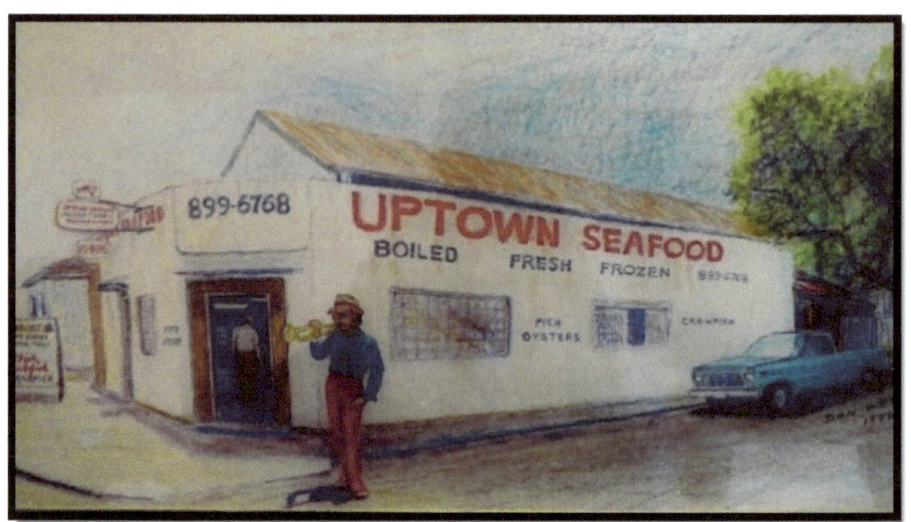

Title: Uptown Seafood
Size: 9x17 inches
Medium: Mixed media on paper
Copyright by Dan Wetta, 1986

That bugler seems to have gone around New Orleans before hurricane Katrina, to blow taps for places that were not going to survive the storm.

My brother, "JJ," used to have crawfish boils all the time, but I never could bring myself to eat crawfish until I was maybe sixty years old.

My brother, Raymond, has a crab boil every month or so, but I don't like crabs either. Maybe it's a good thing I moved to Virginia.

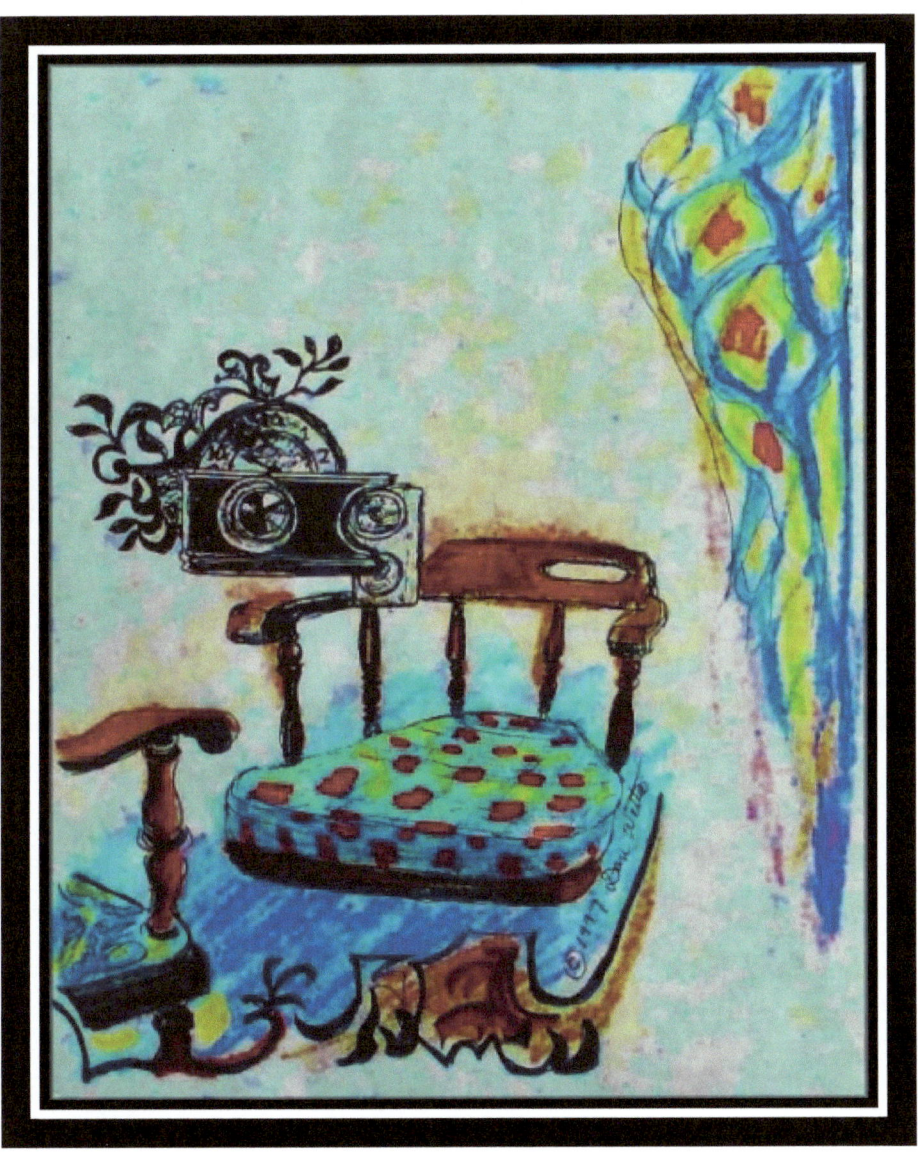

Title: Antique Chair with Blanket (doodle)
Copyright by Dan Wetta, 1997

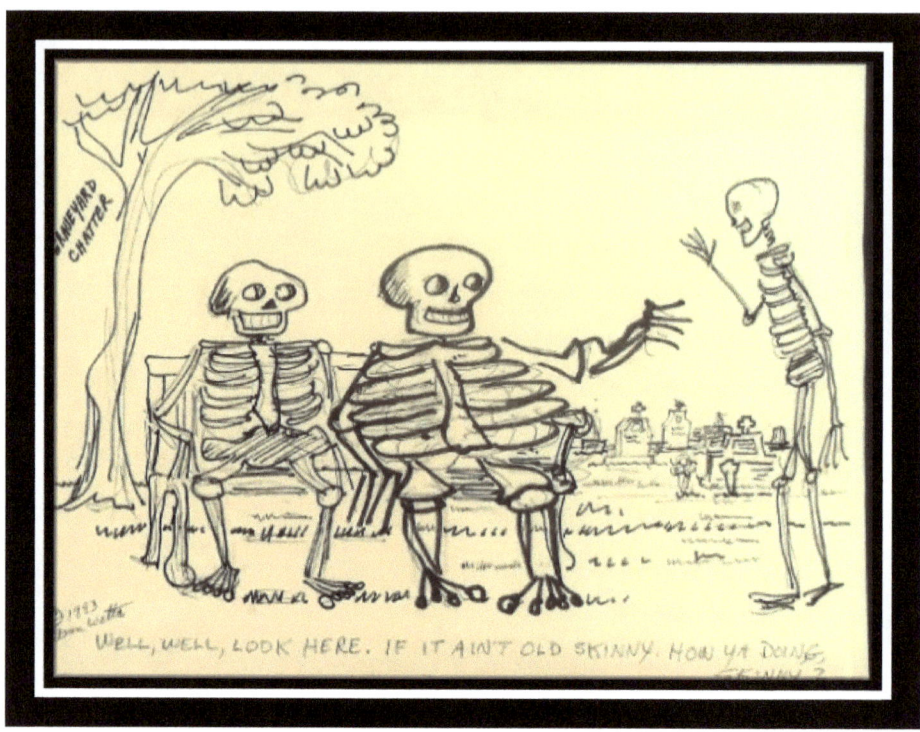

Title: How Ya Doing, Skinny? (cartoon)
Copyright by Dan Wetta, 1993

"Well, well, look here! If it ain't Old Skinny. How Ya' Doing, Skinny?

This is another "Crazy Bones" cartoon of graveyard chatter.

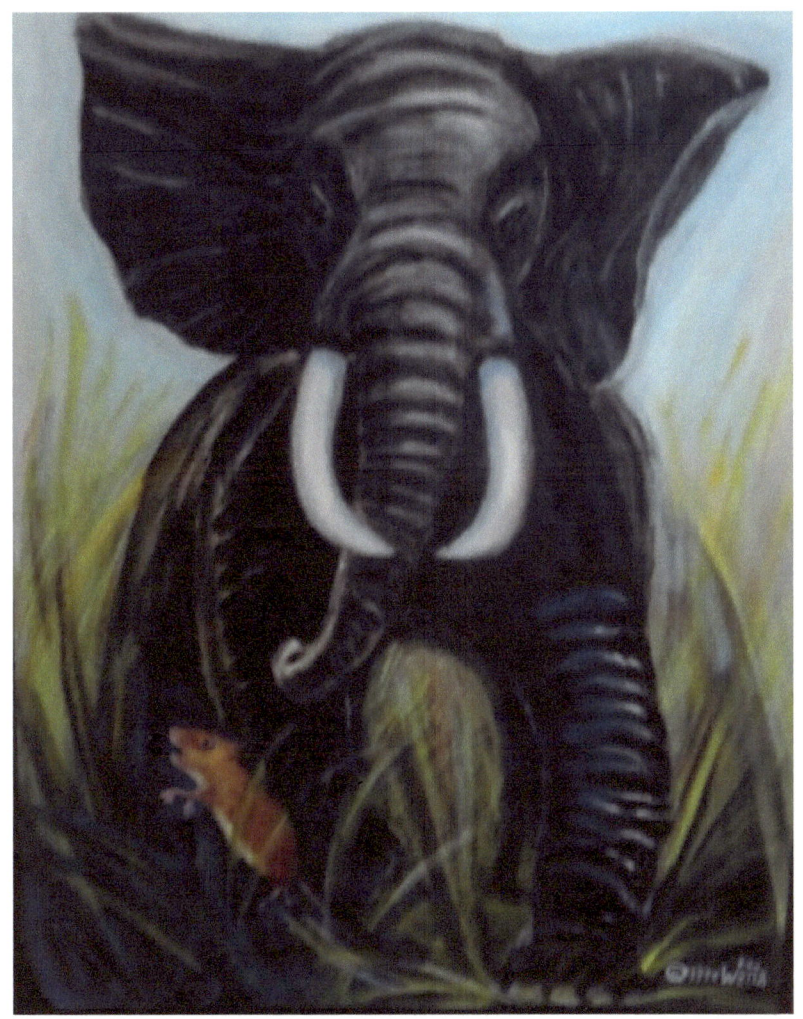

Title: Elephant vs Mouse
Size: 24x30 inches
Medium: Acrylic on canvas
Copyright by Dan Wetta, 1995

Two thousand years ago, the Greek philosopher, Pliny, said that elephants are afraid of mice, and this belief still persists.

However, in 2007, a TV show called "Myth Busters" went to Africa and placed a mouse in the path of some elephants.

On one occasion, an elephant backed off, as if afraid. On a second occasion, an elephant side stepped away from the mouse. Thus, the myth busters concluded that elephants were indeed afraid of mice.

However, it could be that elephants are gentle giants who avoid stepping on mice for fear of crushing them.

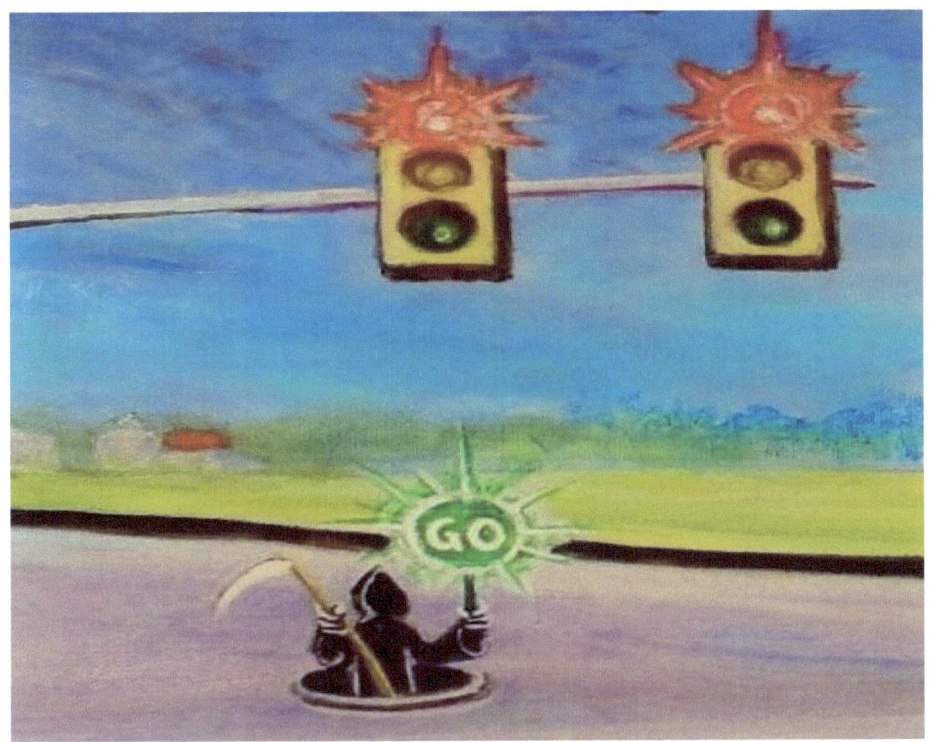

Title: Mixed Signals
Size: 18x24 inches
Medium: Acrylic on canvas
Copyright by Dan Wetta, 1996

There had been a lot of accidents at this intersection of By-Pass Road and Commons Way, so my neighbors were asking: "How many people gotta die before they put up a traffic light?"

They finally put up traffic signals, and when I was half-way through my sketch of this intersection, The Grim Reaper poked his head up through a sewer manhole with a counter signal.

He never gives up.

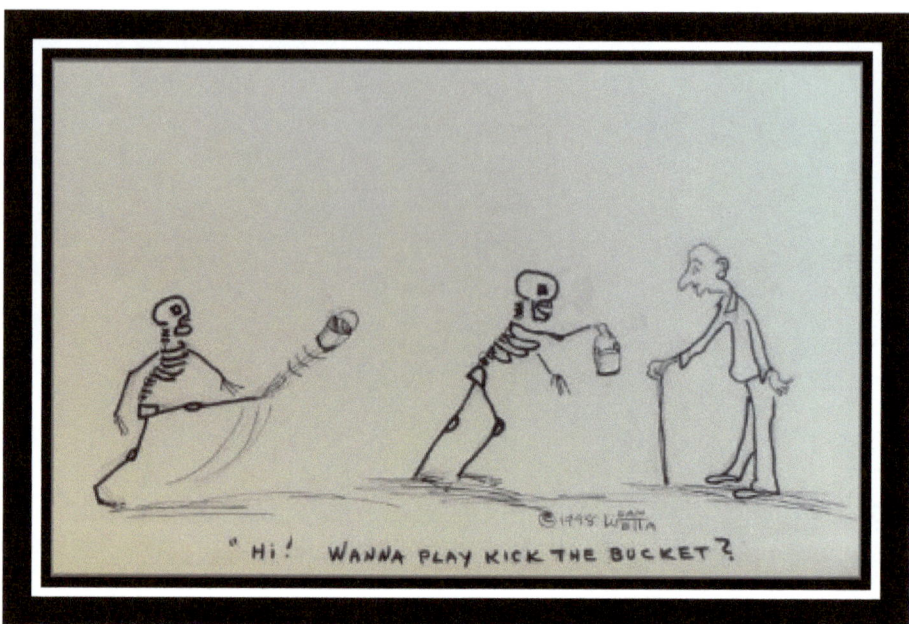

Title: Kick the Bucket (cartoon)
Copyright by Dan Wetta, 1998

"Wanna play 'Kick the Bucket'?"

"Kick the Bucket" is a gruesome idiom that probably stems from the time when somebody with a hangman's noose around his neck stood on a bucket, then someone kicked it from under him.

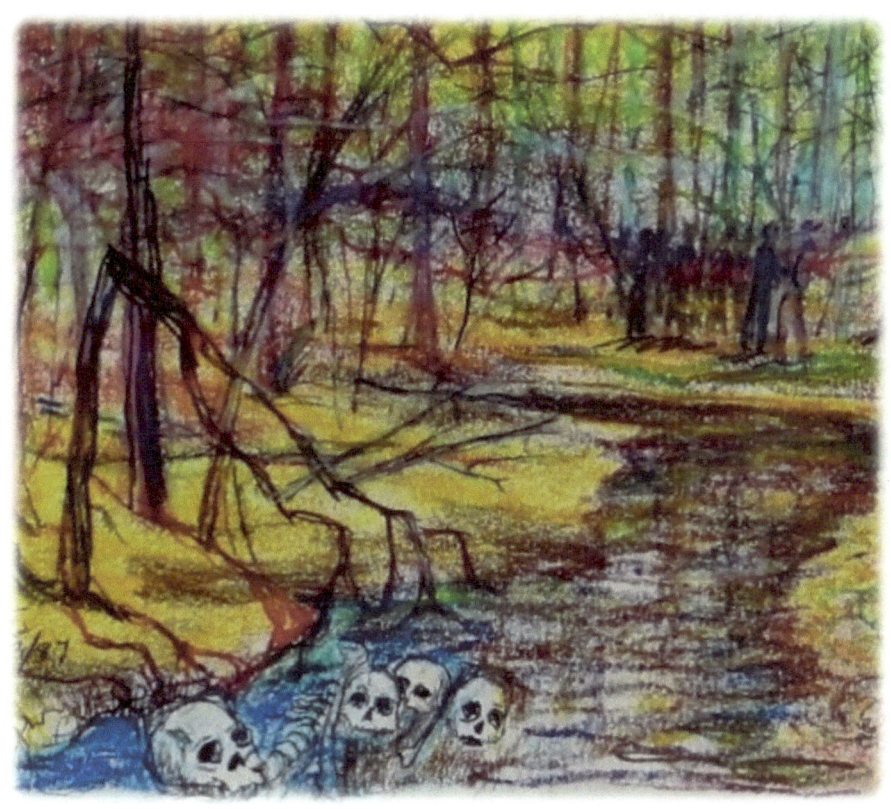

Title: Skulls in Stream
Size: 11x17 inches
Medium: Mixed media on paper
Copyright by Dan Wetta

Skulls in a stream? Looks like I woke up from a nightmare, did a quick drawing, and then went back to sleep.

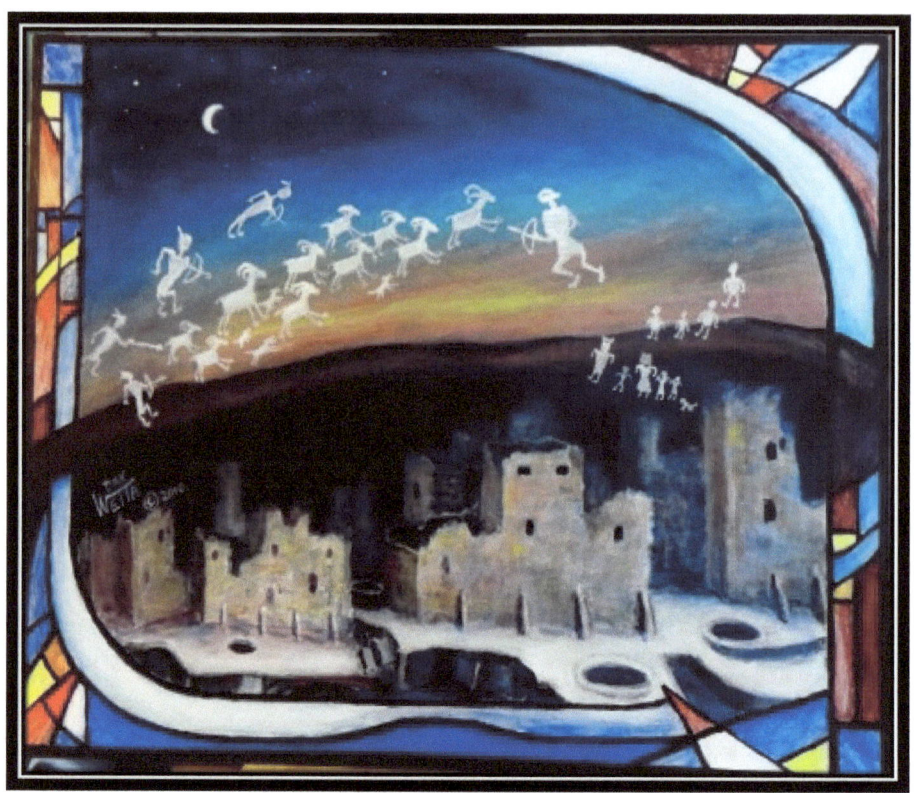

Title: Anasazi
Size: 24x30 inches
Medium: Acrylic on canvas
Copyright by Dan Wetta, 2010

"Anasazi" means "Ancient Ones." The Anasazi cliff dwellers of the American Southwest originally hunted deer and big-horn sheep, and later they began to farm.

They date from 900 to 1450 A.D., after which they disappeared, and nobody knows where they went.

However, their ethereal rock paintings leave us a clue: They believed that all creatures have a spirit and are part of the Great Spirit, so perhaps their spirits remain at the cliff sites to this day – where they are now hunting deer and big-horn sheep in the sky.

Chapter 7: You May Not Want To Go Here!

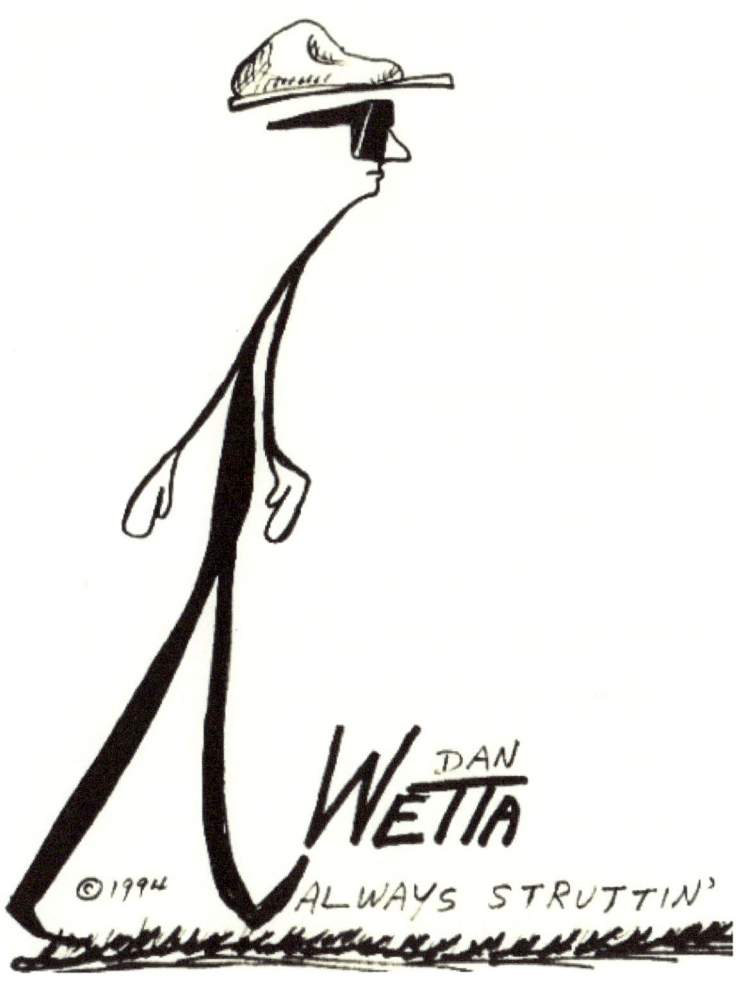

You may not want to go here, because this chapter contains drawings that are very corny or just plain dumb.

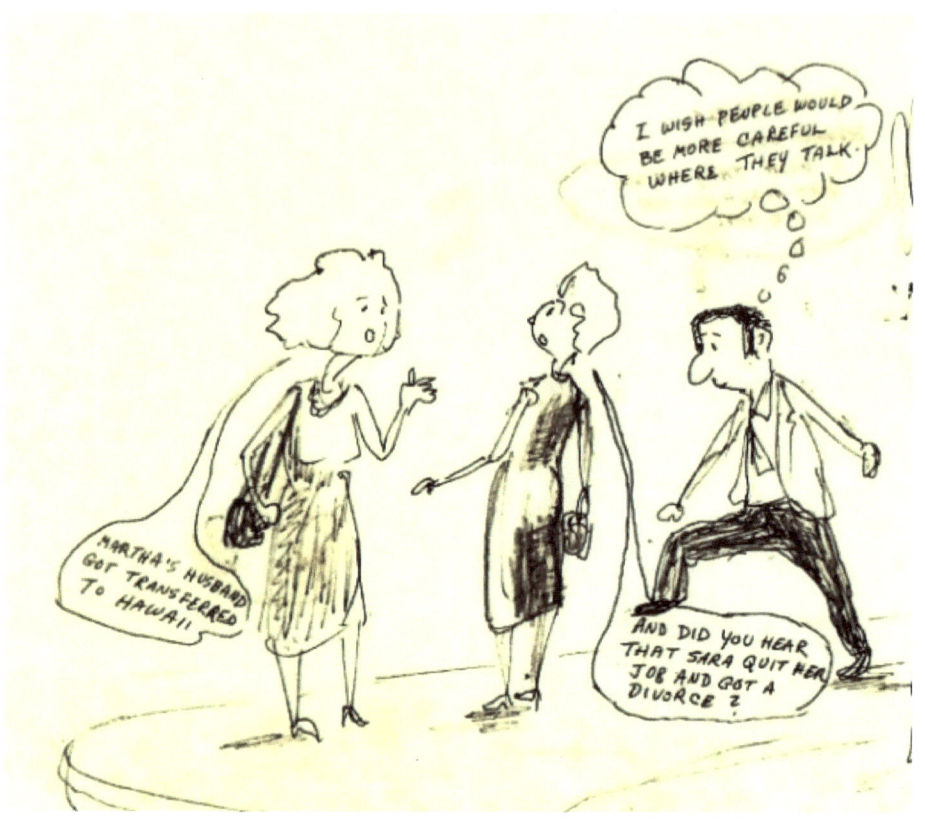

Title: Be Careful Where You Talk (cartoon)
Copyright by Dan Wetta, 1998

"I wish people would be more careful where they talk!" says the frustrated man, as he tries to step over the "talk bubbles" of the ladies gossiping.

And if you like gossip: The lady on the left is saying, "Martha's husband got transferred to Hawaii." The lady on the right is adding, "And did you hear that Sara quit her job and got a divorce?"

This man does need to be careful where he steps!

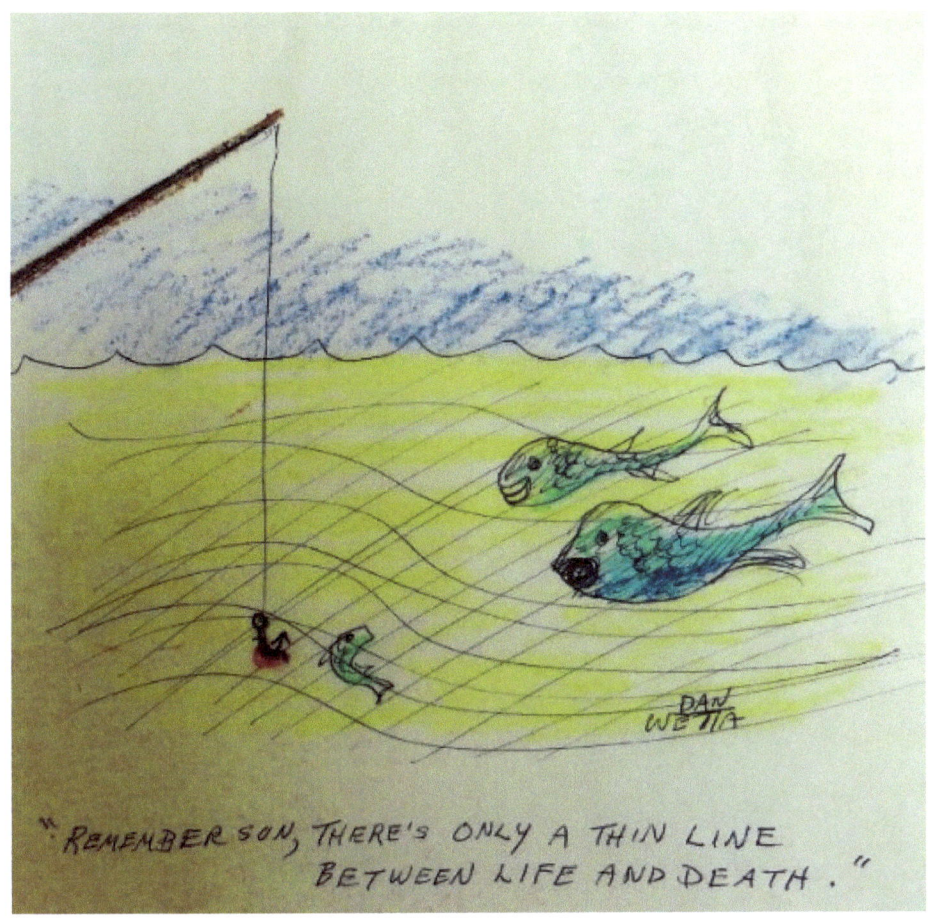

Title: Thin Line (cartoon)
Copyright by Dan Wetta

"Remember, son, there's only a thin line between life and death," admonishes the papa fish to his inexperienced son!

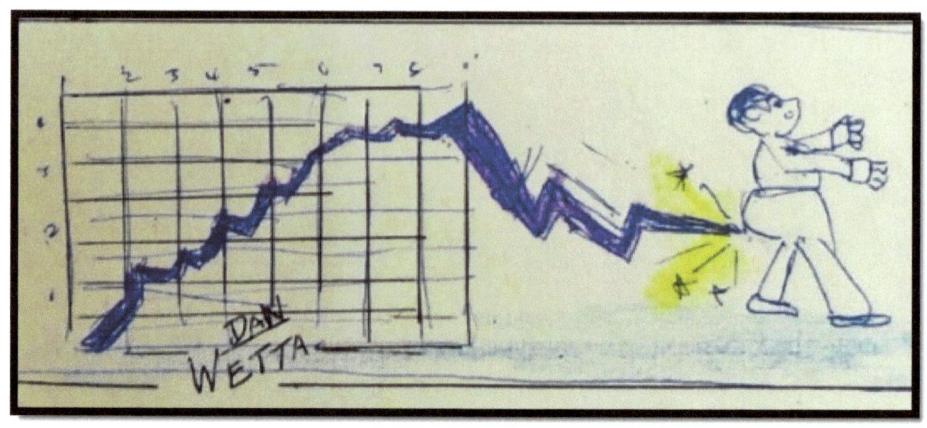

Title: Off The Chart (cartoon)
Copyright by Dan Wetta

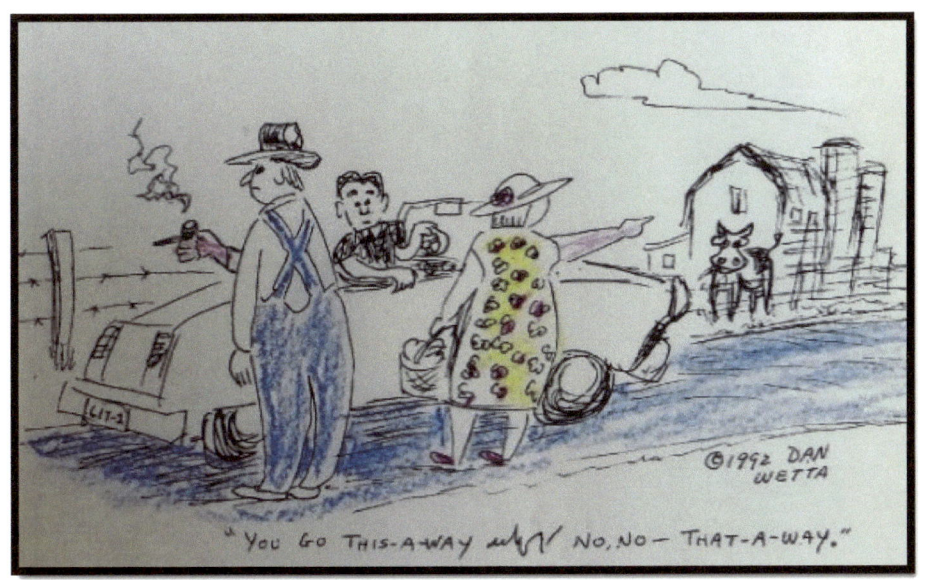

Title: This-a-Way (cartoon)
Copyright by Dan Wetta, 1992

"You go this-a-way."
"No, no, that-a-way."

Now you know why men don't like to ask for directions.

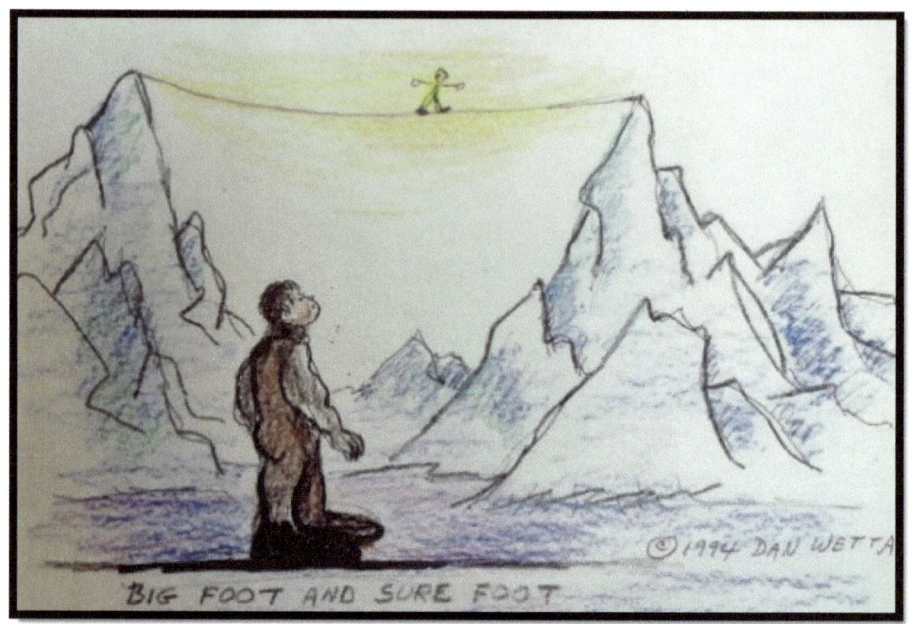

Title: Big Foot and Sure Foot (cartoon)
Copyright by Dan Wetta, 1994

On the wire, Sure Foot takes the higher road.

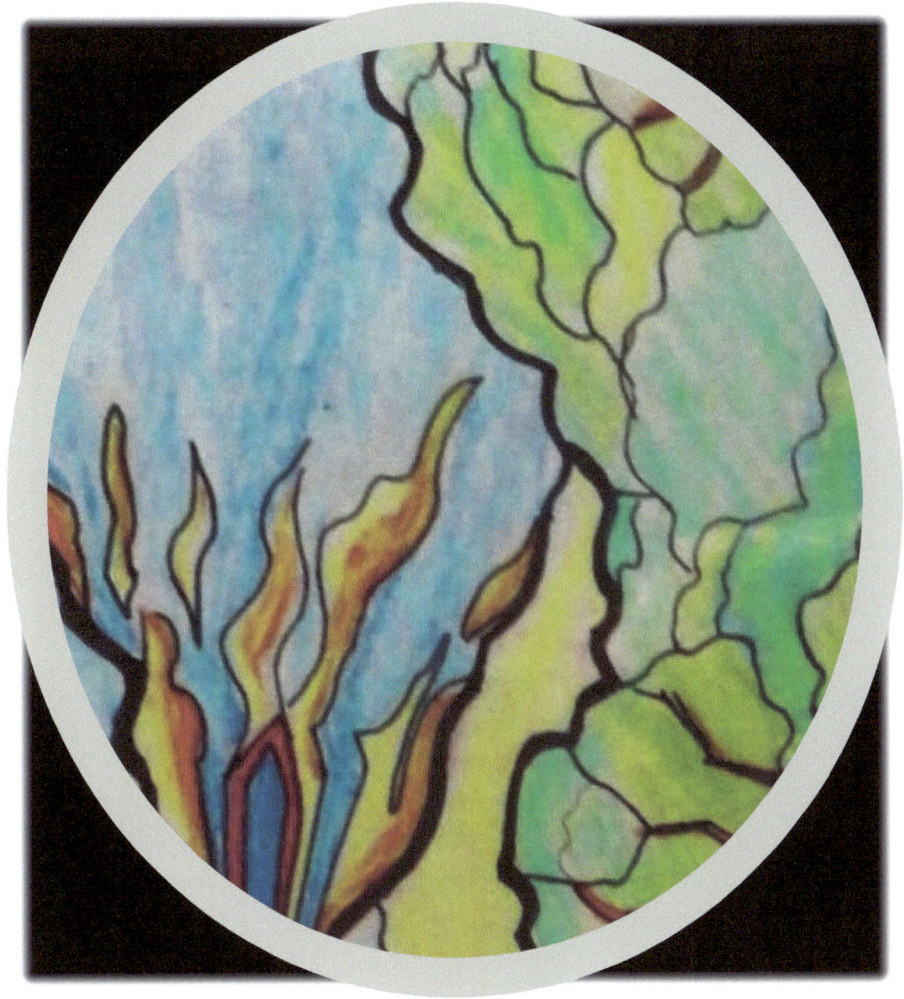

Title: Abstract Three: "Eve Reminiscing."
Copyright by Dan Wetta, 1997

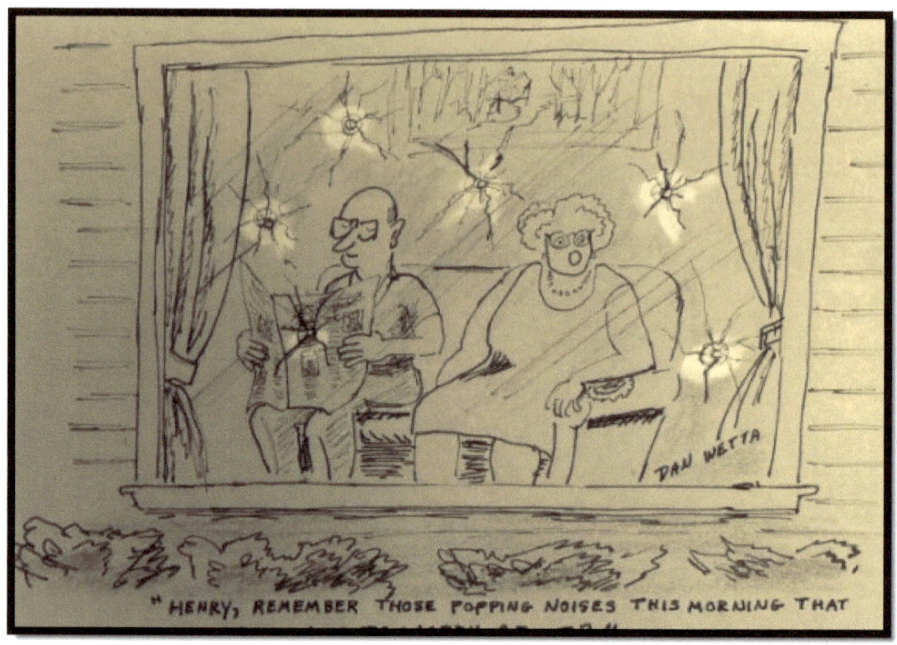

"HENRY, REMEMBER THOSE POPPING NOISES THIS MORNING THAT

Title: Window Holes (cartoon)
Copyright by Dan Wetta

"Henry, remember those popping noises this morning that you said not to worry about?"

Those yellow spots on the window are supposed to be highlighting bullet holes in the window, but when my son asked me why I drew all those spider webs on the window, I knew this cartoon was a flop.

However, I decided to put it in this book to demonstrate how we all see things differently.

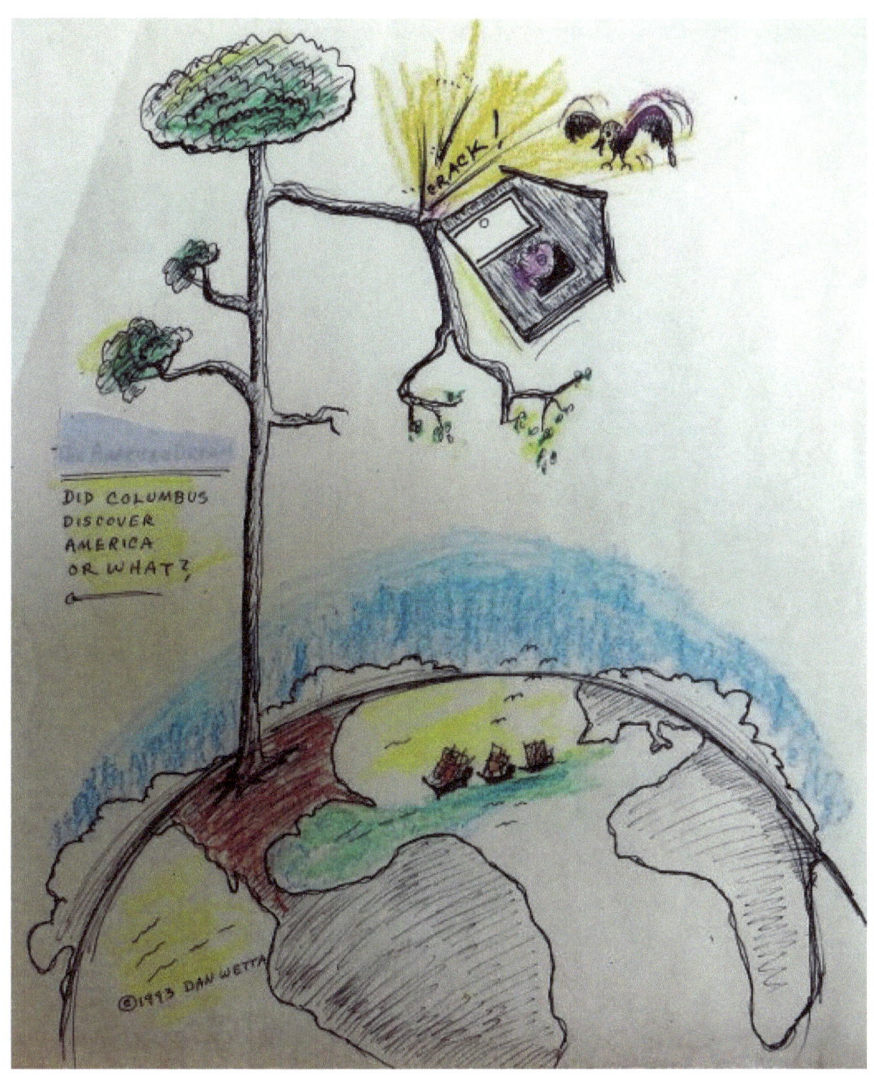

Title: Nina, Pinta and Santa Maria (cartoon)
Copyright by Dan Wetta, 1993

The cartoon asks, "Did Columbus discover America, or what?" That man would not be able to live in an American tree house if Columbus had not discovered America! The crow squawks its unhappiness about the man in its birdhouse.

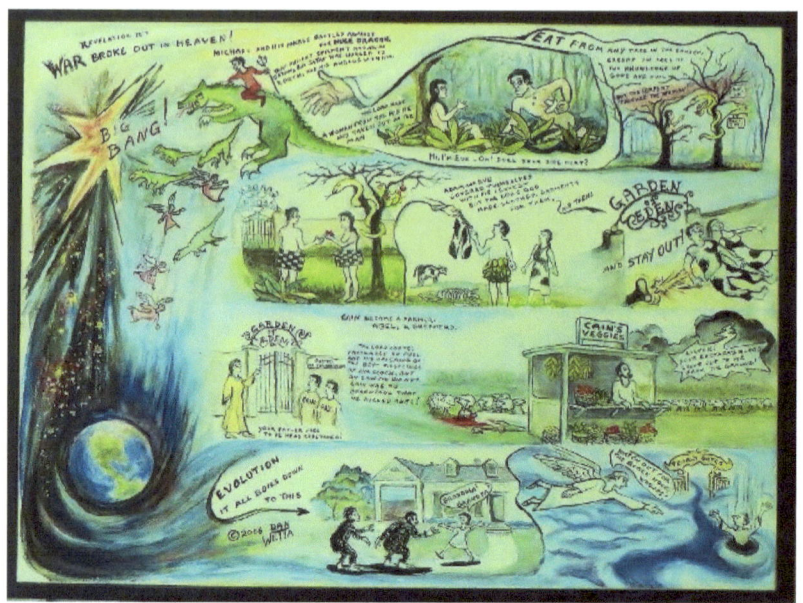

Title: Summary (cartoon)
Size: 30x40 inches
Medium: Acrylic on canvas
Copyright by Dan Wetta, 2006

This is a compilation of several of my cartoons expressing commentary about Bible stories (especially the creation stories) and evolution theory. The depictions on this canvas have been separately illustrated throughout the volumes of art in this series.

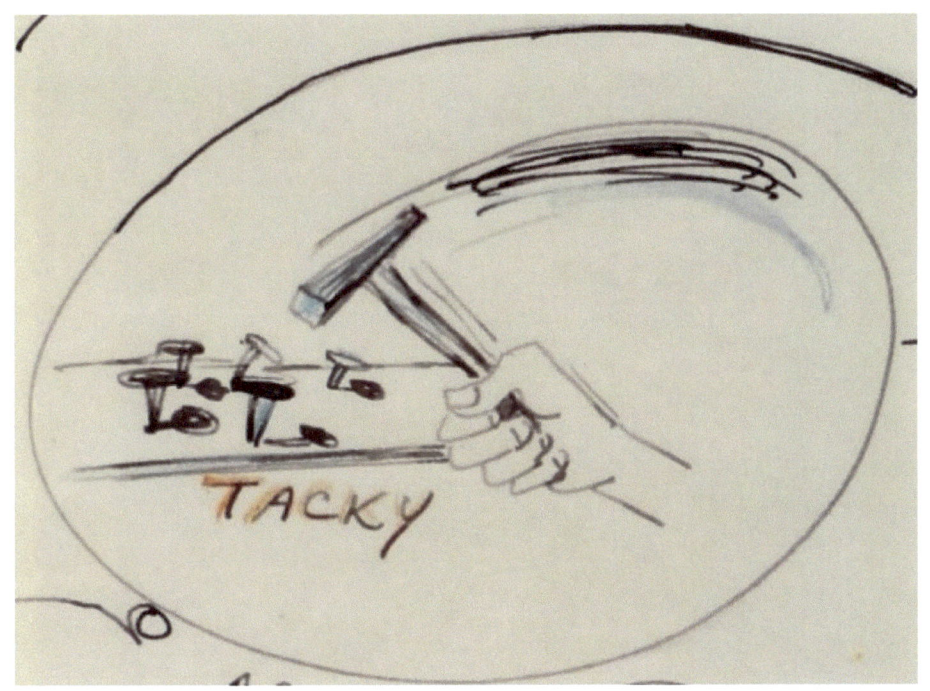

Title: TACKY (doodle)
Copyright by Dan Wetta

I guess this is more of a pun than a doodle.

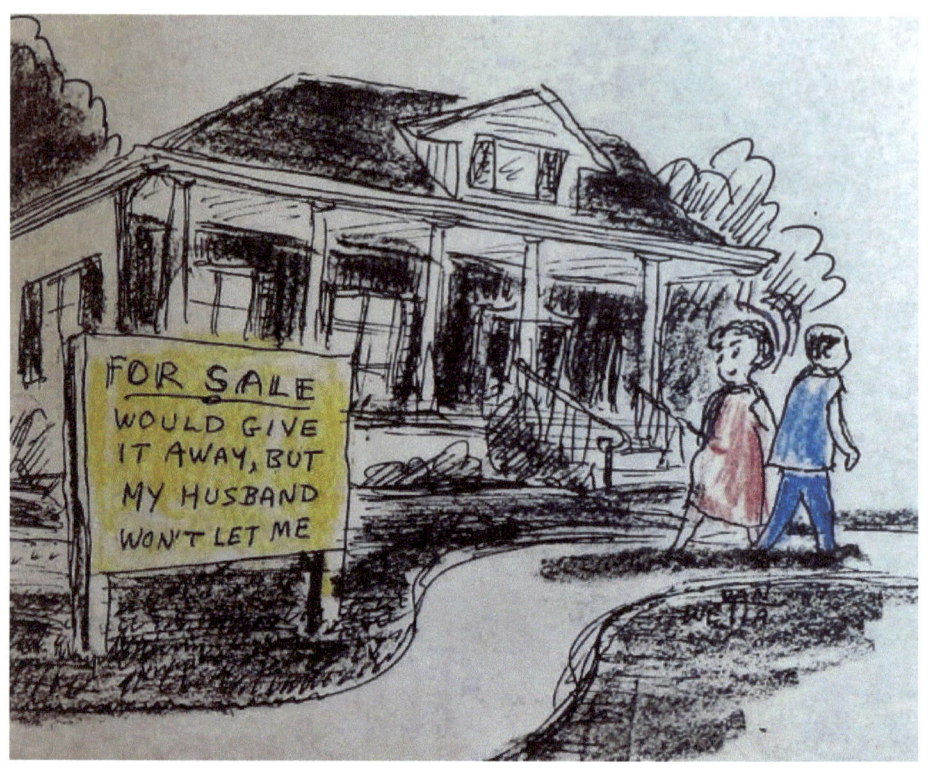

Title: For Sale (cartoon)
Copyright by Dan Wetta

"For Sale: Would Give It Away But My Husband Won't Let Me"

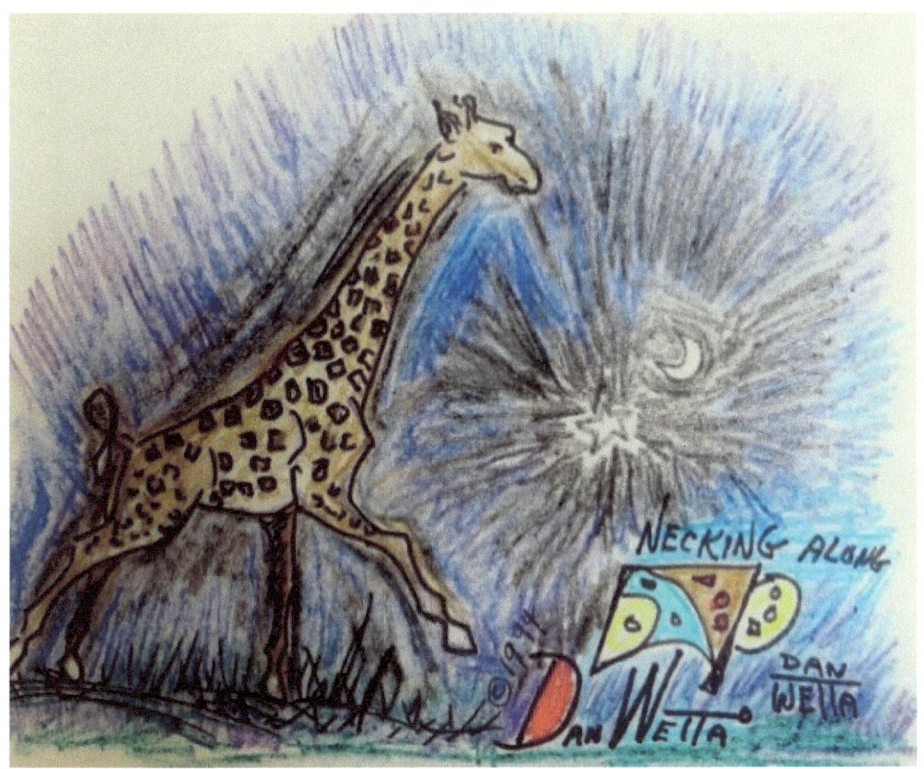

Title: Necking Along (cartoon)
Copyright 1994, Dan Wetta

I should have given the giraffe a longer neck, but I like the colors.

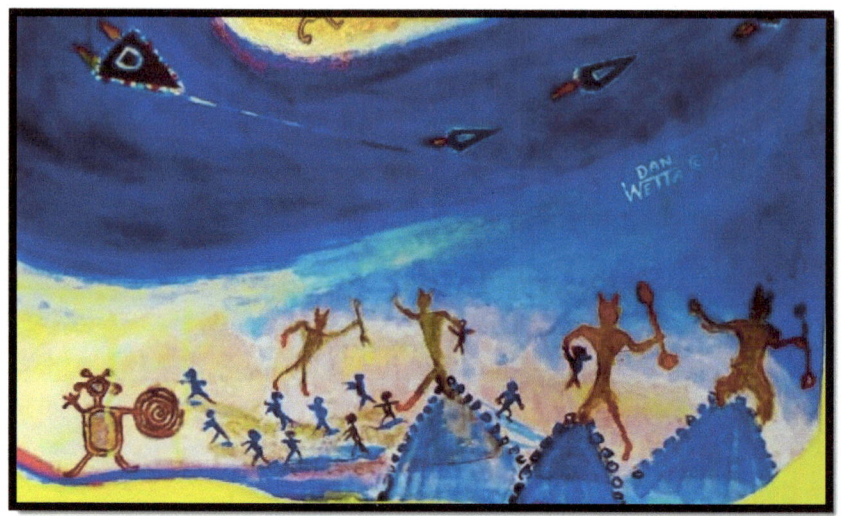

I have reproduced a pictograph that American Indians made 30,000 years ago to show how they were invaded by aliens from space.

They have a legend about a battle in the sky above their pueblo on the Snake River in west central Idaho, followed by an invasion of star beings who wreaked havoc upon them. The pictograph shows giants emerging from their triangular shaped air ship with strange weapons.

I think that this ancient pictograph about giants and the legend about this space invasion confirms what Genesis 6:4 says: "The Nephilim were on the earth in those days…and also afterward."

Some bible scholars say that Nephilim refers to giants, and other scholars say that it means "The ones who came down from above."

Something else to think about:

Since there were no airplanes in the sky until about a hundred years ago, it is not likely that the legend of triangular-shaped airships is a figment of their imagination.

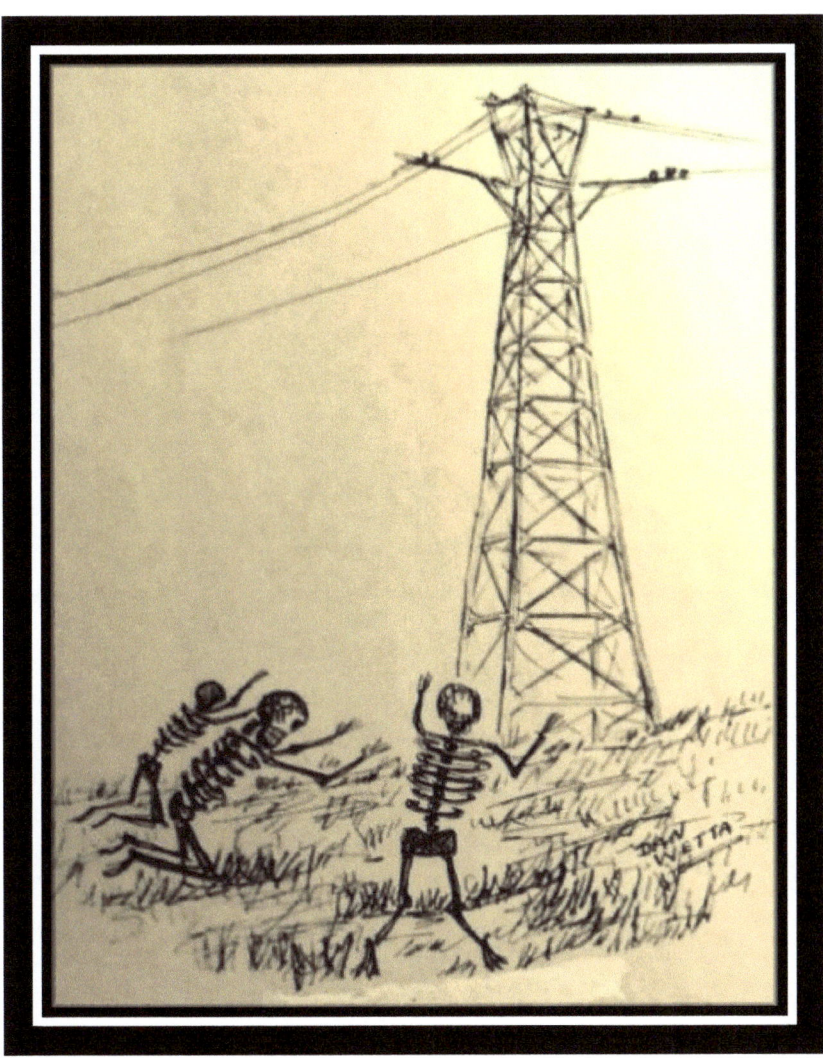

People will believe anything. So will skeletons.

This trio thinks the hi-voltage tower is a giant skeleton from the sky. (Undated cartoon).

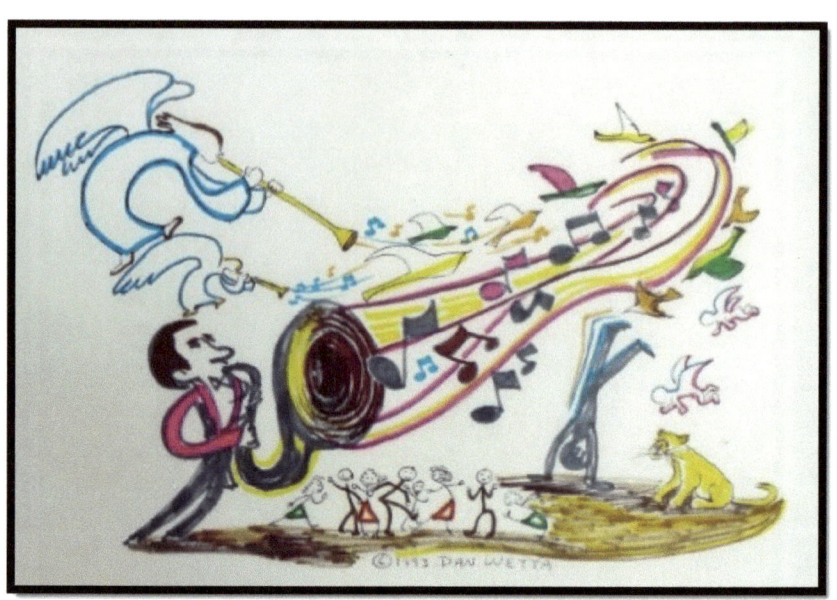

Title: Saxophone Player (cartoon)
Copyright by Dan Wetta, 1993

Do you ever wonder what would happen if a saxophone player ever got into heaven?

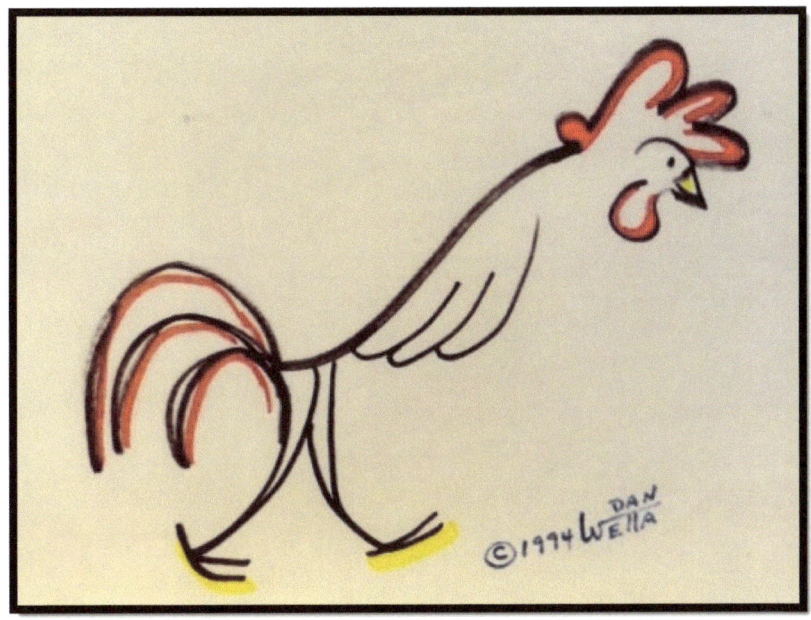

Title: Rooster Down in the Dumps (cartoon)
Copyright by Dan Wetta, 1994

A) Is this rooster down in the dumps?

B) Is this rooster in deep thought, trying to figure out the answer to his problem?

C) Is this rooster worried about climate change?

D) None of the above

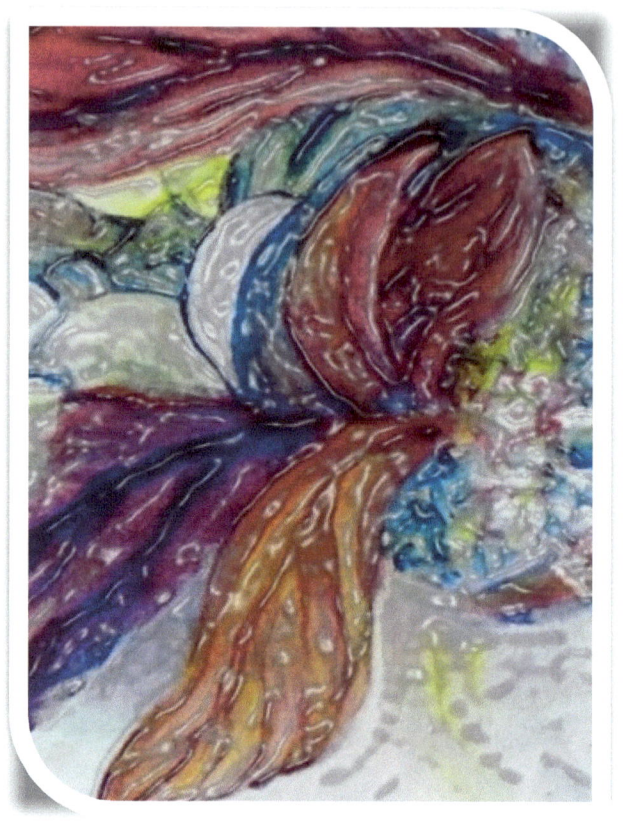

Abstract Forty One
Copyright by Dan Wetta, 2012

This abstract is from my painting, "Flowers in the Swimming Pool."

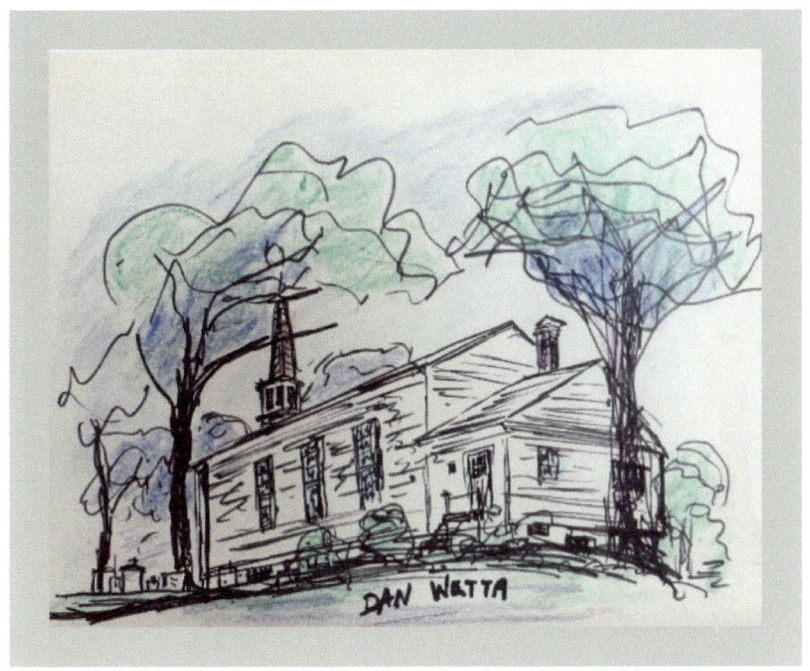

Title: St. David's Episcopal Church

This is a rough sketch that I did of historic St. David's Episcopal Church in Aylett, Virginia, but I never got around to doing a finished acrylic painting of it.

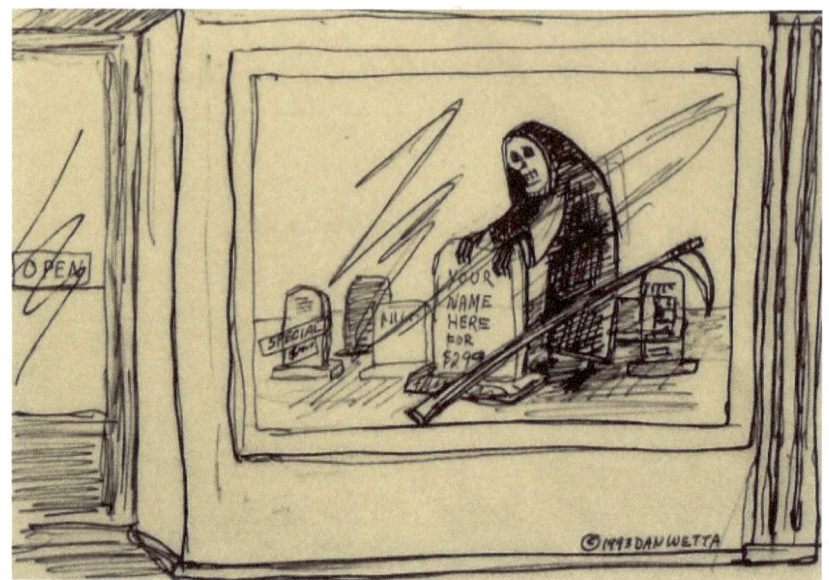

Title: Carve Your Name In Stone (cartoon)
Copyright by Dan Wetta

Don't trust this guy!

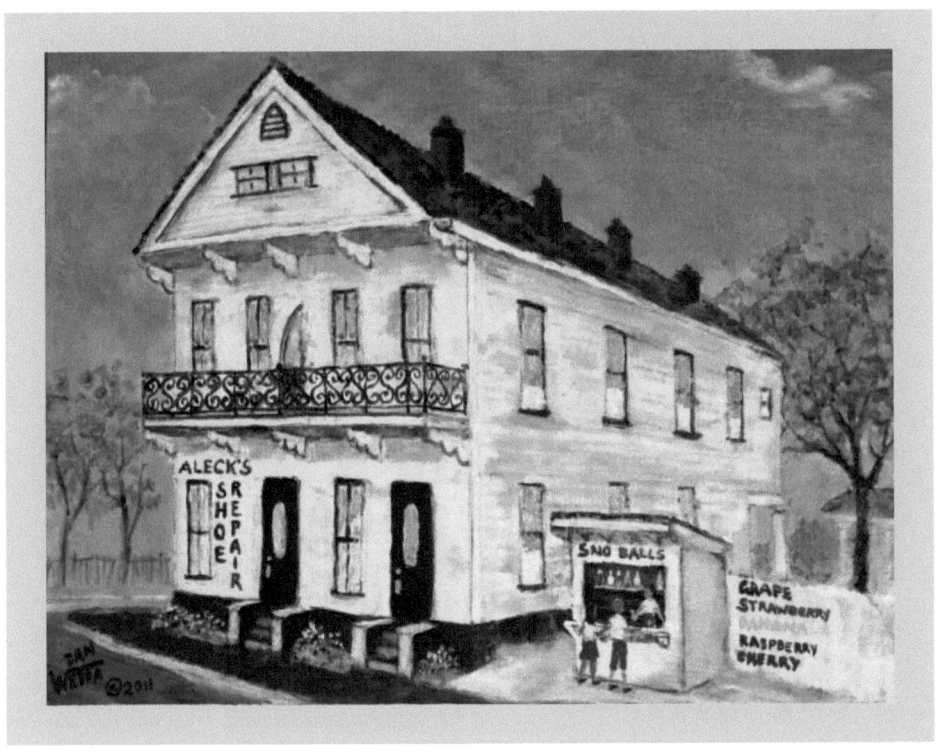

Washington Avenue Revisited

    I just had some more memories of how life was when I lived in this house on Washington Avenue in New Orleans during the 1930's.

    There used to be a family barroom on just about every other street corner in New Orleans. Sometimes my daddy would give one of us children ten cents and a pitcher and say, "Go to Sam's Bar and get me ten cents worth of beer." Sam would fill the pitcher up with draught beer, and we would bring the pitcher of beer back home. One time my sister Anna Marie was carrying a glass pitcher of beer, and she fell down on the way home. The glass pitcher broke, and Anna Marie got back up holding nothing but the glass handle of the pitcher. She came home and gave the handle to daddy. To this day, I still tease Anna Marie about that.

Sometimes I would sit at the kitchen table with Daddy and drink a half glass of beer and eat crackers and cheese. On one rainy night, when raindrops were running down the kitchen window, we tried mind control to make those defy gravity and run *up* the window, but, of course, that did not work.

Then we experimented with mental telepathy. We tried to read each other's mind, but that did not work out either.

We got the news from the radio back then, and my daddy told me that they were experimenting with television, but it was several years later before I saw a TV. Shortly after I was discharged from the Army, I was walking on Broad Street in Richmond, Virginia, when I noticed a crowd of people looking into a store window. A black-and-white TV was on display, and it was turned on. It was my introduction to television, probably in 1948.

We kids never went to the doctor, because Mama had a home remedy for everything from chicken pox to mumps. Daddy had his own home remedies for us as well! He liked it when the kids got sick with the flu, because he made us hot gin and tonic to restore us to health. Of course, he had to sample it for us!

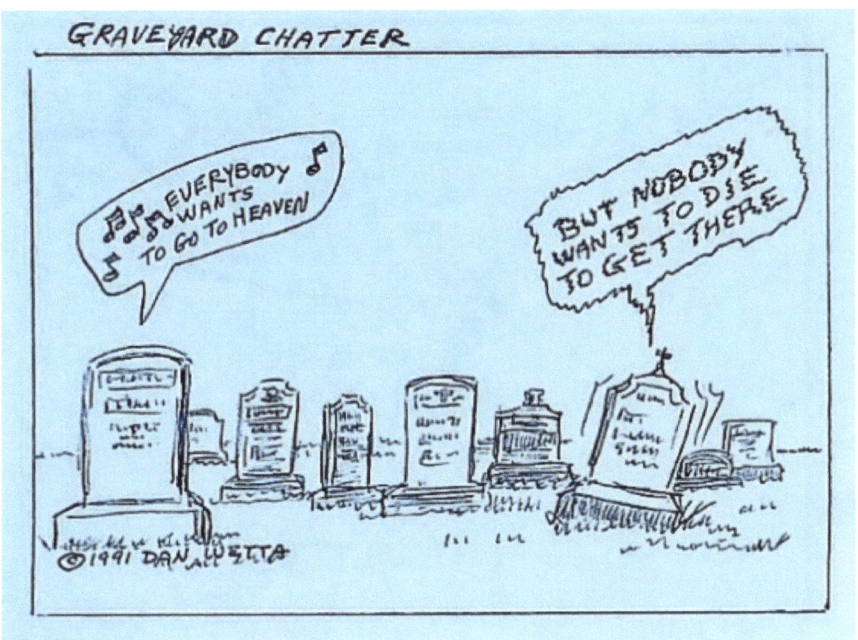

Title: Everybody Wants to go to Heaven (cartoon)
Copyright by Dan Wetta 1991

But General Douglas McArthur said, "Old generals never die, they just fade away."

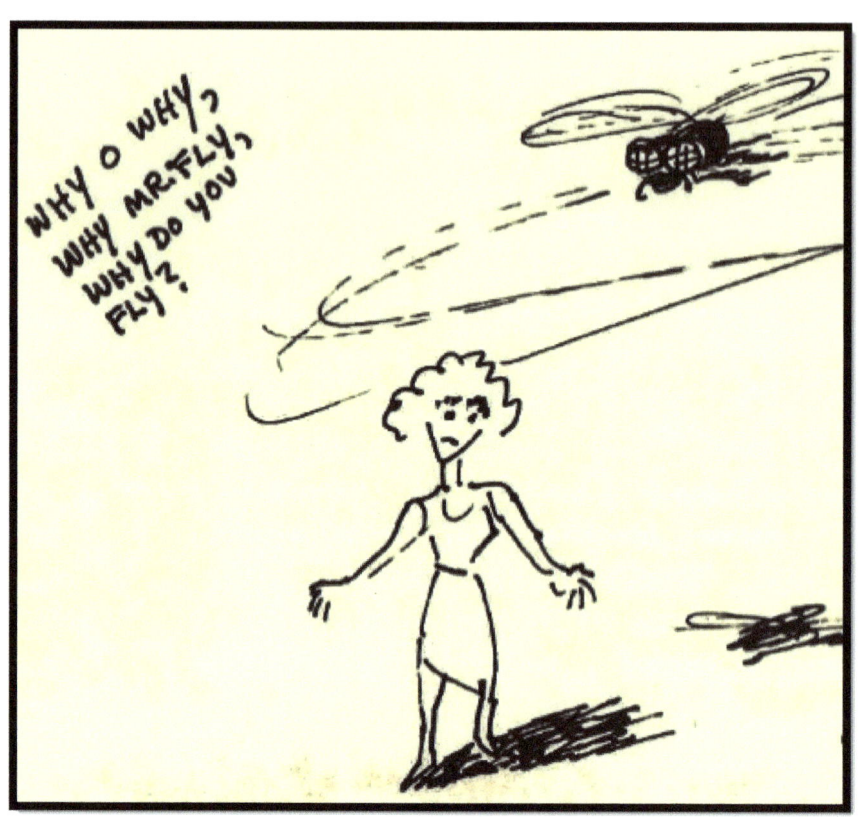

Title: The Fly (cartoon)
Copyright by Dan Wetta

I'm beginning to see why they don't allow flies in heaven.

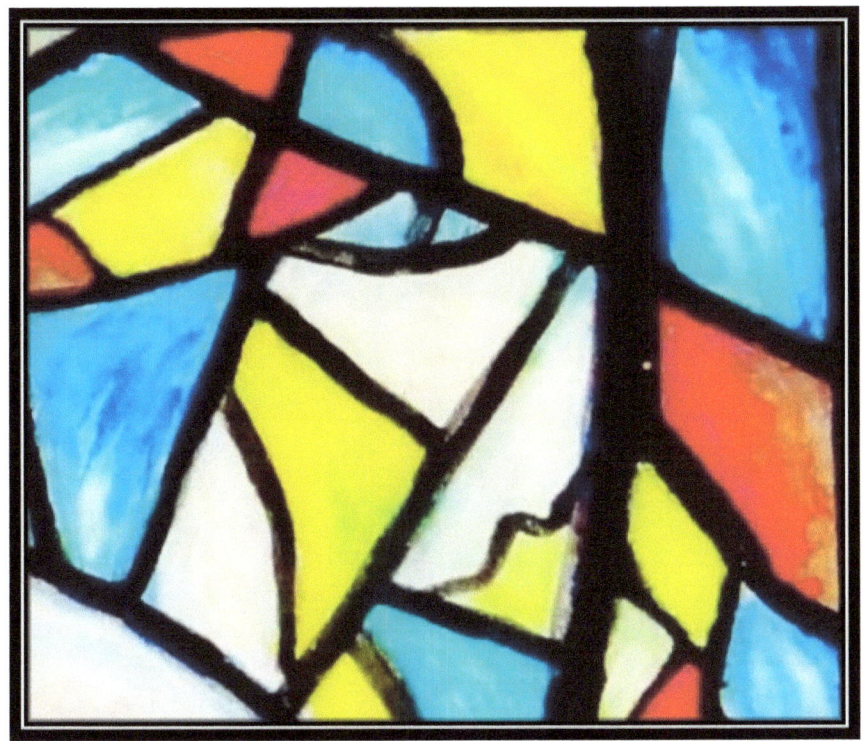

Title: Abstract Eleven
Copyright by Dan Wetta 2001

This abstract is a section of my painting: Stained Glass Birds.

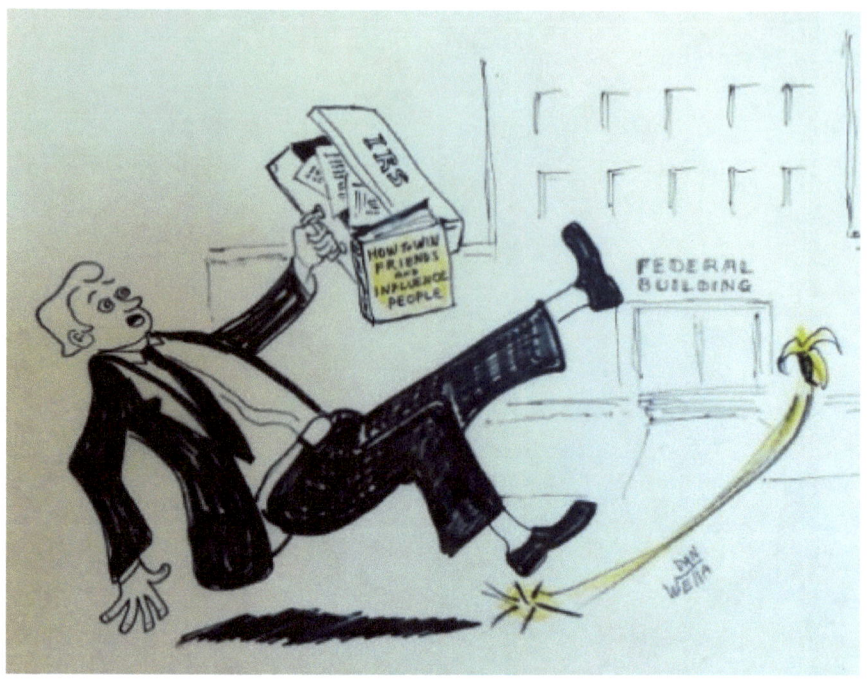

Title: Your Friendly Tax Collector (cartoon)
Copyright by Dan Wetta

This is a slapstick gag. For some reason or other, prat falls like this usually get a laugh, depending upon who is falling on his butt.

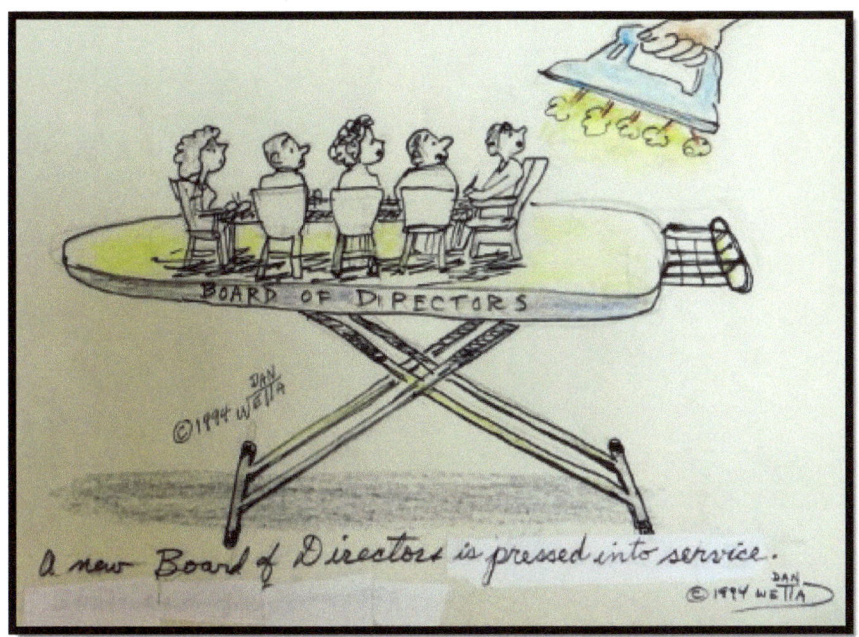

Title: Board of Directors (cartoon)
Copyright by Dan Wetta 1994

If you have ever lived in a condominium association or a gated community, there were probably times when you would like to have been the one holding that hot iron. Not all the time, but there are times.

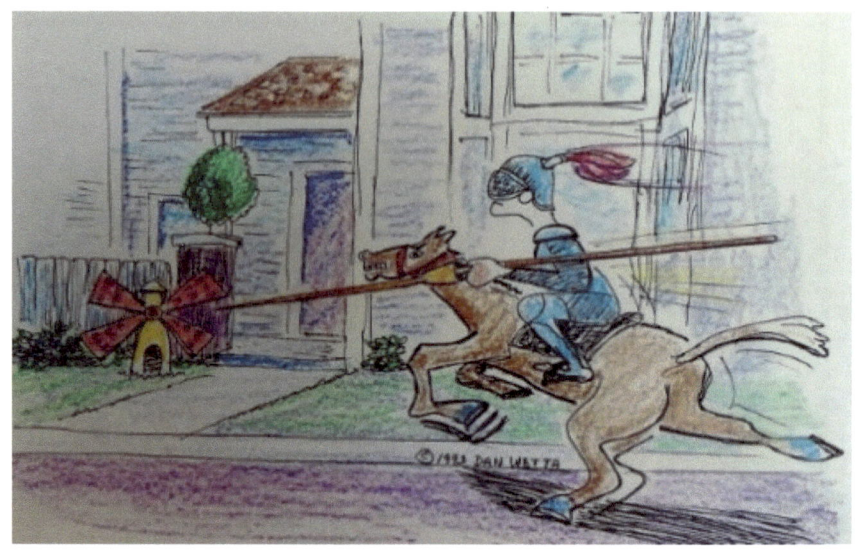

Title: Get Rid of the Wind Mill! (cartoon)
Copyright by Dan Wetta 1993

Before you buy a condo or house in a gated community, read the rules first!

One time, a member of a certain condominium association put an ornamental windmill outside her condo, and the board of directors went bananas. THAT WAS AGAINST THE RULES!

They actually hired a knight in armor to attack and destroy it. (Wink!)

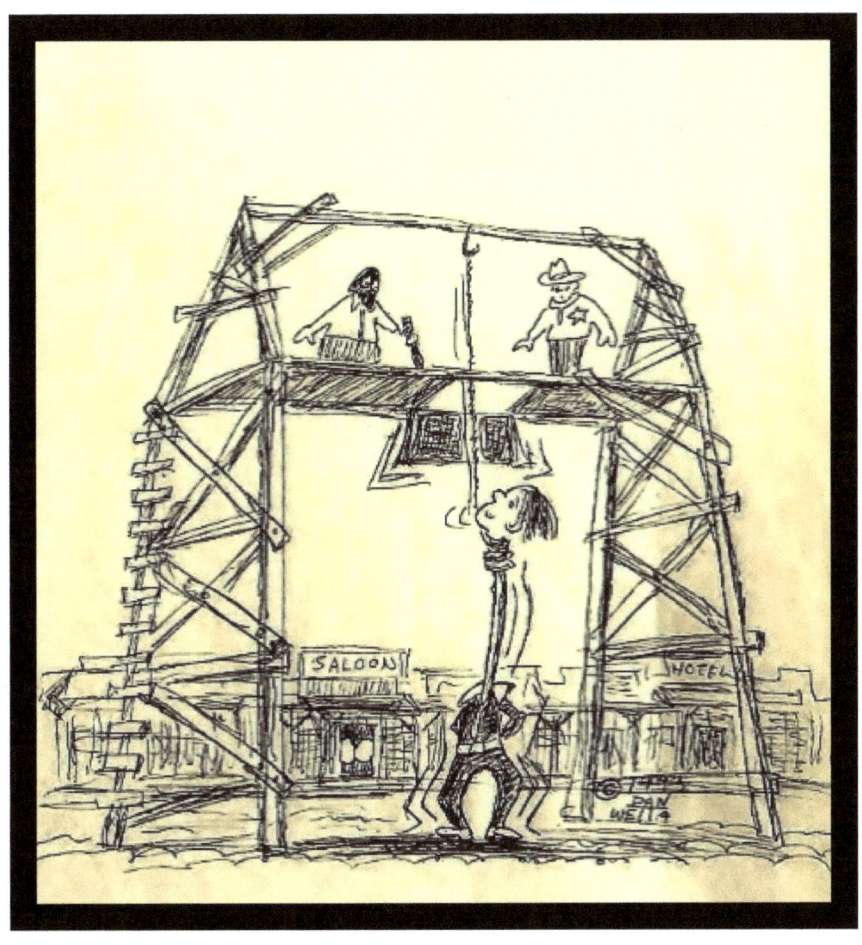

Title: Old Rubber Neck (cartoon)
Copyright by Dan Wetta 1993

The day they tried to hang old Rubberneck…

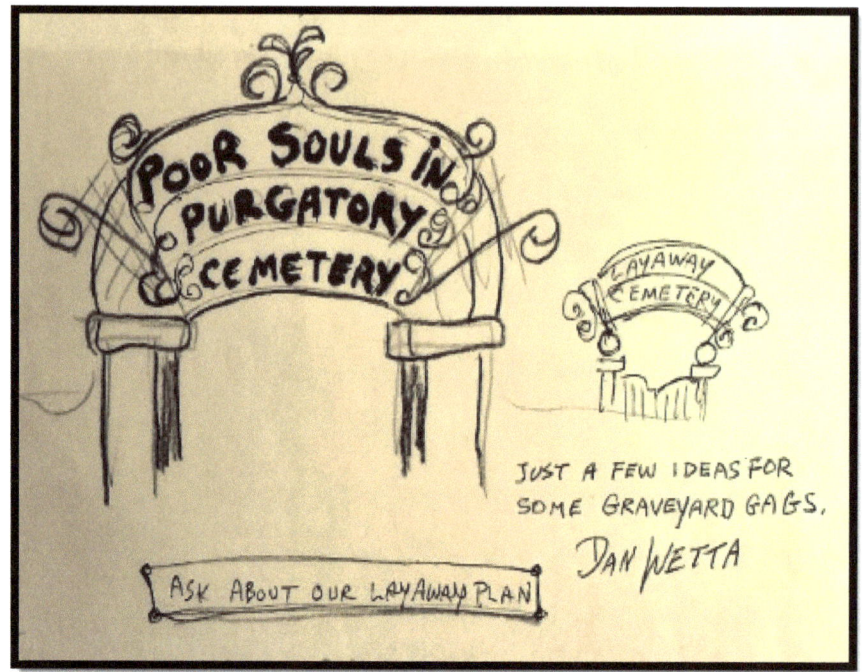

Title: Graveyard Humor (cartoon)
Copyright by Dan Wetta

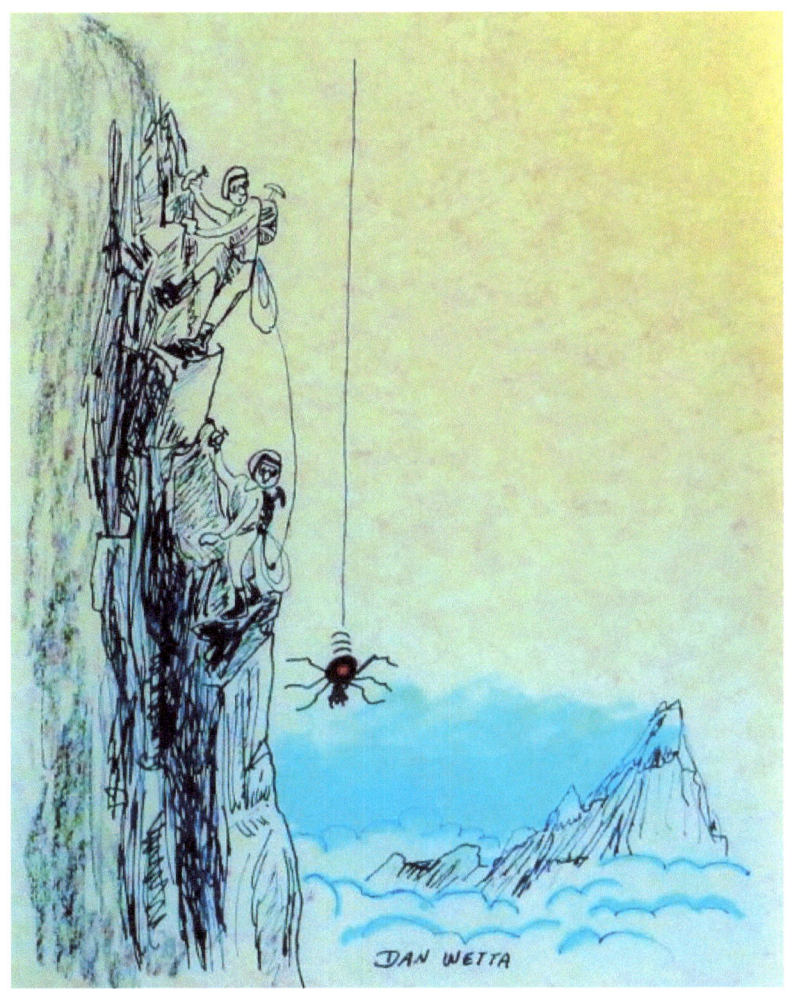

Title: Mountain Spider (cartoon)
Copyright by Dan Wetta 1997

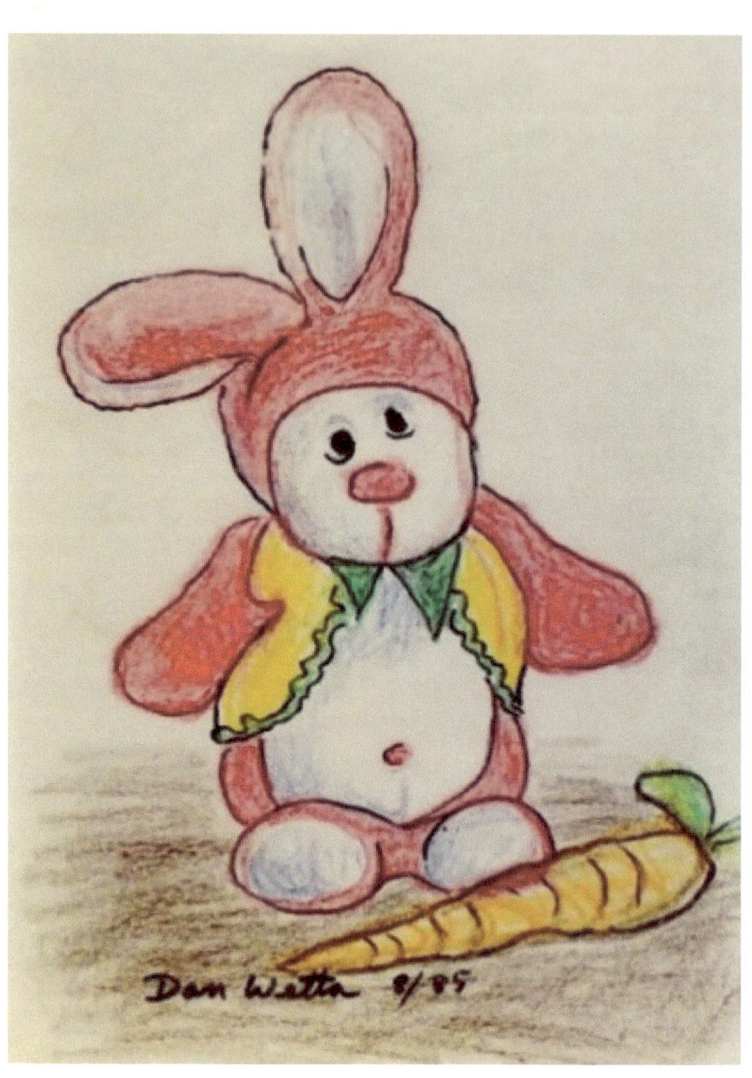

Title: But I Don't Like Carrots (cartoon)
Copyright by Dan Wetta 1985

Like people, some rabbits don't like carrots either.

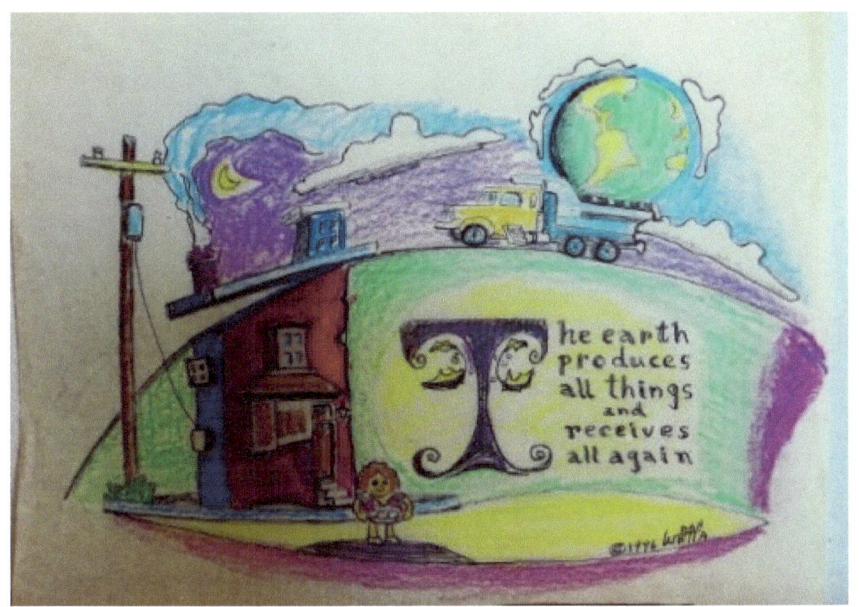

Title: The Earth (drawing)
Copyright by Dan Wetta 1996

"The earth produces all things and receives all again." I don't remember where I got this quote from. Do you know if it is from the bible?

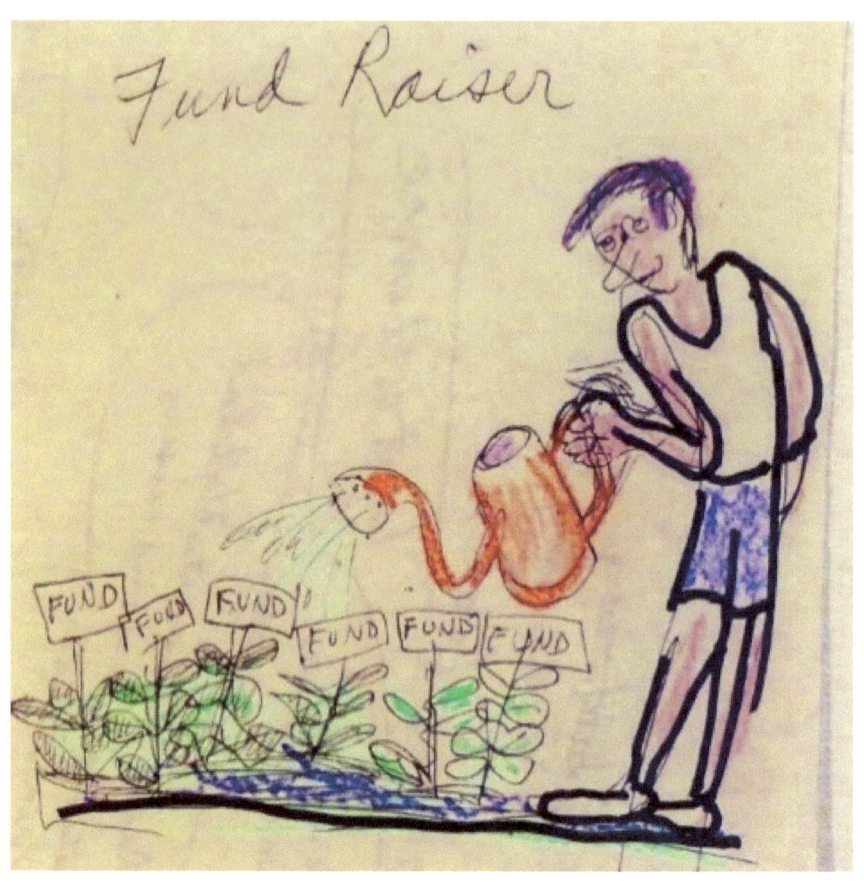

Title: Fund Raiser (cartoon)
Copyright by Dan Wetta

This is a corny gag, but the guy watering the plants looks dumb enough to think it'll work.

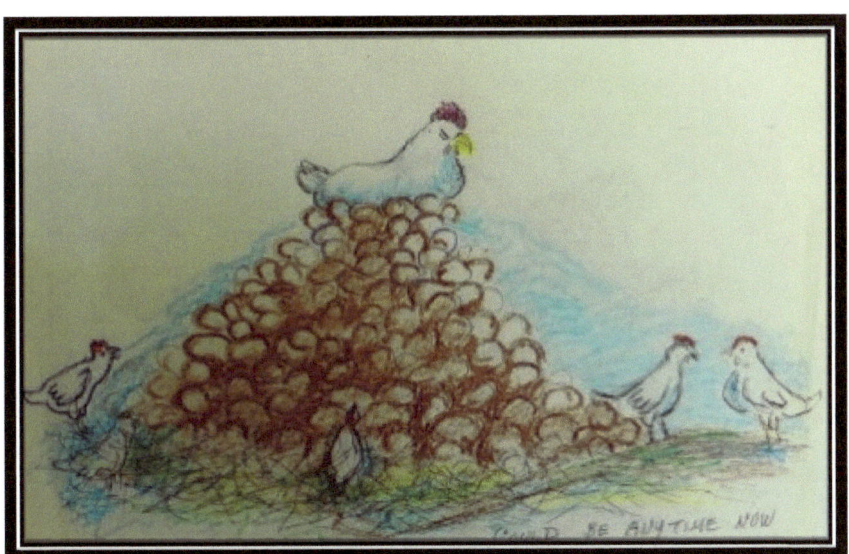

Title: Brown Eggs (cartoon)
Copyright by Dan Wetta 1989

Talk about a population explosion!

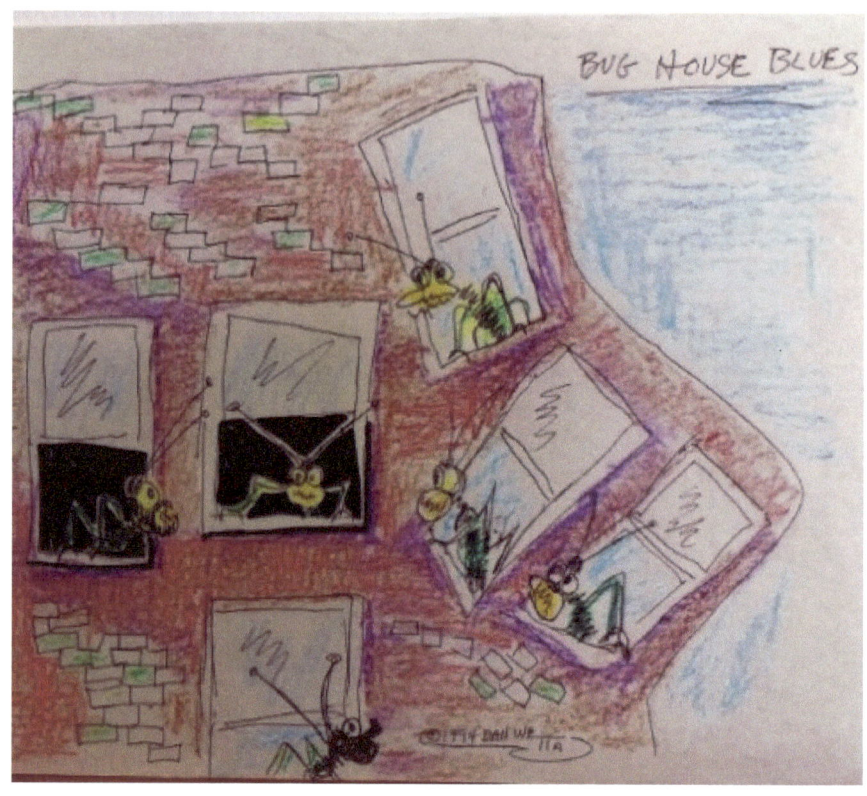

Title: Bug House (cartoon)
Copyright by Dan Wetta 1994

    Do you ever wonder what grasshoppers gossip about? Grass? Who can hop the farthest? Pesticide on Mr. Johnston's lawn?

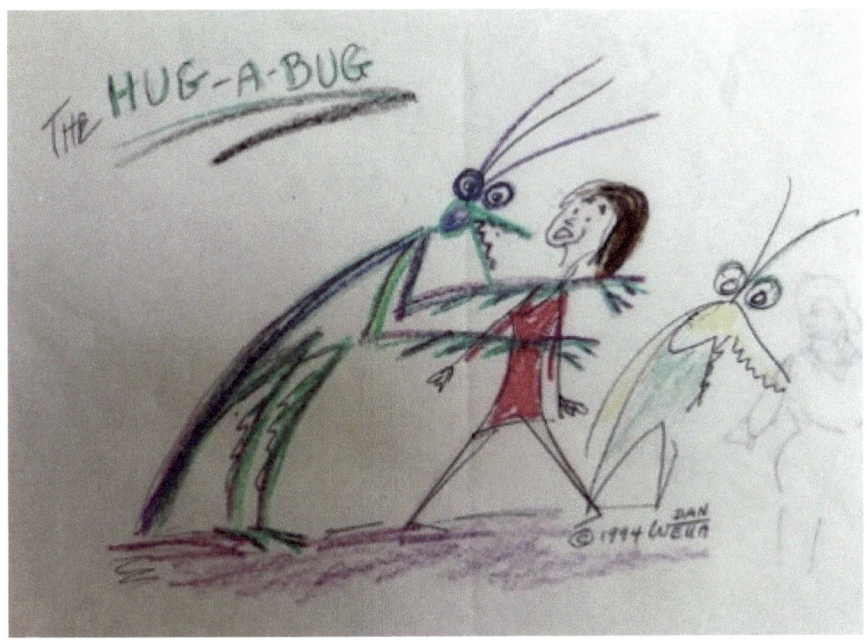

Title: Hug-A-Bug (cartoon)
Copyright by Dan Wetta 1994

That lady doesn't trust Hug-A-Bugs, and I don't blame her.

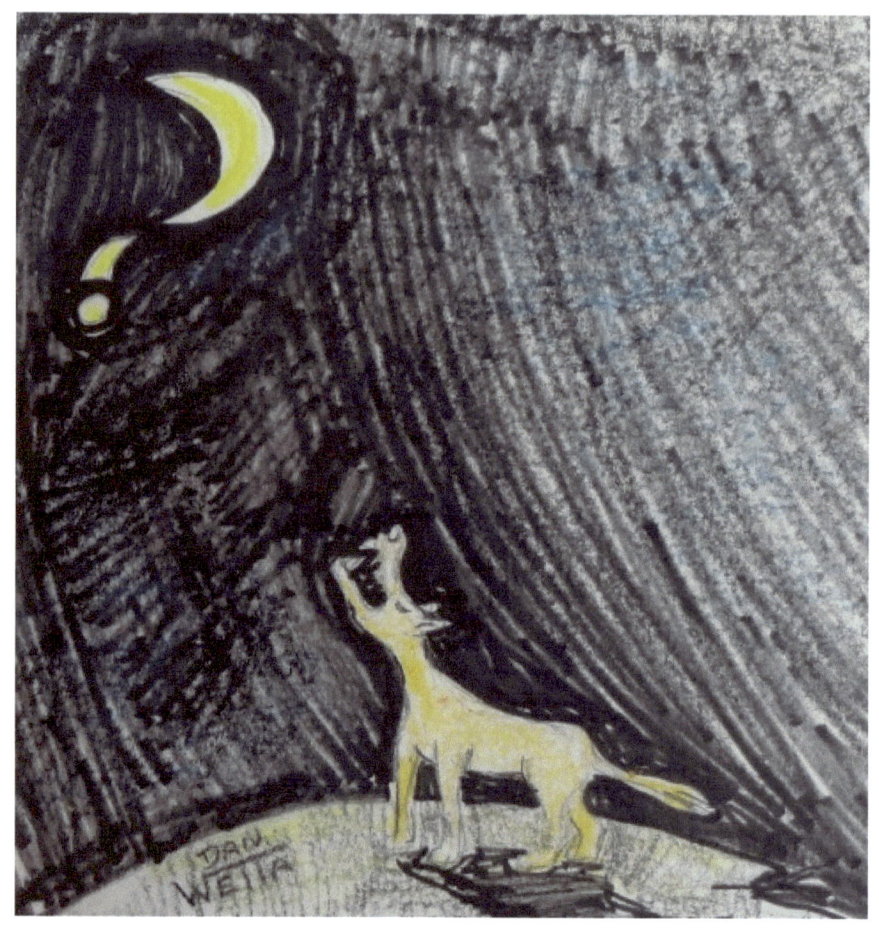

Title: Owooooooooo (cartoon)
Copyright by Dan Wetta

Do you know why they holler at the moon?

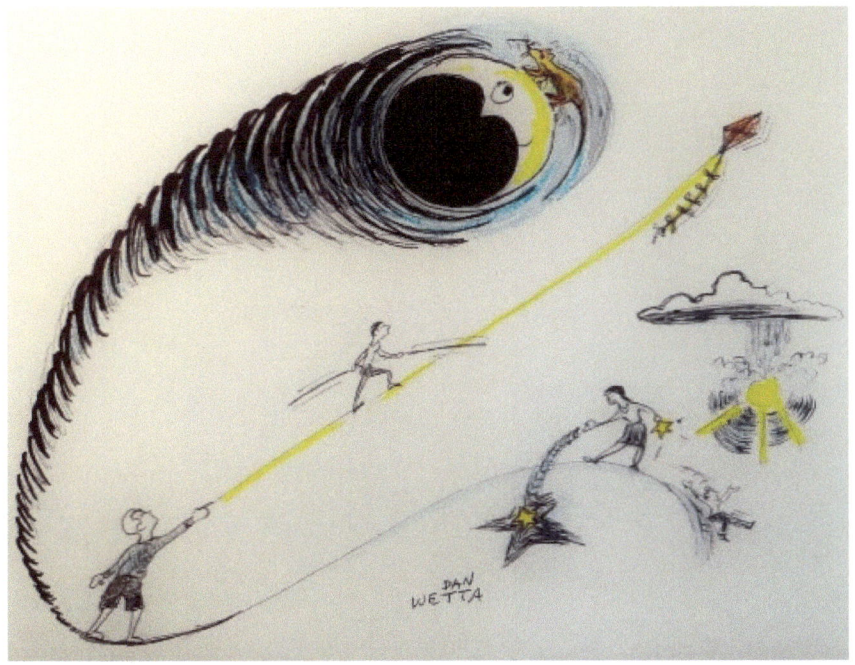

Title: Moon Doodle (cartoon)
Copyright by Dan Wetta

If a cow can jump over the moon, rats are probably up there too.

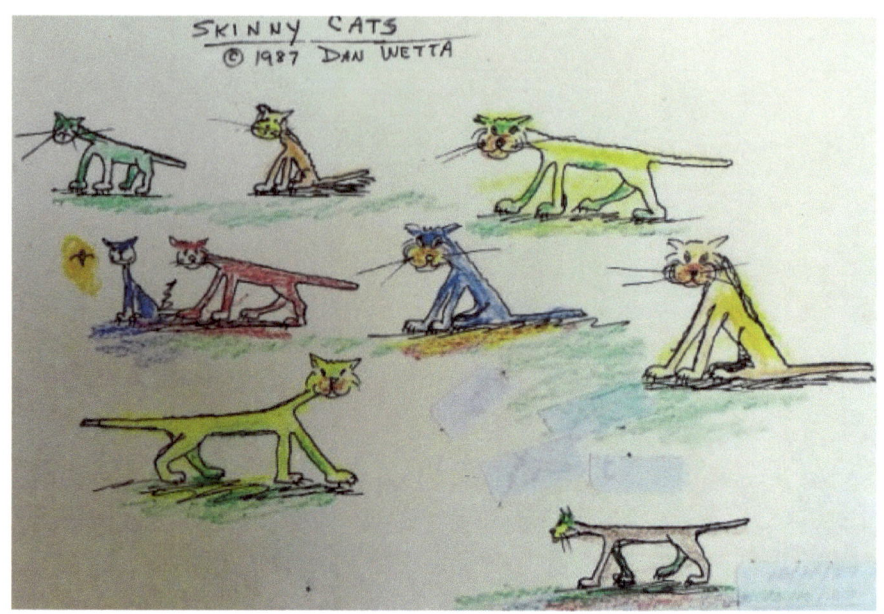

Title: Skinny Cats (cartoon)
Copyright by Dan Wetta 1987

Another "Cat-toon"

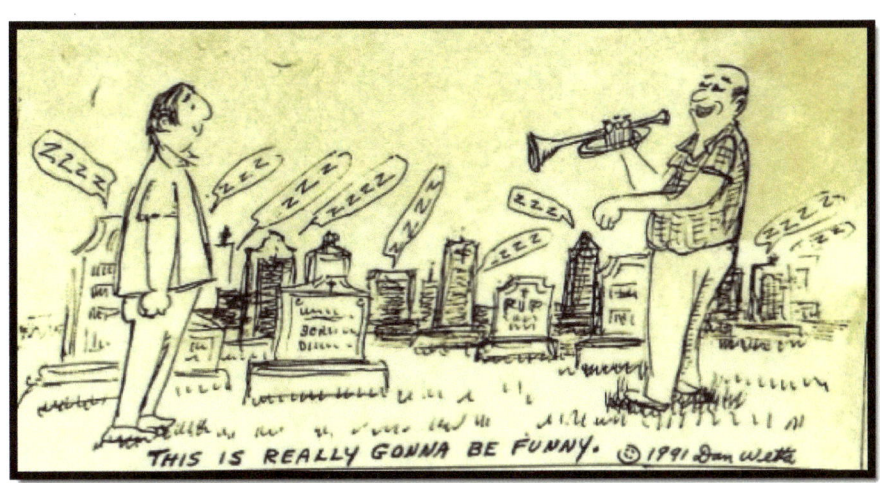

Title: Graveyard Bugler (cartoon)
Copyright by Dan Wetta 1991

They would both do you know what in their pants if those dead souls did arise from their graves.

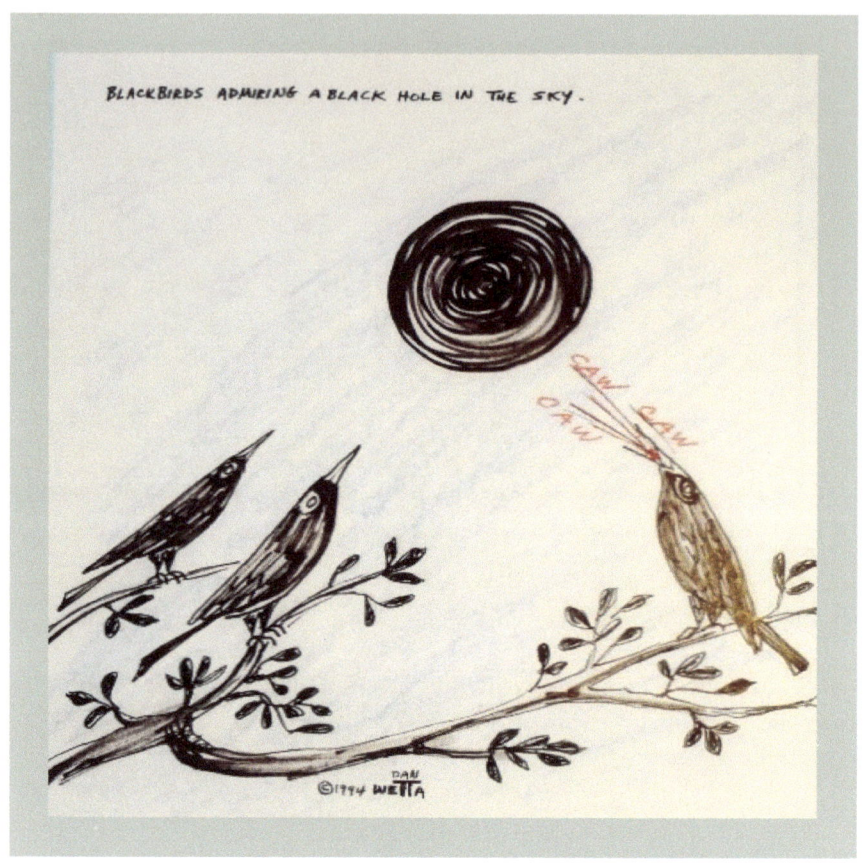

Title: Two Black Birds Admire Black Hole in Sky (drawing)
Copyright by Dan Wetta

But the brown bird thinks it is funny. The Spanish laugh is "ja ja ja." The gringo laugh is "ha ha ha." The Santa Claus laugh is "ho ho ho." A belly laugh is "haw haw, haw." So, naturally, the brown bird laugh is "caw caw caw."

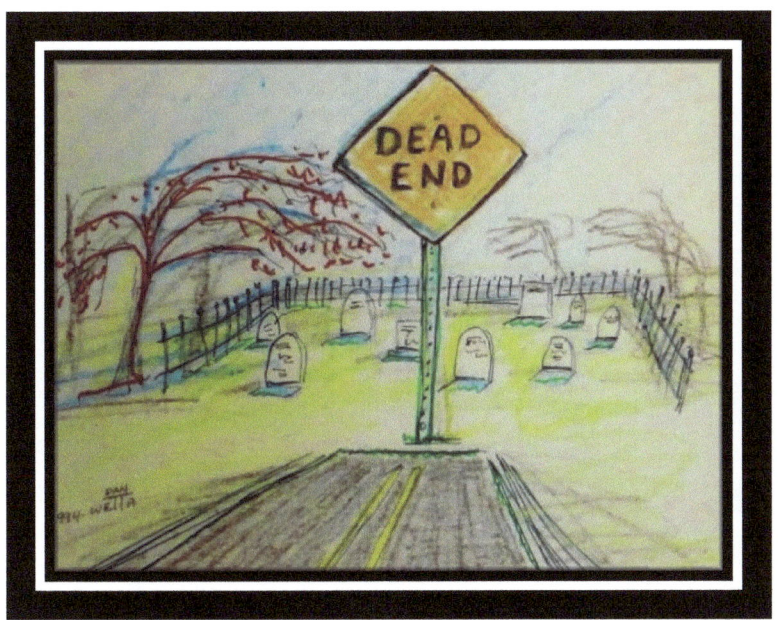

Title: Dead End (cartoon)
Copyright by Dan Wetta, 1994

Dan Wetta, Artist and Cartoonist

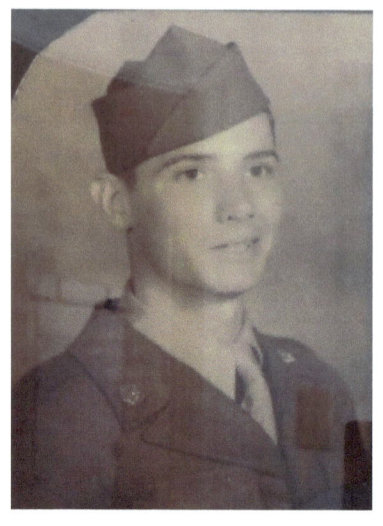

I was born on October 10, 1927, and I grew up during the Great Depression of the 1930's. I enlisted in the army in 1946 and was stationed at Camp Lee, Virginia, near Richmond, where I met my wife and settled down.

My father was a commercial artist, a steel and copper plate engraver for Dameron Pierson Stationery company in New Orleans. He was foreman ot their printing department. One of his tasks was to engrave printing plates to create paper money for Central and South American countries.

I began drawing and painting as a child, but did not want to become a commercial artist like my father because I wanted to paint things that interested me, so I made a living as an accountant-auditor.

I have exhibited at the Virginia Museum of Fine Arts, and was a member of the Richmond Artists' Association for about fifteen years.

We used to have fun exhibiting at malls until one day a City of Richmond Sales Tax Agent came by with a note pad and began writing down the names of artists who did not have a sales tax license.

When I got the city license, the IRS required me to file a quarterly FICA tax form, and the State said I had to have a business license, and then the malls got worried about liability, so they made us buy liability insurance.

Rules and regulations were taking up so much of my painting time that I said, "To heck with it, and I quit exhibiting." As a result, I have acumulated quite a few paintings over the years. This is why my life's collection of work is pretty much intact, and I decided to exhibit through books.

www.ingramcontent.com/pod-product-compliance
Lightning Source LLC
Chambersburg PA
CBHW040819180526
45159CB00001B/2